The Medusa Effect

SUNY SERIES IN PSYCHOANALYSIS AND CULTURE

Henry Sussman, editor

The
Medusa
Effect

REPRESENTATION AND EPISTEMOLOGY
IN VICTORIAN AESTHETICS

THOMAS ALBRECHT

Published by
STATE UNIVERSITY OF NEW YORK PRESS
ALBANY

© 2009 State University of New York

For information, contact State University of New York Press, Albany, NY
www.sunypress.edu

Production by Eileen Meehan
Marketing by Michael Campochiaro

Cover image: Burne-Jones, Edward (1833–1898). The Baleful Head. 1886–87. Staatsgalerie, Stuttgart, Germany. Photo Credit: Art Resource, NY.

Library of Congress Cataloging-in-Publication Data

Albrecht, Thomas, 1965 Jan 26–
    The Medusa effect : representation and epistemology in Victorian aesthetics / Thomas Albrecht.
        p. cm. — (SUNY series in psychoanalysis and culture)
    Includes bibliographical references and index.
    ISBN 978-1-4384-2867-3 (hardcover : alk. paper)
    ISBN 978-1-4384-2868-0 (pbk : alk. paper)   1. Psychoanalysis.
2. Medusa (Greek mythology)   3. Horror.   I. Title.
    BF173.A5774 2009
    809'.9164—dc22   2009003223

10 9 8 7 6 5 4 3 2 1

To J. Hillis Miller,
with gratitude and in friendship

Contents

Acknowledgments

I am grateful to everyone who read portions of this book at the various stages of its inception and development: Megan Becker-Leckrone, Ellen Burt, Philip Leider, Stefan Mattessich, J. Hillis Miller, Patience Moll, Tom Pepper, Matt Potolsky, Julia Reinhard-Lupton, Molly Rothenberg, Heather Schwartz, Barbara Spackman, and Andrzej Warminski, and I thank them for their nuanced and careful readings and their helpful comments and suggestions. I especially wish to thank Barbara Spackman for directing the dissertation that was the original basis of this project. I also want to thank my students in the various "Medusa" and "Fatal Woman Fantasies" seminars I taught at the University of California, Los Angeles, and at Tulane University for their critical and creative interactions with the texts and ideas that make up this book.

The development of this project benefited greatly from the two years I spent as an Andrew W. Mellon postdoctoral fellow at the Humanities Consortium and the Center for Modern and Contemporary Studies at UCLA, and I thank Ken Reinhard, Vince Pecora, and Daniel Gross for their intellectual friendship and good conversation during those years and afterward. I also wish to thank the German Academic Exchange Service (DAAD) for a research grant that allowed me to spend a semester in Berlin. I am grateful to my teachers and fellow students in what was at the time the Department of English and Comparative Literature at the University of California, Irvine, where I completed my graduate studies in Comparative Literature. I also thank the Humanities Core Course Program at UC Irvine and the English Department at Tulane University for providing me with supportive institutional homes during the writing and revising of this book. I am grateful to Dean George L. Bernstein, Dean Carole Haber, and the School of Liberal Arts at Tulane University for awarding me with two grants to cover the costs of procuring the necessary copyright permissions. I also wish to thank my Research Assistant (and former student) Brett Long for his work on the manuscript, and the

Tulane University Provost's Office and Associate Provost Brian S. Mitchell for making that work possible.

Finally and foremost, I wish to thank Henry Sussman, editor of the series Psychoanalysis and Culture at SUNY Press, and James Peltz, Associate Director at SUNY Press, for their generous support, assistance, and patience during the writing and revising stages of this project. It has been and continues to be my great pleasure to work with both of them.

An earlier version of chapter 1 was previously published under the title "Apotropiac Reading: Freud's 'Medusa's Head'" in *Literature and Psychology* 45:4 (1999), 13–25, and is reproduced by permission of the publisher. A slightly abbreviated version of chapter 4 was published under the same title in *English Literary History* 73:2 (2006), 437–463, © The Johns Hopkins University Press, and is reprinted with permission of The Johns Hopkins University Press.

Introduction

The Medusa Effect

DANTE GABRIEL ROSSETTI'S REFLECTIONS OF MEDUSA

It is a very straightforward work.

—Dante Gabriel Rossetti, on "Aspecta Medusa"

In explaining what I mean in this book by Medusa effect, I begin with an extended example, a reading of a poem and a proposed painting by Dante Gabriel Rossetti. In July 1867, Rossetti received a commission from Charles Peter Matthews, a Scottish brewer and art collector, for a painting of Perseus showing Andromeda a reflection of Medusa's severed head in a large basin, intended by Matthews for display in the drawing room of his home in Havering, Essex. Matthews commissioned the painting, to be called "Aspecta Medusa" (literally, Medusa Beheld), after having been shown preparatory sketches by Rossetti (Figures 1 and 2) and after having approved the reflection theme and Rossetti's overall design.

Taking his motif from "representations of it on vases & in wall-decoration of classic times," Rossetti had been working on the subject for several years.[1] But he never completed the actual painting, as Matthews eventually cancelled the commission, writing to Rossetti, "I cannot all get over the horror and repugnance with which I have always regarded that which according to your original design, is to be one of the chief features in it—I mean of course the *severed* head of Medusa. And I cannot help thinking that the repulsive portion of your design would admit of some modification."[2]

In response to the cancelled commission, Rossetti declined to modify his design and attempted instead to reassure Matthews that his misgivings were unfounded. In a letter to Matthews of November 12, 1867, he defends his planned treatment of the reflection motif against the charge that it would willfully aim to provoke horror and repugnance in the viewer:

FIGURE 1. Dante Gabriel Rossetti, Study for *Aspecta Medusa*. Birmingham Museum & Art Gallery. Photo: Birmingham Museums & Art Gallery Picture Library.

[Medusa's] head, treated as a pure ideal, presenting no likeness (as it will not) to the severed head of an actual person, being moreover so much in shadow (according to my arrangement) that no painful ghastliness of colour will be apparent, will not really possess when executed the least degree of that repugnant reality which might naturally suggest itself at first consideration. I feel the utmost confidence in this myself, as the kind of French sensational horror which the

FIGURE 2. Dante Gabriel Rossetti, Study for *Aspecta Medusa*. Victoria and Albert Museum, London. Photo: Victoria & Albert Museum, London / Art Resource, NY.

realistic treatment of the severed head would cause is exactly the quality I should most desire to avoid. (C 3:590)[3]

Beyond the contrast between Pre-Raphaelite idealism and "French" naturalism, what is striking about Rossetti's description is the implied analogy between the proposed painting and the reflection the painting depicts: just as Perseus shows Medusa's head to Andromeda in the form of a reflection in water, the painting will present the severed head "so much in shadow" to its viewer. In the case of the reflection as in the case of the painting, a horrifying object that should not be shown or looked at directly—Medusa's head in the first case, the decapitated head of a corpse in the second—is to be shown and seen obliquely. Rossetti evokes an implicit series of analogies that follows from this first analogy: between Perseus and himself, between Andromeda and Matthews, and between Medusa's head and "the severed head of an actual person." So at one level, the depicted scene can be interpreted as an allegory about the very painting in which it appears. The painting may *show* a severed head, Rossetti suggests to Matthews, but it will not *be* a Medusa's head to those who look at it. For the spectator, any feeling of horror potentially provoked by seeing the decapitated head will be tempered by Rossetti's artistic presentation of the subject, just as for Andromeda, the petrifying power of Medusa's head is negated by Perseus's reflection of the head in water. Complementing this specific analogy between the scene and the proposed painting, Rossetti's description also evokes a more general set of analogies: between Perseus and the artist, between Andromeda and the viewer, between Medusa's head and "repugnant reality," and between the head's reflection and visual art. At this latter level, the painting, like many of Rossetti's paintings, can be interpreted as an allegory about painting itself: about its Apollonian function, for instance, or its potential power to convert repugnant reality into "pure ideal."

Given the reflection motif's thematic emphasis on vision and mirroring, it is not surprising that Rossetti would choose it as the subject of a painting. Nor is it surprising that he would choose it as an allegory about painting. The motif obviously lends itself to a visual representation, and it also lends itself to commenting on painting and visual representation as such, a use to which Rossetti alludes when he writes to Matthews that his objection to the painting "has given me matter for reflection" (C 3:590). Rossetti's problem as an artist (how to present decorously the decapitated head of a corpse) is strikingly similar to Perseus's predicament evoked in the picture (how to show Andromeda Medusa's head without petrifying her). And Perseus's solution by means of the reflection anticipates Rossetti's own solution: his shadowy presentation will obscure and simultaneously idealize the reality of the corpse's head.

The implicit parallel between the picture and the mirroring it depicts is also reinforced by a general emphasis throughout the Perseus myth on the themes of vision and visibility. As Jean-Pierre Vernant has noted about the myth,

> One theme is central [in Perseus's story]: the eye, the gaze, the reciprocity of seeing and being seen. This theme appears already in the sequence of the three Graiai with their single tooth and eye . . . [and] is found again in the *kunee*, the magical instrument of invisibility concealing from all eyes the presence of the one whose head it covers, and also in the detail that Perseus turned his eyes away at the moment of Medusa's death. He does this when he cuts the monster's throat, and later too,

when he brandishes her head to turn his enemies into stone and pru-
dently looks in the opposite direction. The theme finds its full development in those version, attested from the fifth century on, that insist on
the indispensable recourse to the mirror and its reflection that enables
the young man to see Gorgo without having to cross glances with her
petrifying gaze. (135–36)[4]

While the thematic concern with the eye and the gaze does not necessarily make the Perseus story into an allegory about visual art, it gives one
reason why an artist like Rossetti might appropriate one or another of its
episodes, for instance the reflection of Medusa's head in a body of water,
for such a purpose. Any painting of Medusa's head, insofar as we can safely
look at it, can potentially be interpreted as an allegory about the mitigating
power of art described by Rossetti in his letter to Matthews. Caravaggio's
famous painting of the decapitated Medusa's head makes this association
explicit by depicting the head in the form of its mirror image, as though it
were being reflected in a round convex surface, presumably Perseus's mirror
shield (Figure 3).

Rossetti's allegory makes apparent that for him, painting's idealizing
and elevating function is simultaneously a protective, neutralizing function.
This is obvious foremost in the use of Medusa's head as an analogy for what
art depicts, for what Rossetti in his letter calls "repugnant reality." It would
seem from the choice of image that this reality has for Rossetti a potential
element of horror or danger, a potentially Medusa-like effect on the viewer.
He refers explicitly to a "French sensational horror which the realistic treatment of the severed head would cause," evoking the canonical association of
Medusa's head with horror as an implicit metaphor for the effect of natural-
ist art, the kind of art that would show reality in all its repugnance, on the
spectator. He also refers to his motif's potentially "painful ghastliness of
colour," suggesting that the viewer must somehow be protected from being
harmed by the painting's subject matter. He then makes explicit that the
interposition of an artistic presentation between subject matter and viewer,
much like the interposition of the reflecting pool between Medusa's head
and Andromeda's gaze, is his means of expelling and purifying the horrifying, painful elements in the subject, and of protecting the spectator: "the
head, treated as pure ideal . . . will not really possess when executed the least
degree of that repugnant reality which might naturally suggest itself at first
consideration." Rossetti describes his painting as a formal execution that as
such would purify or sublimate the horrifying natural reality it depicts—
the reality of a corpse's head—not unlike the water's reflection of the deadly
Medusa's head, which transforms a lethal object into an aesthetic object for
Andromeda's contemplation.

When Rossetti wrote to his mother, Frances Polidori Rossetti, to tell
her about Matthews commissioning the Medusa painting, he appended to

FIGURE 3. Caravaggio, *Head of Medusa*. Uffizi, Florence. Photo: Nicolo Orsi Battaglini / Art Resource, NY.

his letter a short poem, also entitled "Aspecta Medusa," noting, "Some lines of mine which I write opposite will explain the [painting's] subject":

> Andromeda, by Perseus saved and wed,
> Hankered each day to see the Gorgon's head:
> Till o'er a fount he held it, bade her lean,
> And mirrored in the wave was safely seen
> That death she lived by.
>   Let not thine eyes know
> Any forbidden thing itself, although
> It once should save as well as kill: but be
> Its shadow upon life enough for thee. (C 3:557)

The juxtaposition of the poem with the proposed painting is an example of a so-called double work of art, a practice commonly found in Rossetti's oeuvre, where a poem accompanies and interprets a given picture or, conversely, a picture illustrates and comments on a given poem.[5] Here, the poem's first stanza describes the scene to be shown in the painting, and the second stanza provides an explanation of the scene's significance. In an 1870 letter to A. C. Swinburne, Rossetti specifies that he had originally intended the poem to accompany the painting "as an inscription" (C 4:394), and while the painting was ultimately never completed after Matthews withdrew his commission, Rossetti did publish the poem on its own in the collected *Poems* of 1870 under the title "Aspecta Medusa (For a Drawing)." The planned juxtaposition of painting and poem, and the explicit moral provided in the poem's didactic second stanza, make clear that the reflection scene is to be taken as an allegory. The references to eyes and shadow suggest that Rossetti possibly intends the scene as an allegory about painting or visual art, as the painting itself and the accompanying passage from the letter to Matthews imply as well. The phrase "Its shadow upon life" in particular would seem to be, among other things, a reference to the phrase "being so much in shadow" from Rossetti's description of the presentation he intends for the severed head in the painting. The interpretation of the poem as an allegory about painting would follow as well from the addition of the phrase "For a Drawing" to its title, which specifies that Rossetti has written the poem in order to supplement the proposed painting and its preparatory sketches (rather than, say, having made the drawings in order to illustrate the poem).[6] To have written it "for" the picture may also mean in this case to have written it about pictures in general, given the implied exemplarity of the picture in question.

But the apparent simplicity and didacticism of the poem is deceptive, and the second stanza turns out to be less straightforward than it might seem, and more like the oblique reflection of which it is a gloss. The parallel between the two companion pieces, the painting and the poem, goes beyond their shared motif and their shared cautionary message. For as in the painting, there is in the poem an implicit parallel between the scene that is depicted and the depiction itself. In the first stanza Perseus shows Andromeda Medusa's head "mirrored in the wave," while concurrently the poem shows what it calls the "forbidden thing itself" to its reader figuratively, in the image of the Gorgon's head. So just as Medusa's head is rendered by Perseus in the form of its reflection, the forbidden thing and the admonitory lesson about the thing ("be / Its shadow upon life enough for thee") are rendered by the poem in the form of images, in the allegorical figures of Perseus, Andromeda, the Gorgon's head, the wave, the reflection, the forbidden thing, and the shadow. This mode of indirect presentation characterizes the explicitly allegorical first stanza and also the second stanza, which might initially seem to be more straightforward than the first, but which is ultimately no less figurative. The phrase "forbidden thing itself" is as much a figure as "the Gorgon's head," and the many images saturating the second stanza (the knowing eyes, the thing that "once should save as well as kill," the thing's shadow upon life) reiterate the figurative nature of the stanza and of the entire poem. Evidently the poem will only show figures to its reader, just as Perseus only shows Medusa's head to Andromeda in the form of its reflection. Whatever mysterious and presumably dangerous referent, if any, is behind such images as the Gorgon's head and the forbidden thing, the reader will only know it or see it in the form of those and other images. So the poem, it would seem, is following its own advice and is itself an example of the very lesson it teaches.

Underlying the complex and diffuse set of analogies Rossetti plays on between the reflection, the painting, the description of the painting in the letter to Matthews, the poem's first stanza, the poem's second stanza, and the poem as a whole, there is a fundamental parallel between the painting and the poem: both work with shadows, in one case literally, in one case figuratively. Both are indirect presentations of something Rossetti will not show or say directly. The protective capacity of the poem's figurative shadows (that is, poetic language) is perhaps less obvious than the protective capacity of the painting's literal shadows (which is explained in the letter to Matthews). Like painting, poetic language and imagery would seem to be for Rossetti a potential form of idealization, a sublimating force akin to what Walter Pater describes in his essay "Aesthetic Poetry":

> Greek poetry, mediæval or modern poetry, projects, above the realities of its time, a world in which the forms of things are transfigured. Of that transfigured world this new poetry takes possession, and sublimates beyond it another still fainter and more spectral, which is literally an artificial or "earthly paradise." (*Selected Writings*, 190)

What Rossetti adds to Pater's notion of aesthetic poetry's double transfiguration of the material world is the identification of poetic sublimation as a form of defense against that world, a world his Medusa metaphor defines as inherently threatening. The poem's second stanza explicitly depicts direct, unmediated confrontations with repugnant realities and forbidden things as dangerous, and indirect confrontations mediated by art as safe: "And mirrored in the wave was safely seen / That death she lived by." The reflection of Medusa's head depicted in both painting and poem is thus a self-reflective figure for the protection the painting and the poem are each providing in their respective mediums.

As a figure that reflects as much on what the poem is doing with figurative language as on what the painting is doing with shadows, Medusa's mirroring indicates that Rossetti's allegory in the painting and poem goes beyond the Apollonian or sublimating function of certain forms of visual art (for instance, Pre-Raphaelite art) and is also, on a wider and more fundamental level, about representation as such, about the act of fashioning visual or verbal images as a means of protecting oneself against some kind of threat.[7] More specifically, it indicates that the allegory is about the protective effect of those images that portray the threatening thing itself. Such an interpretation of "Aspecta Medusa" suggests itself in that Perseus effectively creates an image or representation of Medusa's head, namely the reflection, in order to protect Andromeda against its petrifying power. It is substantiated by the traditional narrative and pictorial accounts of Medusa's decapitation in which Perseus looks into an angled mirror or polished shield so as to avoid looking at Medusa directly and being petrified, for instance the version told by Apollodorus in Book 2 of the *Library*:

> The Gorgons . . . turned to stone such as beheld them. So Perseus stood over them as they slept, and while Athena guided his hand and he looked with averted gaze on a brazen shield, in which he beheld the image of the Gorgon, he beheaded her. (157–59)

Another standard account, Book 4 of Ovid's *Metamorphoses*, also highlights the act of mirroring and its significance as a means of protection:

> All through the fields and along the roadways [Perseus] saw statues of men and beasts, whom the sight of the Gorgon had changed from their true selves into stone. But he himself looked at dread Medusa's form as it was reflected in the bronze of the shield which he carried on his left arm. While she and her snakes were wrapped in deep slumber, he severed her head from her shoulders. (125)

In both accounts, the emphasis is on Perseus using the reflective shield in order to create what is specifically characterized as a representation: "he beheld the *image [eikon]* of the Gorgon" (the Greek word *eikon* means likeness, image, or portrait), and "he himself looked at dread Medusa's *form [formam]* as it was reflected in the bronze of the shield" (the Latin word *forma* means form, figure, or shape, and also image, likeness, or model). It is through fashioning an image of Medusa that Perseus protects himself from Medusa's danger. This association between image making and protection is also evoked in Caravaggio's Medusa painting (Figure 3), which is simultaneously a shield (one in which the viewer can "safely" see an image of Medusa's newly decapitated head as if it were being reflected) and a painting of a shield.[8] In Ovid's and Apollodorus's accounts of the decapitation, the reflection of Medusa in the mirror shield is not only a means of protection, however, but also the means of defeating Medusa. It is the ruse by which Perseus avoids seeing Medusa directly and by which he is able to kill her, as it allows him to see where to strike so as to cut off the head. Rossetti alludes to this latter association—between representing a threat and over-coming it—in the image of the head's reflection in water, which as a kind of reenactment recalls its earlier reflection in Perseus's shield at the moment of the decapitation.

It would seem, then, that Rossetti's allegory in "Aspecta Medusa" exceeds the immediate contexts of the proposed painting and of visual art in general, and extends to a larger epistemological problematic in which poem and painting are both implicated. This larger context is implied by the image of the mirror, a frequent and equivocal motif in Rossetti's work, which in "Aspecta Medusa" functions specifically as a figure for protective and transfiguring representations, both visual and verbal.[9] It is also implied by the overall imagery in the second stanza: for instance, by the images of the eye, the "forbidden thing itself," and the shadow, all of which have general epistemological connotations. The injunction "Let not thine eyes know the forbidden thing itself" indicates that for Rossetti, the sight of Medusa's head is not only a figure for something horrifying or dangerous, for the idea of death, say, or for repugnant realities such as a severed head. It is somewhat more specifically a figure for a dangerous revelation or insight, one that Rossetti insists must be faced and rendered indirectly, in the form of literal or figurative reflections and shadows. Like the mirror's reflection of Medusa, the indirect presentation of the insight is a form of protection against—and a means of overcoming—the threat to oneself that is posed by the insight. This is the epistemological lesson of "Aspecta Medusa," as it is stated in the poem's second stanza and of which both the poem and the painting are demonstrations. And so the forbidden insight, whatever it might be literally, is accordingly rendered by Rossetti only in the form of one or another figure: as the Gorgon's head, as a corpse's head, as the head's reflection in the fountain, as "Any forbidden thing itself," as the forbidden thing's shadow upon life, as death, and so on.[10]

In "Aspecta Medusa," Rossetti tellingly juxtaposes these various images, which are all variations on an image of death, with accompanying images of life: he does this in the phrase "shadow upon life," for instance, and also in the phrases "That death she lived by" and "It once should save as well as kill." These pairings are significant,[11] and constitute a series insofar as they each designate a similar kind of economy: a life given in return for a death, someone's life saved by another's death. In the context of the Perseus myth, the lines "That death she lived by" and "It once should save as well as kill" specifically refer to Perseus's use of Medusa's head to petrify the sea-monster Ketos and thereby to save Andromeda's life. It is in that sense that Andromeda is said to have lived by Medusa's death and to have been saved by something that kills. But these lines and their (playful, ironic) juxtaposition of life and death also have a wider epistemological significance. By clustering simultaneous references to Medusa's death and Andromeda's life around the central motif of reflecting Medusa's head, Rossetti indicates that the representation of a terrifying insight is not only a way of protecting oneself from it and of negating its power, but is moreover a way of literally or figuratively restoring oneself to life in the process. This sacrificial restoration of life by means of a death is suggested, for instance, in the figure of the saved Andromeda, whom Perseus has delivered from certain death by using as his weapon the head of a corpse, "That death she lived by." It is also suggested in the phrase "It once should save as well as kill," which refers specifically to the killing of Ketos and the saving of Andromeda, and more generally to the vivifying potential of Medusa's fatal power, but which also evokes the prior killing of Medusa upon which any beneficial capacity of her head depends. Finally, it is suggested in the admonition "be / Its shadow upon life enough for thee," which implies an interdependent relation between the reader's life and the thing's shadow. The implication is that the forbidden thing as such must somehow die—that is, become a shadow—so that the reader can safely live. The shadow is a figure for death and is also a figure for an image or representation, so the line establishes a correlation between representing the forbidden thing and killing it, and then defines both kinds of "shadowing" as protective and life-preserving, in accordance with the definition of shadow as a form of shelter. In the context of the overall allegory, all three examples, and in particular the third, make the case that the representation of dangerous insights is also literally or figuratively a form of killing, a sacrifice of someone or something through which one is oneself reaffirmed and revived. More than a gesture of self-protection, then, the making of images is apparently a gesture of self-empowerment, as demonstrated by the figure of Perseus triumphantly holding up the spoil of the severed Medusa's head and making an (indirect) display of it for Andromeda to see. It seems from Perseus's gesture, insofar as it reflects back on the poem in which it appears, that the poem is not only a defensive prohibition but also a kind of brandish. "Aspecta Medusa" celebrates the victorious Perseus as a figure for the triumph of life. In so doing it also celebrates by implicit analogy Rossetti's own survival and triumph over the presumably lethal revelations he has faced and ultimately triumphed over, revelations he then reflects for his readers and viewers in the protective forms of the allegorical poem and painting.

Concurrent with this celebration, however, the image of the shadow also casts some ambivalence on the poem's epistemological message, and specifically on the indirect representation of "Any forbidden thing itself" which the poem ostensibly prescribes and exemplifies. As an example of—and a reflexive figure for—such an oblique representation, the shadow has connotations not only of shelter and protection, but also of obscurity and ignorance, delusion and deception, and transience and insubstantiality. Despite its ostensibly anti-Platonic moral ("be / Its shadow upon life enough for thee," an apparent reversal of Socrates's lesson in the Allegory of the Cave in *The Republic*), Rossetti's poem remains at the level of its imagery very much situated within a Platonic scheme, one that fundamentally distinguishes between a "thing itself" and its representations. And within the context of any such scheme, the figure of the "shadow upon life" conveys all the implicit negative connotations associated with the representation as opposed to the thing: with the shadow as opposed to life, the imitation as opposed to the real, the sensual as opposed to the spiritual, the copy as opposed to the original, the sign as opposed to the meaning, appearance as opposed to truth, and so on. So while it may be read as an affirmative image, for instance in the spiritualizing sense that Pater attributes to aesthetic poetry's "fainter and more spectral" world, the shadow less reassuringly also suggests a condition of being a step dangerously removed from life or truth, a state not unlike that of the prisoners in the Allegory of the Cave, who mistake the shadows they see for realities, or that of Tennyson's Lady of Shalott, who describes herself as "half sick" of the shadows of the world that appear in her mirror. It echoes the "unreal shapes" and "shadows, which the world calls substance" that are woven by Fear and Hope in Shelley's sonnet "Lift not the painted veil," a poem whose cautionary and ambiguous moral several readers have heard echoed in "Aspecta Medusa."[12] And it recalls the predicament of the speaker and unrequited lover in Rossetti's poem "The Mirror," who compares his own mistaking his beloved's feelings to a man expectantly identifying himself with the "forms that crowd unknown / Within a distant mirror's shade," only to discover "his thought betray'd" by the shadowy images he sees, and to find that he "must seek elsewhere for his own" (*Works*, 194). At the level of these kinds of connotations, the shadow in Rossetti's poem is perhaps no less ominous than Medusa's head itself, and the reader is left in the dilemma of having to choose between the illusory effect of the one and the fatal effect of the other.

As Rossetti alternately associates representation with sublimation and protection, on one hand, and with a potentially dangerous illusion, on the other hand, he also suggests through the image of Medusa's head a wholly other insight about representation, specifically the recognition that there is no tenable alternative to our showing and seeing only shadows. To know or to see the forbidden thing in any other way but via its shadow, the Medusa image makes explicit, is not only inadvisable or forbidden, but is simply impossible insofar as it is synonymous with death (that is, with the instant annihilation of the self and of the senses). As a specifically epistemological figure, Medusa's head is indicative of a truth or thing than can only ever be known or seen figuratively, in the form of images, as any direct seeing of it is not a form of knowing. One could no more see Medusa's head directly than know one's own death. In its literal impossibility, Medusa's head is therefore fundamentally different from an image like the sun in Plato's Allegory of the Cave, which is also a metaphor for the "thing itself." In Plato's case, the sun *can* ultimately be seen directly, albeit with great difficulty and pain, implying that the thing it represents (that is, the good) can be apprehended directly. As part of the allegory, Socrates tells Glaucon about the prisoner who has been liberated from the cave and has made his way into the light, seeing first shadows and "images of men and other things in water, then the things themselves. . . . Finally, I suppose, he'd be able to see the sun, not images of it in water or in some alien place, but the sun itself, in its own place" (*Republic*, 516b 188). Socrates's account of the prisoner's gradual progress reverses the story told in "Aspecta Medusa" insofar as it moves from someone seeing various reflections of a thing to seeing the thing directly, "in its own place." For Socrates, the movement from seeing the sun's reflection to seeing the actual sun (which is allegorically to say, to apprehending the good as such) becomes a necessary imperative: "Once one has seen [the form of the good], however, one must conclude that it is the cause of all that is correct and beautiful in anything . . . so that anyone who is to act sensibly in private or public must see it" (517b-c 189). "Aspecta Medusa" makes the opposite argument, since it advocates on behalf of our restricting ourselves to seeing only the shadows of things rather than the things themselves. But in substituting the image of Medusa (that which can only ever be seen in images of it in water or in some alien place) for the image of the seeable sun as the paradigmatic figure for the thing that we would ultimately see and know, Rossetti's epistemological allegory does not just reverse Socrates's argument. It essentially breaks with that argument's (metaphysical, mimetic) foundation, the opposition between the thing and its shadow.[13] Rather than just insisting that we should look at shadows instead of the things themselves, Rossetti questions whether the things could ever be seen as anything but shadows. So the poem's cautionary moral given in the second stanza may insist contra Plato that we *should* limit ourselves to shadows and reflections of the forbidden thing for the sake of safety, but the Medusa image in the first stanza implies that we *could* in fact do nothing else. As Rossetti's exemplary metaphor for what it is that we would ultimately know, Medusa's head—the thing that by definition can only ever be known or seen as a shadow, never as a "thing itself"—suggests that in seeing and knowing what we do, we only see and know shadows and reflections. This suggestion is reiterated by the image of the "forbidden thing itself" in the poem's more "literal" second stanza, which is as much a figure—that is, a shadow—as Medusa's head in the first stanza. In showing his reader these two figures, Rossetti is evidently not only being cautious and protective, in accordance with the ostensible moral of his poem; judging from the Medusa image, it would seem that he could show—and we could see—nothing else.

The recognition that we inevitably see and show only shadows shifts the epistemological problematic of "Aspecta Medusa" away from the ambiguity between conceiving of representation as a protective and self-empowering defense, on one hand, and conceiving of it as a potentially harmful delusion, on the other. Both of the latter positions depend on the tenable distinction between the thing and the representation of the thing. The first position, the one ostensibly advocated by the poem, presumes the existence of a forbidden thing itself that would be distinct from its shadow, a thing from which like Andromeda we could safely avert our gaze and look toward its reflection in the pool of water. The second, more Platonic position, which is also alluded to in the poem, makes the opposite argument insofar as it tells us to turn from the illusory shadow toward the thing itself, rather than vice versa. But it presumes the same distinction between the shadow and the thing, and it presumes as well our ability to turn from one to the other, just as Socrates in *The Republic* presumes an intelligible distinction between being in darkness and being in sunlight, and between the shadows on the walls of the cave and the real things of which those shadows are only reflections. In contrast, Rossetti's Medusa image, insofar as it is the figure for which there exists no thing, no corresponding nonfigurative referent, is irreducible to either a shadow or a thing, or to the entire opposition between the thing and the shadow. As such, it destabilizes both positions that "Aspecta Medusa" ostensibly takes on the question of representation (since both depend on the validity of the opposition) and displaces the poem's epistemological problematic altogether.

The ambivalence about representation in "Aspecta Medusa," it would seem then, goes beyond an awareness of the potential deceptiveness of images, of their potential disjunction from reality or truth. The latter awareness, despite the Platonic skepticism it casts on Rossetti's activity as an artist, is fundamentally affirmative, since it presumes an accessible reality or truth against which images could reliably be measured, and against which illusions could reliably be discredited. The epistemological insight introduced into "Aspecta Medusa" by the Medusa image is that the dangerous truths which representations represent, sublimate, and protect against are always already in one or another way represented. That is to say, they are contained within one or another form of representation, for instance in a poem or painting, rather than being something external and prior to representation. This insight runs counter to Rossetti's statements that explicitly locate the dangerous object or truth outside of representation, for instance his letter to Matthews, which refers to "the severed head of an *actual* person" (my emphasis), the potential horror of which the idealizing painting would mitigate against. Rossetti's formulation implies that the person and the head "actually" precede their representation by the painting. But of course no actual person and no actual severed head exist prior to Rossetti's painting of them. So it is not the case that the painting protects the viewer against the horror of an external threat, even though such a model of representation is precisely what the letter to Matthews and the second stanza of "Aspecta Medusa" construct. Rather, the horror is an internal aspect of the painting itself, as is its mitigation. This is the case in the poem as well. Just as there exists no severed head prior to its representation in Rossetti's painting, there is no "forbidden thing itself" prior to its figuration in the poem as the forbidden thing, as the thing's shadow upon life, as Medusa's head, or as the head's reflection in the fountain. Insofar, then, as both the poem and the painting are thematically about a danger and the representation of that danger, the image of Medusa's head (something which is by definition impossible outside of its own representation) implies that the danger in question inheres in the representation itself, not in an object or insight that precedes its representation and that impinges on the artist, reader, and viewer from the outside. And as something that is always necessarily an image, which is to say literally or figuratively a reflection in Perseus's mirror or in a pool of water, Medusa's head also suggests— consistent with Rossetti's statements in the letter to Matthews and in the poem's second stanza—that the containment of the given danger inheres in representation as well. Thus Rossetti supplements the epistemological problematic he ostensibly constructs (an external threat is represented by art in a way that protects, affirms, and possibly also deceives the artist, viewer, or reader) with a second problematic, one wherein the threat and its mitigation are both aspects of representation itself.

The emphasis of the second problematic on an internal aspect of representation, rather than on the external object of representation, should not be an occasion to simplify Rossetti's poetics into clichés and received ideas about "autonomy of art," "formalism," or the categorical separation of art from reality or life.[14] As the figure of the water mirror makes clear, Rossetti depicts art (and specifically his own art) as a mimesis, albeit one that does not aim accurately to reflect reality as much as to idealize and transfigure it (this is stated explicitly in the letter to Matthews). The water mirror is thus a figure for the affirmative and sublimating power of art, and is also indicative of an external reality that art would reflect and idealize. Supplementing this image is the image of Medusa's head, which specifies that what art reflects is always already in one or another way a reflection. As such a reflection, Medusa's head is not only a figure for the thing that art represents but also, like the water mirror, a figure for representation. In the latter capacity, it is like the figure of the shadow: a means for Rossetti to suggest that despite its protective function, representation is not without its own danger; this latter danger does not lie outside of representation, for instance in the gruesome reality of a severed head, but lies within it, just as according to the poem, saving and killing are both simultaneous properties of the one Medusa's head.

THE MEDUSA EFFECT

The tripartite structure I trace in my reading of "Aspecta Medusa" is what this book calls the Medusa effect. The first part of the structure posits a subject's visual confrontation with a dangerous object. This object is the means by which the subject attains some kind of terrifying insight, an insight into its own mortality, for example, or into the nature of its own sexuality or morality or existence or epistemological authority. This insight threatens in one or another way to destabilize or even to destroy the subject. The second part of the structure is the interposition by the subject of a protective representation of the object, for instance an idealizing painting, or a literal or figurative reflection of the object in water. By means of this representation, the dangerous object would be mirrored safely, the threat of the insight would in one or another way be mitigated, and the imperiled subject would be protected and ultimately revived, much as Perseus in the Medusa myth effectively protects himself by creating a reflection of Medusa's head in his polished shield. Rossetti's poem depicts and also performs both the first and second part of the structure in the allegorical image of Perseus mirroring the decapitated Medusa's head for Andromeda in a pool of water.

The third and final part of the structure is a second insight, an insight that takes place *in* the protective representation, rather than prior to it. Like the first insight, it is the recognition of a certain danger. But the danger it recognizes is of a different kind than the first. It is not a terrifying external object that exists outside of the representation. Instead, it is a danger that inheres within the representation and that pertains to the representation itself, for instance the threat that the representation is in one or another way illusory, deceptive, or unstable. "Aspecta Medusa" implies this kind of danger, for example, in its use of the word *shadow* as a figure for the oblique representations it both prescribes and performs. In this choice of metaphor, the poem calls the reliability of representations (including presumably the representations it itself performs) into question, even while it ostensibly tells its reader that he or she should limit himself or herself to seeing and showing only representations, not the "forbidden thing" itself.

This structure, then, is what I call the Medusa effect: an external threat is mitigated by means of its representation, which in turn prompts in the representation a critical insight into its own nature. It suggests that while the act of representing a dangerous object or insight may protect a subject from the threat of that object or insight, it is not without inherent dangers of its own.

This book finds versions of the Medusa effect in a series of mid- and late-nineteenth-century European writings on aesthetics and in Freud's essays on infantile sexuality and sexual theories. The specific examples I discuss are Freud's writings on the male castration complex, including his 1922 essay fragment on Medusa's head; Nietzsche's *Birth of Tragedy* (1872); Walter Pater's essay "Leonardo da Vinci" (1869); Algernon Charles Swinburne's essay "Notes on Designs of the Old Masters at Florence" (1868); and George Eliot's gothic novella *The Lifted Veil* (1859).[15] In each case, the author, narrator, or protagonist is confronted with some kind of horrifying recognition: in Freud's texts about male infantile sexual development, for instance, the little boy recognizes castration's "reality" when he first sees the genitals of a girl or woman; in *The Birth of Tragedy*, the Greeks are confronted with the appearance of terrifying Dionysian festivals and revels, and thereby catch a glimpse into what Nietzsche calls the Dionysian abyss; Swinburne and Pater write about being powerfully fascinated with the frightening existential insights they say are revealed to them in works of visual art by Michelangelo and Leonardo; and in *The Lifted Veil*, George Eliot's anxious protagonist gains insight by means of his telepathic powers into his own and other people's egotism and sense of isolation from one another, while Eliot concurrently has an unsettling recognition via her story that an awareness of others' feelings and thoughts (such as works of literary realism would make possible) does not reliably prompt sympathy and compassion in the reader or viewer.

In each case as well, the author or character responds to this recognition by representing it in a way that would somehow mitigate the threat it poses to himself or herself: in Freud's essays, this protective representation takes the form of what Freud calls symbols and fetishes, figures which indirectly testify to the repressed trauma of the original castration complex in ways that are ambiguous but ultimately reassuring; in *The Birth of Tragedy*, it is the Apollonian artwork and the Apollonian *Schein* (illusion or appearance) which interposes itself between the Greeks and the Dionysian, and by which the frightful Dionysian essence is both contained and also safely intimated; in Swinburne's and Pater's essays, it is the exposition by the critic of the artworks under discussion which would protect against the threat those works pose to the viewer; and in *The Lifted Veil*, Eliot introduces a *Doppelgänger* of her protagonist into her story, a female scapegoat figure onto which she then projects all the misanthropy and antipathy of which she would purge both the protagonist and the narrative.

Thirdly and finally, each example includes a moment of self-reflection, a moment of critical reflection on the act of representation that it performs or describes. As already shown in my reading of Rossetti's poem, this reflection on the representation itself significantly complicates the initial two-part model, the model wherein a threatening insight prompted by an external object is subsequently mitigated by means of its representation. Not only does it complicate this model, however, but it also goes on to destabilize (or at least potentially destabilize) the larger project of each text or writer in question, since each of those projects depends in one or another way on an act of representation, whether explicitly or implicitly. This destabilization of the larger project is compactly exemplified in Rossetti's poem. As I suggest in my reading, the poem is structured by a Platonic scheme that fundamentally distinguishes between the "thing itself" and its representations. Its moral, the ostensibly anti-Platonic lesson that one should restrict oneself to looking at oblique reflections and shadows of the thing itself and not look directly at the thing, depends on the stability of the distinction between thing and representation. In accordance with his own prescription, Rossetti offers this moral not in literal form, but in the form of a series of allegorical images, which is to say a series of representations. Among other ways, he figuratively represents it in the image of the forbidden thing's shadow and in the image of Medusa's head reflected in water. The shadow is a figure for representation, while Medusa's head is a figure for what representation represents. Both of these images, even as they serve to illustrate Rossetti's point, also run counter to the logic of the poem's argument: counter to the anti-Platonic argument, in the case of the shadow, and counter to the Platonic scheme that underlies that argument, in the case of Medusa's head. The image of the shadow, for its part, has negative implications for the anti-Platonic argument insofar as it suggests a form of illusion or copy that is categorically devalued vis-à-vis the thing itself. As such, it opens up the possibility of reading a Platonic counterargument into the poem, one that would be opposed to Rossetti's manifest message. Yet at the same time, the shadow has positive implications for Rossetti's underlying Platonic scheme because it implies the existence of a thing of which it is the mere image, and thereby affirms the poem's fundamental opposition between thing and image. As a figure for the thing, meanwhile, Medusa's head has an unequivocally destabilizing effect on Rossetti's Platonism. Insofar as it represents a thing that by definition can only ever take the form of images (reflections and shadows), it undermines the fundamental opposition between thing and image on which Rossetti's lesson—regardless of whether one ultimately reads it as anti-Platonic or Platonic—is based.

My reading of Rossetti's poem attempts to show two things: one, that Rossetti critically reflects by means of his choice of metaphors on the representations his poem describes and performs, and two, that by means of this self-reflection, the poem acknowledges certain destabilizing consequences (and also empowering consequences) for its own ostensible argument. This latter acknowledgment is not stated explicitly, and it is not necessarily something that Rossetti can be said consciously to intend. However, it demonstrably does take place in the text, and one could say, speaking in a psychoanalytic idiom, that it is an unconscious recognition (the unconscious manifesting itself here in the form of the literary text).

In discussing writings by Freud, Nietzsche, Swinburne, Pater, and George Eliot, this book proposes that each text or set of texts similarly reflects in one or another way on the representations it performs and describes, representations that are originally prompted as a defense against a perceived external threat. It further proposes that in each case, this reflection on representation culminates in a moment of self-recognition, a recognition about the project and kind of project in which it is engaged. In themselves, these projects are very different from one another: Freud posits the theory of a universal and primal castration complex, and then attempts to construct a far-reaching hermeneutic system by means of which he could reliably link a vast and diverse series of psychiatric symptoms and cultural symbols "back" to this complex; Nietzsche posits a primal Dionysian essence that precedes and ultimately exceeds any of its formal representations; Pater and Swinburne both identify the specific dangers they find in Leonardo's and Michelangelo's art, and then attempt rhetorically to mitigate this danger by means of their expositions of selected works; and Eliot attempts to formalize a literary ethics that would respect and acknowledge the otherness of other people. Because each of these projects necessarily depends in some way on representation and acts of representation—for instance, psychoanalytic symbols, Freud's interpretation of those symbols, Apollonian artworks that mirror or veil the Dionysian, Nietzsche's own verbal accounts of the Dionysian, Pater's and Swinburne's descriptions of the artworks they discuss, Eliot's figures for the consciousnesses of other people, and so on—the reflection on representation is implicitly a reflection on the nature of the project as a whole, for example on its internal coherence or stability. This is the case whether the given project is aesthetic, ethical, mimetic, hermeneutic, expository, analytical, taxonomic, or some combination thereof.

This book would demonstrate that the texts by Nietzsche, Pater, Swinburne, and Eliot on aesthetic topics reflect no less critically on the representations they describe and perform than do Freud's writings. Victorian writings on aesthetics and Victorian literature more generally have long been identified by their commentators with a preoccupation with the themes of knowledge and epistemology.[16] More specifically, they have been identified with a preoccupation with dangerous forms of knowledge and with insights that are somehow threatening, whether sexually, aesthetically, ethically, racially, socially, economically, or politically.[17] The texts and authors I discuss in the book are very much situated within this tradition, as Rossetti's injunction "Let not thine eyes know / Any forbidden thing itself" compactly suggests. Eliot announces an interest in the themes of knowledge and initiation by means of her title, *The Lifted Veil*, and her story bears out this interest in the central motif of gaining access to the consciousness of another person. Nietzsche defines the Dionysian as a traumatic recognition about human nature, including one's own nature, and about the nature of existence in general. And Swinburne and Pater claim to be drawn to Leonardo's and Michelangelo's artworks because of the existential and tragic insights those works provide, insight that are thematically akin to what Nietzsche calls the Dionysian. In the case of each of these examples, the knowledge in question poses an explicit danger. In *The Birth of Tragedy*, the revelation of Dionysian truths threatens to overwhelm and annihilate the Apollonian Greeks. Pater and Swinburne both claim to feel dangerously disoriented and disconcerted by the works they look at, and Swinburne also finds a distinctly sexual threat in Michelangelo's female portraits. In *The Lifted Veil*, the protagonist's clairvoyance reveals a moral threat: the shallowness, antipathy, misanthropy, and narcissism in the consciousnesses of the people around him, in his own consciousness, and in the consciousnesses of the reader and Eliot herself.

The texts I discuss in this study thus each reproduce commonplace Victorian motifs of traumatic initiations and dangerous knowledge. But as my reading of "Aspecta Medusa" anticipates, I argue that they also reveal a specific preoccupation with their own representations of those initiations and that knowledge. My claim is that much like Rossetti's poem, each of my other examples of what I call the Medusa effect reflects implicitly on the stability and reliability of its own representations, and considers in particular their destabilizing and empowering epistemological effects.

This book proposes that the image of Medusa is a recurring and exemplary means by which the texts I examine reflect on representation itself (on its purposes, for instance, or its objects, or its inherent dangers). As I point out earlier in this introduction, the connection between Medusa and representation would seem more or less to suggest itself, most obviously because Medusa is by definition something that only ever appears—or that can only ever be seen—in the form of one or another representation, a point to which Caravaggio's Medusa painting explicitly calls attention (Figure 3). In the myth, the reflection of the head is a central motif. In the classical literary accounts of Medusa's story, for instance, including those by Ovid and Apollodorus cited earlier, and also those by Pherecydes, Lucan, Lucian, and Nonnos, Perseus reflects the head in a polished shield or mirror before decapitating it.[18] In addition, the subsequent episode of the victorious Perseus mirroring the decapitated head in a body of water, a kind of reenactment alluding to the first reflection, frequently appears in classical visual art, specifically in Greek vases, Roman wall paintings, and grave reliefs.[19] Rossetti derives his version of the reflection episode from a Pompeian fresco. And two of his Pre-Raphaelite contemporaries take up the episode as well: Edward Burne-Jones in *The Baleful Head* (1887), one in a series of paintings that collectively make up his Perseus cycle, and William Morris in "The Doom of King Acrisius" (1868), a long narrative poem devoted to the Perseus myth.[20] The central place the myth gives to the motif of reflection thus underscores the myth's potential relevance to the topic of representation as such.

If the representation of dangerous knowledge and insights is indeed a particular theme in Victorian literature, it follows that the reflection of Medusa's head in a shield or in water would serve as a privileged figure for such representation. Medusa's head is canonically not only a figure of horror, but more specifically is a figure for horrifying or dangerous knowledge, as suggested by the specification that it is something that should not be *seen*.[21] In the texts I discuss in this book, each threatening insight is explicitly portrayed as a moment of seeing: Freud's little boy sees female genitals; the Greeks are said by Nietzsche to stare into the Dionysian abyss; Swinburne and Pater describe themselves looking at artworks; and Eliot's protagonist has clairvoyant visions of other people's thoughts and feelings. Rossetti specifies the connection between seeing, knowing, and danger in his injunction, "Let not thine eyes know / Any forbidden thing itself." So it is not surprising that seeing Medusa would serve these texts as an image for revelations that are figured as both dangerous and specifically visual, and that Medusa's reflection would in turn serve as an image for the protective representation of those revelations.

Medusa lends herself as a figure for dangerous insights not only because she poses a distinctly visual threat, however, but also because of her gender. In the texts discussed in this book, the traumatic visual initiation into knowledge is repeatedly depicted as a confrontation by an anxious male character or author with the face, mind, or body of a woman (Nietzsche's *Birth of Tragedy* is the one exception to this pattern). The terrifying recognition that is revealed—the recognition of the author's or character's mortality or castration, say, or the recognition of human antipathy, narcissism, sexuality, or evil—is in each case made intelligible through the figure of a dangerous woman: the castrated and castrating little girl, the castrated and castrating mother, and Medusa in Freud's writings; a set of Michelangelo's female portraits in Swinburne's essay; Leonardo's painting of Medusa's head in Pater's essay; and the protagonist's female *Doppelgänger* in *The Lifted Veil*. I comment on the significance of each of these figures in the individual chapters. For now, I am simply interested in establishing and accounting for the recurrence of a Medusa motif in the texts I discuss: the texts' shared equation of dangerous knowledge—its danger and also its intelligibility—with the image of a woman accounts for the choice of Medusa as one paradigmatic figure for such knowledge, as much as does their equation of dangerous knowledge with visual revelations.[22]

I call this book *The Medusa Effect* not only because Medusa is a recurring reference or allusion throughout, but also because the doubleness of the structure outlined above (a representation of danger protects against that danger, but also poses a danger itself) is like the characteristic doubleness of the mythological Medusa figure itself. In the canonical narrative and pictorial versions of the myth, Medusa regularly combines two opposed qualities, such as beauty and horror, beauty and death, or attractiveness and repulsiveness. Apollodorus, for example, describes her as both monstrous ("the Gorgons had heads twined about with the scales of dragons, and great tusks like swine's" [157]) and beautiful ("the Gorgon was fain to match herself with the goddess [Athena] even in beauty" [161]). William Morris evokes this tradition in "The Doom of King Acrisius" when he describes Medusa's head as "so beautiful and dread" (277).

One version of Medusa's doubleness that recurs frequently is her dual function as a source of danger and as a defense against danger: on one hand, she threatens to turn Perseus to stone, for example, and on the other hand, he is able to use the petrifying power of her decapitated head as a

weapon or shield against his enemies. This double aspect of threat and protection is a defining element of the Medusa figure as far back as the myth's
earliest articulations. In the *Odyssey*, for instance, Medusa provokes fear
in Odysseus during his descent into the Underworld, but in the *Iliad*, her
head appears twice as a protective talisman, once on Agamemnon's shield
and once on Athena's aegis.[23] In Euripides's *Ion*, Creusa recounts how Athena gave "Two drops of Gorgon's blood" to Erichthonius, of which "One
is poisonous, the other cures disease" (228).[24] Rossetti twice alludes to this
tradition in "Aspecta Medusa," first in the line "That death she lived by,"
and then in the phrase "It once should save as well as kill."

This book proposes that Victorian writings about dangerous revelations reproduce Medusa's canonical double quality of threat and protection, killing and saving, and poison and cure. On one level, they reproduce
these combinations of opposite elements as an explicit theme, as Rossetti
does in his poem, for instance. On another level, they also reproduce them
as a textual structure, the structure I call the Medusa effect. They represent
a given threat in the image of Medusa or a Medusa-like woman, and by
means of that representation defend against and ultimately overcome the
threat, much as Perseus overcomes Medusa by creating a reflection of her.
However, the representation that serves as their means of defense is also
revealed to be itself inherently dangerous. In this double quality, representation ultimately turns out to be much like the decapitated Medusa's head.
Perseus can manipulate the head as shield or weapon, but this is always
a hazardous operation because he runs the risk that it will turn against
him or that he will turn it back against himself, as he does for example in
an episode recounted in Ovid's *Metamorphoses* in which he inadvertently
petrifies one of his own men in a battle with the followers of Andromeda's
suitor Phineus.

My interest in this book is by means of close readings of exemplary
works to trace different versions of the structure I call the Medusa effect.
(I say exemplary because the works I discuss are each explicitly or implicitly figured as exemplary of a larger project, and are each also exemplary
of a shared epistemological problematic that characterizes both Victorian
aesthetics and Freud's writings.) In view of the book's title, it is important
to specify that my interest is not to follow the image of Medusa per se. All
but one of my examples make explicit reference to Medusa, and George
Eliot, the one exception, alludes to the Medusa myth in several places in
her novella. But none is primarily concerned with the Medusa figure or the
Medusa myth for its own sake; all use Medusa as an image with which to
illustrate or represent some other idea (castration, Dionysus, narcissism,
death, and so on). This is the case even for Freud and Rossetti, whose texts
are most explicitly about Medusa; I have already shown this in my reading of "Aspecta Medusa," and I demonstrate it as well in my reading of
Freud's essay "Medusa's Head" in chapter 1. Thus my own primary concern

is also not with the figure of Medusa. This book offers neither a thematic or chronological study of nineteenth-century or Victorian versions of the Medusa myth, nor a comprehensive survey of such versions.[25] My concern is rather with the textual structure and rhetorical effect to which I have assigned, for the specific reasons outlined in the previous paragraphs, the name Medusa effect. Just as my reading of "Aspecta Medusa" is intended to preview, condense, and exemplify my more elaborate readings of the other works discussed in this book, so those works in turn exemplify a general Victorian preoccupation with dangerous knowledge, with its figurative representation, and with the dangers inherent in the act of representation. This preoccupation is of course in no way limited to texts that refer or allude to Medusa. Nor do all Victorian texts in which a Medusa appears share this preoccupation. But the Medusa figure has already proven in my reading of "Aspecta Medusa" to be a useful mirror in which to make visible the epistemological problematic I trace and construct in this book.

I begin the book with a reading of Freud's essay "Medusa's Head" for two principal reasons. The first has to do with the nature of Freud's text. Like "Aspecta Medusa," "Medusa's Head" is manifestly about the Medusa myth, and thus will help to confirm the book's unifying premise that Medusa serves in the context of Victorian aesthetics and epistemology as a privileged figure by which texts reflect on epistemological and representational questions. (Like other commentators have done before me, I provisionally include Freud here in the category "Victorian," in my case not so much because some of his ideas and assumptions reflect the values of Victorian and Hapsburgian bourgeois society, but because his texts reproduce literary commonplaces that are distinctly Victorian, for instance the motifs of the Fatal Woman, the imperiled and potentially "feminized" male protagonist, and the traumatic initiation of this protagonist by means of the revelation of a woman's body.)

Moreover, the Freud texts I discuss provide an exceptionally compact example of my problematic, what I call the Medusa effect. In these texts, Freud recounts various versions of a narrative in each of which a little boy catches sight of female genitals, recognizes them as proof for the "reality" of the paternal castration threat, represses or disavows this recognition, and ultimately comes to find disguised representations of it in artworks, cultural artifacts, and dream symbols, for instance the mythological image of the petrifying Medusa's head. The representations of the boy's traumatic insight in the form of symbols are explicitly a means of veiling (but also of indirectly revealing) his horrifying awareness of the "truth" of castration, not unlike Perseus's allegorical reflection in Rossetti's poem of Medusa's head in the fountain, and not unlike what Nietzsche calls the Apollonian artwork. In Freud's expositions of the boy's castration complex, this representation then prompts a second representation, one that essentially reverses the first: Freud interprets the manifest symbol and replaces it with what he asserts is its latent meaning, the boy's original view of the female genitals, which for Freud is to say—via an interpretative sleight of hand—his original view of castration. So just as the boy represents the idea of castration by means of a symbol, so Freud in turn represents the symbol by means of its latent meaning, the idea of castration. And just as the boy's initial representation of castration and castration fear in the disguised form of symbols serves to mitigate a sexual threat, so Freud's successful interpretation would serve to mitigate any external or internal skepticism about psychoanalysis or about his authority as an interpreter.

My reading of Freud's texts would demonstrate, however, that Freud not only empowers himself through the interpretation he performs, but that he also finds himself subjected by means of this interpretation to what I am calling the Medusa effect. In his texts, the Medusa symbol, its alleged latent meaning, and the link Freud establishes between them become the occasion for an epistemological reflection on the tenuous nature of the interpretation itself. Freud's use of figurative language puts into question both the primacy of castration fear over the alleged castration symbol, and the hierarchy of latent meaning over manifest figure. Thus Freud ultimately confronts the recognition that his interpretation is merely an arbitrary, ungrounded, and bilateral set of tropological substitutions between what he calls a symbol and what he calls that symbol's meaning. He is forced to acknowledge that his own interpretation is an open-ended substitution of one set of arbitrary figures for another, rather than a unilateral movement from symbol to underlying meaning, and to consider the consequences of this recognition for psychoanalysis.

My second reason for beginning with Freud has to do with my own methodology in this book. Starting with the chronologically most recent text is not as counterintuitive as it might seem, given that my project is not to construct a genealogy or to tell a literary-historical narrative. Rather, it is to build a problematic that is epistemological, rhetorical, and psychoanalytic. The preceding pages will have explained the epistemological nature of the problematic: the texts I discuss in this book share a preoccupation with the themes of knowledge, initiation, and perception, and also with the question of how it is that they know what they do (briefly put, they know what they know by means of reflections and shadows of "forbidden things"). The problematic is rhetorical insofar as the texts' representations of their object (and of their own knowledge of that object) take the form of figures and tropes, and these figures in turn become the occasion for a critical (sometimes anxious, sometimes empowering) reflection by the texts on their own authority, specifically their epistemological authority (in the case of Eliot's *The Lifted Veil*, it is both its epistemological and its ethical authority that are at stake). And finally, my problematic is psychoanalytic in that I use Freudian concepts to talk about literary texts, especially those concepts that are important in "Medusa's Head" and in the Freud essays that sur-round it. One of these concepts is what Freud calls *fetishism*. According to Freud, a fetish is a totemic object that has both a terrifying and a reassur-ing meaning for the fetishist. Fetishism is by Freud's definition a structure in which the effects of danger and protection coincide and are simultane-ously, paradoxically maintained. This structure has obvious parallels with the canonical Medusa figure, described previously, and also with what I am calling the Medusa effect. All three function in this book as unifying threads that tie the different chapters and different readings together. The Medusa effect reproduces the paradoxical logic of Freudian fetishism, and manifests itself as a textual structure that variously characterizes each of the works under discussion, much as fetishism manifests itself as a structure in the fetishist's unconscious. And those works in turn reveal a fetishistic relation to their own recognition of the Medusa effect, which is to say that they acknowledge it on one level, and that they disavow and negate it on another, much as Freud's fetishist recognizes and also disavows his own potential castration.

Like the Medusa effect itself, this fetishistic relation to the Medusa effect (that is, to one's epistemological insights into the stability and insta-bility of one's conclusions) emerges in writings on art and aesthetics by Nietzsche, Swinburne, Pater, Rossetti, and Eliot, and it also emerges in Freud's own texts (including his texts about fetishism). Freud is by his own admission not exempt from the symptoms he describes and interprets, and one general aim of this book is to demonstrate that psychoanalytic concepts like fetishism (or symbolization, condensation, displacement, projection, the unconscious, and so on) are useful not only for reading works of litera-ture but also for reading psychoanalytic texts, in particular the very texts in which Freud introduces and defines those concepts.

A more specific aim of this book in using Freudian concepts like fetish-ism to talk about literary and psychoanalytic texts is to support the book's unifying argument: to show that, figuratively speaking, there is more than one Medusa haunting each of the texts I write about. In the case of Freud's essays on male castration fear, for example, there are the female genitals and the boy's "recognition" of those genitals as castrated, which are respectively represented as Medusa's head and the act of seeing Medusa's head. And then there is Freud's recognition of the fundamental groundlessness of his own interpretative system, which is also figured as his seeing Medusa's head. In Freud's text, Medusa alternately functions as a figure for both recognitions. The first Medusa figure designates the recognition of a traumatic sexual threat and also functions to mitigate that threat by ultimately transforming it into an affirmation. The second Medusa figure designates the recogni-tion of an epistemological threat that confronts Freud in his interpretation of the first Medusa. It is by means of the first Medusa's interpretation as a sexual threat that this second Medusa becomes intelligible—legible, real-ly—to Freud and the reader. The chapter which follows would demonstrate that the first Medusa and its virtuoso interpretation are then also the means by which Freud would disavow the threat that the second Medusa poses to himself and to psychoanalysis, the fetish by which he would ward off the Medusa effect.

CHAPTER ONE

Apotropaic Reading

Freud's *Medusenhaupt*

On horror's head horrors accumulate.
—*Othello* (III,iii)

MEDUSA'S HEAD AND THE CASTRATION COMPLEX

Finally, the curiosity of the child engaged our interest . . .
—"The Infantile Genital Organization"

Freud's brief notes about Medusa's head are dated May 14, 1922. According to the editors of the *Internationale Zeitschrift für Psychoanalyse und Imago*, who posthumously published the manuscript in 1940 under the title "Das Medusenhaupt" ("Medusa's Head"), Freud's text is a companion piece to Sandor Ferenczi's note on the same topic, published in 1923 as "Zur Symbolik des Medusenhauptes" ("On the Symbolism of Medusa's Head"). Freud's editors propose that unlike Ferenczi's completed text, Freud's manuscript "appears to be a sketch for a more extensive work" (*Standard Edition*, 18:273). Just as the decapitated Medusa's head evokes the body from which it was cut,[1] they suggest, so Freud's manuscript evokes "a more extensive" body of work. Unpublished and fragmentary, it is itself a kind of Medusa's head, separated from and evoking an absent, imagined text. It is a part detached from a whole whose existence Freud's editors can only posit through an interpretation of the part. This chapter reflects on the synecdochical evocativeness of Medusa's head and of Freud's text about it, an evocativeness to which both the text's editorial commentary and its title allude. Although it is ostensibly a minor piece in Freud's oeuvre, "Medusa's Head" implies a much larger body of Freud's work. It not only implies the "more extensive work" about Medusa that was never written, but the more extensive work that was: Freud's published writings on such fundamental topics as the castration complex, the Oedipus complex, symbolism and symbolic interpretation, displacement and condensation, and fetishism. In reflecting on the theme of Medusa's head, Freud also reflects on the project of psychoanalysis more generally.

Freud opens "Medusa's Head" by noting, "We have not often attempted to interpret individual mythological themes, but an interpretation suggests itself easily in the case of the horrifying decapitated Medusa's head" (18:273). He interprets the Medusa myth as a symbolic representation of a traumatic and repressed childhood experience, the little boy's first look at female genitals that confirms to the boy the terrifying possibility of his own castration and thus inaugurates his castration complex:

> To decapitate = to castrate. The terror of Medusa is thus a terror of castration that is linked to the sight of something. Numerous analyses have made us familiar with the occasion for this: it occurs when a boy, who has hitherto been unwilling to believe the threat of castration, catches sight of the female genitals, probably those of an adult, surrounded by hair. . . . (18:273)

The two opening claims of this paragraph might give the reader reason to pause, as they would seem to contradict one another. To decapitate, Freud writes in the first sentence, equals to castrate.[2] According to this equation, the decapitated Medusa's head symbolizes a cut-off penis. But in the next sentence, Freud puts forth a different equivalence: "the terror of Medusa is thus a terror of castration that is linked to the sight of something." The contradiction is in the word *thus*, since the second equivalence does not follow from the first. In the second sentence, the viewer's terror at seeing Medusa symbolizes the boy's castration fear that is prompted by his sight of female genitals. So here Freud equates Medusa's head with the female genitals, not with a penis. In the childhood scenario to which the Medusa myth is said to refer, the female genitals are seen by the boy as the place from which a penis has been cut off (this is why they terrify him). So according to the line of interpretation offered in the first sentence, Medusa symbolizes a penis, while according to the line of interpretation offered in the second, she symbolizes the absence of a penis.

In Freud's account of the little boy's sexual development, the first sight of female genitals is said to be terrifying because it inaugurates the boy's fear of being castrated. According to the numerous versions of this scenario recounted in Freud's essays on infantile sexuality, the boy has earlier been confronted by his parents or by a parental substitute with a threat that his penis may be cut off but has refused to believe in such a possibility up until the moment he first sees female genitals. When he then sees the female genitals, he understands the girl's or woman's lack of a penis to be due to a castration, thereby also confirming to himself that such a castration could in fact happen to him as well. The perception thus activates his castration complex. The revelation of castration's "reality" is terrifying to the boy because by this point in his sexual maturation, what Freud calls the phallic phase, he has developed a powerful, narcissistic investment in his own penis. The boy's attachment to his penis is taken by Freud to be too self-evident to warrant any explanation; no other evidence appears to be necessary besides the statement that it is provided to the boy by nature (21:153). Freud provides two different narratives to explain the boy's developmental passage from the phallic stage to the castration complex, narratives in which the sight of female genitals plays an important role.

According to the first of these narratives, the boy's investment in his penis manifests itself in sexual investigations: "He wants to see [his penis] in other people as well, so as to compare it with his own" (19:143). At this stage of his development, the boy attributes a penis to all human beings; his investment in his own penis is reflected in his inability to imagine anyone without this "essential component" (19:142, 9:215–16). According to Freud, he simply overlooks the anatomical distinction between the sexes. When confronted with the sight of female genitals (sometimes those of a sister or playmate, sometimes those of an adult), the boy may deny the absence of a penis, believe that he sees a penis all the same, or gloss over the discrepancy between what he sees and what he imagines by the idea that the girl's or woman's penis is still small and will grow (19:143–44, 9:216). Eventually, however, the boy is confronted by a parent or another adult authority figure with an actual or imagined threat that his penis will be cut off. This threat is usually a response to the masturbation that accompanies his anatomical inquiries during the phallic stage. It recalls to the boy his earlier perception of female genitals and he unconsciously constructs the theory that the castration with which he has been threatened has actually been carried out on the girl or woman whose genitals he has seen: "The lack of a penis is regarded as a result of castration, and so now the child is faced with the task of coming to terms with castration in relation to himself" (19:144). For the boy, the parental threat retroactively activates the heretofore insignificant memory of having seen female genitals. The memory in turn confirms the possibility that the castration threat may actually be carried out. The boy attributes the anatomical difference between himself and the girl or woman to the theory that her penis has been cut off and concludes that this could potentially happen to him as well. When he draws this conclusion, he enters the castration complex.[3]

Freud's alternate narrative of this process reverses the order of the boy's discovering the anatomical sex distinction and the parental castration threat. In the second version, the boy is first confronted with a warning that his penis will be cut off, usually in response to his masturbation, but does not believe the threat or obey it. This is because he has hitherto been given no evidence that would compel him to accept the loss of his penis as a "real" possibility. It is not until his first sight of female genitals, which in this version comes after the castration threat has been uttered, that the threat is believed and that the castration complex takes effect:

> The observation which finally breaks down [the boy's] unbelief [in castration's "reality"] is the sight of the female genitals. Sooner or later the child, who is so proud of his possession of a penis, has a view of the genital region of a little girl, and cannot help being convinced of the absence of a penis in a creature who is so like himself. With this, the loss of his own penis becomes imaginable, and the threat of castration takes its deferred effect. (19:175–76)[4]

The loss of his own penis becomes imaginable to the boy through the image of the female genitals he sees. This is because he sees the girl ("a creature who is so like himself") as an image of himself (that is to say, as an image of what he could become) and because he sees her genitals as a deficient version of his own. Freud seems to find it no more necessary to provide an explanation for the boy's response to seeing the girl's genitals than he does in positing the boy's inherent attachment to his penis; the boy "cannot help being convinced" that the girl used to have a penis much like his own and that it has been taken away from her. This version of the boy's initiation into the castration complex, like the former one, requires two events for the complex to be activated: the parental castration threat and the boy's sight of female genitals.[5] Both versions relate these consecutive events in a structure of deferred action; in each story, the second event retroactively gives a new, threatening significance to the temporally prior event, which had hitherto been considered harmless or meaningless.[6] Freud goes on to say in the essay "The Dissolution of the Oedipus Complex" that the boy's castration complex has several potential consequences: it may lead the boy into perversion (homosexuality or fetishism) or it may inaugurate the repression of the boy's oedipal desire for his mother. In response to the confirmed castration threat, Freud theorizes, the boy forms a super-ego, enters the latency period, and may eventually go on to occupy a place in normal adult heterosexual relations.

In "Medusa's Head," Freud seeks to establish a figurative relation between the castration complex and the Greek myth. He interprets the motif of the viewer's being turned to stone by looking at Medusa's head as a symbolic reenactment of the castration complex's primal scene, the boy's look at female genitals. Medusa's head symbolizes the female genitals as they are seen by the boy subsequent to the castration threat, while the petrified viewer symbolizes the terrified boy: "The terror of Medusa is thus a terror of castration that is linked to the [boy's] sight of . . . the female genitals"

(18:273).[7] Taken as a whole, the Medusa myth serves for Freud as proof of an original childhood trauma and of its repression: "Legends and myths testify to the upheaval in the child's emotional life and to the horror which is linked with the castration complex—a complex which is subsequently remembered by consciousness with corresponding reluctance" (9:217).

Yet what makes Freud's essay such a complex and ambiguous text is that while on one hand Freud interprets Medusa's head as an image of "castrated" female genitals, on the other hand he also proposes an entirely opposite interpretation, namely that the head is a penis symbol. He makes the latter interpretation in the formula "To decapitate = to castrate," an equation I referred to earlier, and in his claim that the snakes on Medusa's head are symbolic substitutes for the penis:

> The hair upon Medusa's head is frequently represented in works of art in the form of snakes, and these once again are derived from the castration complex. It is a remarkable fact that, however frightening they may be in themselves, they nevertheless serve actually as a mitigation of the horror, for they replace the penis, the absence of which is the cause of the horror. This is a confirmation of the technical rule according to which a multiplication of penis symbols signifies castration. (18:273)

This paragraph elaborates both aspects of Freud's double interpretation. On one hand, the conceit of the snaky hair is "derived from the castration complex" insofar as it is a visual reminder of the female genitals seen by the boy, which in "Medusa's Head" are described as "probably those of an adult, surrounded by hair" (in most other essays that narrate this scenario, they are said to be those of a little girl). The interpretation of the snakes as pubic hair is consistent with the interpretation of Medusa as an image of a woman's genitals. On the other hand, the snakes are said symbolically to "replace the penis," a claim that is consistent with the alternate interpretation of Medusa as an image of a penis. Freud juxtaposes not only these two contrasting interpretations of the snakes, but also two contrasting effects the snakes produce on the spectator. On one hand, they are "frightening . . . in themselves" because they refer back to the boy's traumatic sight of the woman's genitals and of the surrounding pubic hair. They are a threatening visual reminder of the woman's lack of a penis, a lack the boy perceives as a threat to his own penis. On the other hand, the snakes have a reassuring effect since they also represent (and thus symbolically restore) the penis "the absence of which is the cause of the horror." As a symbolic replacement of the penis, Medusa's snaky hair mitigates the horror of potential castration. By replacing the woman's absent penis, it effectively also reinforces the boy's own (potentially absent) penis, due to the boy's unconscious identification of his genitals with the woman's genitals he looks at. Through the turn from interpreting the snakes as pubic hair to interpreting them as penis symbols,

Freud emphasizes the reassuring aspect of Medusa, whose phallic snakes counteract the horror of the original revelation of castration's "reality." On the other hand, however, the snakes also remain a figure for that very horror. In an abrupt turn from mitigation back to horror, Freud concludes the paragraph with the "technical rule" according to which a multiplication of penis symbols "signifies castration."[8]

Freud elaborates his double interpretation of Medusa and of Medusa's effects on the viewer in the essay's next paragraph, which addresses the motif of the spectator being turned to stone by his look at Medusa. Like the snakes, the effect of being petrified by looking at Medusa's head is said to have two contradictory meanings. Freud first interprets it as symbolizing the little boy's terror at seeing the female genitals and then interprets it as a symbolic erection:

> The sight of Medusa's head makes the spectator stiff with terror, turns him to stone. Observe that we have here once again the same origin from the castration complex and the same transformation of affect! For becoming stiff means an erection. Thus in the original situation it offers consolation to the spectator: he is still in possession of a penis, and the stiffening reassures him of the fact. (18:273)

On one hand, petrification is symbolically "a terror of castration that is linked to the sight of something," while on the other hand it designates a reassurance insofar as the petrified spectator figuratively becomes the penis the little boy is so anxious about losing. As in the paragraph about the snakes, Freud's interpretation oscillates between castration imagery and penis imagery, and between Medusa's terrifying effects and consolatory effects. Although Freud does not point this out, the doubleness of the interpretation is consistent with the canonical double aspect of the Medusa figure, which traditionally combines opposite associations like beauty and horror, attractiveness and repulsiveness, and danger and protection, as for example in the line "It once should save as well as kill" from Rossetti's poem "Aspecta Medusa."

Freud's essay is remarkable for the sketchiness and abrupt reversals of its opening moves, as well as for the density of its interpretations. Yet at the same time, the diverse, contradictory strands of Freud's double interpretation all uniformly and invariably lead back to one single point of origin: the castration complex's primal scene. In "Medusa's Head," the scene is primal in several senses: it is the origin of the boy's castration complex and it is also the origin—as well as the referent—of the Medusa myth. Each detail in the myth, whether horrifying or reassuring or both, ultimately comes out of and refers back to this "original situation." The boy's look at female genitals, Freud claims, is the original prototype of the look at Medusa's head. Similarly, the snakes on the head "are derived from the castration complex," while the motif of petrification has "once again the same origin from the castration complex." The primal scene is the *Ursache* of the spectator's horror in the myth, Freud writes, meaning it is the cause of the horror but also the primal thing (*Ur-sache*) for which the myth symbolically substitutes. Like Pegasus and his brother Chrysaor springing from the neck of Medusa at the moment of her decapitation, the various details in the Medusa myth are all said to have sprung from an origin (*Ursprung*) in the primal scene. And in the end, Freud's interpretations invariably return them to their beginning in the castration complex.[9] In their uniform and unilateral movement out of and back to the castration complex, the myth's individual details are like the dense multiplication of penis symbols on Medusa's head that according to Freud's "technical rule" at bottom "signifies castration."[10]

MEDUSA AS SYMBOL

Freud refers to Medusa's head as a "symbol of horror" (18:273). In *The Language of Psychoanalysis*, Jean Laplanche and J. B. Pontalis explain that in its broadest use in psychoanalysis, the word *symbol* designates a "mode of indirect and figurative representation of an unconscious idea, conflict, or wish" (442). Etymologically, it derives from the Greek *symbolon*, a means of identification consisting of two halves of a broken token that have been separated and must be fitted back together. According to Laplanche and Pontalis, "the notion that it is the *link* that creates the meaning is thus already present in the original conception" (445). In "Medusa's Head," Freud aims to reestablish the lost link between the Medusa myth and the castration complex, thereby closing the hermeneutic circle and revealing the myth's hidden meaning. Like Perseus bringing the decapitated head from the edge of the world back to its origins in Greece, he wants to bring the myth back to its original other half, to reattach the two separated halves, as one might reattach a severed head to the body from which it was cut. He would do this by establishing the link between the Medusa myth and the castration complex as a metaphorical relationship, a correspondence based on a visible analogy.

Writing in *The Interpretation of Dreams* about dream interpretation as "an artistic activity dependent on the possession of peculiar gifts," Freud notes, "Aristotle remarked in this connection that the best interpreter of dreams was the man who could best grasp similarities; for dream-pictures, like pictures on water, are pulled out of shape by movement, and the most successful interpreter is the man who can detect the truth from the misshapen picture" (4:97n2). Insofar as the successful interpretation of dreams depends on the gift of being able to perceive similarities between outwardly dissimilar things, Freud's interpreter is like the successful user of metaphor as Aristotle defines him in his writings on rhetoric. In the *Poetics*, Aristotle maintains that "the successful use of metaphor entails the perception of similarities" (1459a 57).[11] And in the *Rhetoric*, he adds the criterion that the best use of metaphor derives from the perception of similarities that are not immediately obvious: "Metaphors must be drawn . . . from things that are related to the original thing, but yet not obviously so related—just as in philosophy also an acute mind will perceive resemblances even in things far apart" (1412a 191). Aristotle's description of the successful rhetorician and the acute philosopher also applies to Freud's dream interpreter, who is able to "grasp similarities" between things that are "far apart," for instance between the misshapen dream-pictures and their meanings. Through the allusion to Aristotle's theory of metaphor, Freud suggests that dream-pictures are rhetorically a kind of metaphor in that, like metaphors, they are related to their figural meanings via a visible but unobvious similarity, what rhetoricians call the metaphor's proper meaning (the quality shared by the metaphor and the entity or idea for which it substitutes).[12] This is why Freud's dream interpreter, in order to succeed, must proceed in the manner of Aristotle's rhetorician.[13]

In "Medusa's Head," the symbol of Medusa's head, as Freud interprets it, has a similar metaphorical structure as the dream-picture described in *The Interpretation of Dreams*. Like the dream-picture, it corresponds to its figural meaning (which in its case is the female genitals as seen by the boy) via some form of similarity. This similarity is visible to Freud, the discerning interpreter, whose exposition would in turn render it visible for the reader:

> The terror of Medusa is thus a terror of castration that is linked to *the sight of something*. . . . It occurs when a boy who has hitherto been unwilling to believe the threat of castration, catches *sight of the female genitals*. . . . *The sight of Medusa's head* makes the spectator stiff with terror, turns him to stone. (18:273, my emphases)

The telling repetition of the phrase "the sight of" suggests that Freud's interpretation, like that of the dream interpreter, is based on perceptions. As the interpretation moves from "the sight of something" to the "sight of the female genitals" and then to the corresponding "sight of Medusa's head," its wording implies that Freud actually sees the female genitals and Medusa's head, and that he also sees their similarity (they are both a terrifying sight). It is on the basis of this seeing and of this similarity that his interpretation is able to substitute the figural meaning for the symbol, much as Aristotle's rhetorician is able on the basis of his perceptions to substitute metaphors for the entities or ideas they represent. "*Observe* that we have here once again the same origin from the castration complex," Freud notes in the paragraph about Medusa's petrifying effect, suggesting that he is able visually to compare the viewer's petrification and the boy's shock at seeing female genitals and thus to identify the former as a symbol for the latter (18:273, my emphasis).[14] His diction and formulations imply that it is as much he himself as the little boy in the primal scene or the viewer in the myth who catches sight of "something," of the female genitals and of Medusa's head.[15]

Like the success of Aristotle's rhetorician, then, Freud's success as an interpreter fundamentally depends on his perception, his ability to see the two entities and their similarity. This ability would allow him to substitute Medusa's head as a symbol for the female genitals as perceived by the boy, and in turn to reveal those genitals as the figural meaning of the symbol Medusa's head. Freud indicates the obviousness of the correspondence between the two entities in his remark that an interpretation of the Medusa myth "suggests itself easily" (clearly by Aristotle's standards, the Medusa myth is not the best kind of metaphor for castration fear, since the similarity between the two terms is too self-evident). The obviousness of the correspondences Freud sees between Medusa's head and the "castrated" female genitals, and between the look at Medusa's head and the boy's look at female genitals, authorizes the substitution of each of those four terms for its corresponding counterpart, and moreover authorizes Freud's theory of a castration fear that would underlie all four terms. This is because the look at Medusa's head is not only a symbol for the look at female genitals, and the look at female genitals is not only the figural meaning of the look at Medusa's head. Both looks in turn are also figures for (and thus evidence for) what Freud calls "a terror of castration." Similarly, Medusa's head is not only a symbol of the female genitals as seen by the boy, and those genitals are not only the figural meaning of Medusa's head. Both in turn are figures for castration (not in the sense of an actual event, but in the sense of an idea in the boy's unconscious). Freud implies that he is able to posit the existence of a castration complex because he is able to see it in Medusa's head, in the female genitals, in the look at Medusa's head, in the boy's look at female genitals, and in the correspondences between them. Thus perception not only authorizes the specific interpretation Freud offers here of an "individual mythological theme" but also Freud's more general positing the hidden truth of a castration complex. If castration fear is indeed, as Freud says it is, a "terror that is linked to the sight of something," the sight of something is also what would guarantee Freud's knowledge of a castration complex in the first place.

Because it is based on the perception of visible similarities, the Aristotelian structure underlying Freud's interpretation of Medusa's head and his theory of a castration complex presumes that Freud is in fact able to see the entities he compares and exchanges for one another on the basis of their correspondence. But in Freud's narrative about the boy's initiation into the castration complex, the female genitals are precisely what is consistently and emphatically *not* seen. Freud writes, "When a little boy first catches sight of a girl's genital region, he begins by showing irresolution and lack of interest; he sees nothing" (19:252); and elsewhere, "The perception is promptly obliterated, so that the result is the same as when a visual impression falls on the blind spot in the retina" (21:154). Even though the female genitals are an empirical entity that could be seen, the little boy will not or cannot see them. They are a "something" that the boy only sees as nothing ("he sees nothing"). In Freud's various accounts of the primal scene, the boy does not register them until after the castration threat has been uttered, and at that point he does not see them literally but only as visual evidence of a castration, the kind with which he himself has been threatened. That is, he sees them figuratively, as an image of his own potential castration. Freud writes, "It is not until later, when some threat of castration has obtained a hold upon him, that the observation becomes important [*bedeutungsvoll*] to him: if he then recollects or repeats it, it arouses a terrible storm of emotion in him and forces him to believe in the reality of the threat which he has hitherto laughed at" (19:252). Only after the castration threat does the observation of the girl's genitals become "important" to the boy, as James Strachey's English translation puts it, and only then does it become at all meaningful or significant (*bedeutungsvoll*), as the original German text has it. Only then does it leave any impression on the boy's retina, due to his interpretation (*Deutung*) of what he has seen as castration. Thus the female genitals become visible and meaningful to the boy only as a negative reflection of his own genitals, once he sees them as posing a threat to his penis. Prior to the castration threat, Freud makes explicit, the observation is meaningless and insignificant, as if it had not taken place at all, as if it were a mere placeholder waiting for a meaning to be retrospectively projected onto it. At no point does the boy see the female genitals as such: "the real female genitals," Freud notes in the essay "The Infantile Genital Organization," "never seem to be discovered" (19:145). When the boy "sees" them at all, it is only as a castrated penis. This inability of the boy to register the female genitals as such holds true as well for Freud himself. Like the boys (and girls) whose unconscious sexual theories he hypothesizes,[16] Freud is categorically unwilling or unable in his numerous expositions of the castration complex to see the actual female genitals, or to see female genitals as heterogeneous to male genitals.

If the female genitals are not literally seen by either the boy or Freud, they do not constitute an empirical entity, a "something" for which a proper Aristotelian metaphor could be substituted on the basis of a visible correspondence. They have no literal status in Freud's writings and in the childhood scenarios Freud imagines, only a figurative status. Hence any seeing of them by the boy or by Freud is as much a figure as they are. If the little boy and Freud "see" the female genitals as a castrated penis, this is an interpreted or interpreting perception, not an actual perception.[17] Any literal seeing of the genitals, Freud makes explicit, is like "when a visual impression falls on the blind spot in the retina." Consequently the female genitals, when they become visible to the boy and to Freud, are always already a representation created by the boy's unconscious, a castration figure. And the visibility of this figure, so crucial to Freud's Aristotelian interpretation and to his theory of the castration complex, is equally figurative insofar as castration could no more be literally seen in the girl's genitals than it could be seen literally.

If Freud and the little boy will not see the literal female genitals, Freud also does not see the corresponding term in the Aristotelian analogy, Medusa's head, literally either, because by its own definition it cannot be seen literally. Freud refers to "the sight of Medusa's head" and would posit this sight as a symbol for "the sight of the female genitals" on the basis of their obvious similarity. But he seems to forget that any direct, literal sight of Medusa's head is impossible insofar as it is synonymous with death, with the instant destruction of sight and of any sensory experience. He can have no visible access to a literal Medusa's head, whatever that might be in the first place. He can only ever see Medusa as one or another kind of figure, but that figure can never be a proper Aristotelian metaphor because he would have no visual access to the properties of a literal Medusa, properties that could be the basis for using Medusa as a metaphor or for substituting Medusa in the place of a figural meaning sharing those same properties. So, like Perseus who only looks at Medusa's reflection in his polished shield, not at Medusa herself, Freud only looks at Medusa as she is reflected in the light of his interpretation of her as a castration symbol. As I point out at the end of this chapter's previous section, this is evident in the way that every detail of the myth Freud brings up has already been interpreted in terms of the castration complex and the primal scene. Freud sees Medusa exclusively through the lens of his castration theory, just as he and the little boy only see the female genitals through that same lens. And just as Medusa's head—something that by definition cannot be seen or known literally—could never be a proper Aristotelian metaphor, the castrated female genitals as "seen" by the boy and by Freud could never be a properly figural meaning of such a metaphor. This is because both are by definition figures that are only figuratively seen, not empirical entities that could actually be seen, and thus neither can be substituted for the other on the basis of their visibility or their visible similarity.

It would seem, then, that Freud's poetics in "Medusa's Head" are marked by an internal contradiction, not unlike Freud's interpretation of Medusa's head as both a reassuring penis symbol and a threatening castration symbol. On one hand, they reproduce the traditional Aristotelian structure of metaphor by juxtaposing a symbol and a figural meaning on the basis of a visible correspondence. This correspondence and the symbolic and interpretative substitutions it would make possible are the foundation of all of Freud's conclusions in the essay. On the other hand, both the symbol and its figural meaning would seem to undermine the visible basis of the Aristotelian structure insofar as neither is by definition literally seen or literally visible (in the case of Medusa's head, by definition of the myth, and in the case of the female genitals, by Freud's own explicit definition). This means that two different rhetorical movements simultaneously take place in Freud's text, of which the second would seem to imply the destruction of the first.

In the first movement, Freud's interpretation aims to establish a series of reliable (because visually obvious) correspondences between the myth and its figural meaning, the primal scene. The look at Medusa's head visually corresponds to the boy's look at the woman's genitals, the snaky hair corresponds to the woman's pubic hair and also to the penis the boy expects to see when he first catches sight of the woman's genitals, the viewer being turned to stone corresponds to the boy's shock, and so on. In drawing these correspondences, Freud does not situate the primal scene and the Medusa myth on an equal level; instead, he relates them hierarchically as non-symbolic meaning and symbol, truth and appearance, latent and manifest, original and copy, and so on. The exclusive purpose of the Medusa myth, as far as Freud is concerned, is symbolically to refer back to the primal scene out of which it was born, and the exclusive purpose of the interpretation is to reattach every single element in the myth to its original counterpart in the primal scene. And so every detail in the myth, however ambiguous, is said inevitably to refer back in one or another way to the primal scene or to the fear of castration. This is most explicit in mathematical equations like "To decapitate = to castrate" and "a multiplication of penis symbols signi-fies castration," but it also comes out, for example, in the way the opposed feelings of horror and relief in the myth are both said ultimately to derive from the castration complex. Freud posits the primal scene and the fear of castration as the origin of each detail and as the endpoint of each individual interpretation. The primal scene and castration fear are the "original situa-tion" around which the various figures that circulate in Freud's text are all organized. At bottom, Freud claims, all figures are figures for them. Hence they would be the ground of the interpretation. They would make possible a hermeneutic closure in that the interpretation could account decisively and fully for every detail. In terms of the Aristotelian theory of metaphor, the stability of the interpretation's conclusions depends on the mutual visibility of the symbol and of its figural meaning, on the visual correspondence between symbol and meaning, and on the clearly delineated hierarchy of meaning over symbol. Even as Freud's interpretation moves abruptly back and forth between the Medusa myth and the primal scene, it categorically insists on the primal scene's priority and finality.

At the level of the text's second rhetorical movement, by contrast, Freud does not properly see the terms he substitutes for one another, for instance Medusa's head and the female genitals, but "sees" each of them only through the lens of the castration theory. So when he would exchange them for one another as symbol and meaning, he effectively does so blindly, much like the little boy who is said to be blind when he looks at actual female genitals. Consequently his interpretation is not structured as a proper Aristotelian metaphor, a structure in which one literal entity serves as a metaphor for another literal entity on the basis of a visible common property. Instead, it blindly substitutes what is exclusively a figure for something else that is also exclusively a figure, for instance the figure of Medusa's head for the figure of the castrated female genitals, or the figure of looking at Medusa for the scenario of the primal scene.[18] The relation between the myth and castration, the castration complex, and the primal scene is therefore not that of a figure to a nonfigurative entity or event, but that of one figure to another. Medusa's head is a mythological image that symbolizes not the actual female genitals but another image, one created in the boy's unconscious, what Freud tellingly refers to as "a *representation* of the female genitals" (18:274, my emphasis). It is, in short, a figure taking the place of another figure, a representation taking the place of another representation. Castration, castration fear, and the visibility of castration are as much figures as any of the other figures in the essay's repertoire.

In the blind substitutions Freud makes between elements of the myth and elements of the primal scene, each set of elements refers to the other but neither set has ultimate priority or finality. Freud uses the primal scene to explain the Medusa myth, and he conversely uses the myth to construct and confirm the scenario of the primal scene. As he cannot literally witness the primal scene or see castration, no more than the boy could literally see castration, he can only construct them as figures on the figural basis of the myth. Hence the myth is no less an original or grounding term in "Medusa's Head" than is its alleged origin, the primal scene. Rather than charting a unilateral interpretative movement that begins with the symbol and terminates with the symbol's nonfigurative meaning, Freud's essay continually moves between one set of figures and another. The mythological elements are traced back to the primal scene, and the primal scene is in turn theorized out of the mythological elements and confirmed by those elements. This bilateral movement never culminates in a ground that is truly primal, but only ever ends up with one set of figures that refers back to another set of figures.

The open-ended nature of the substitutions Freud makes between the primal scene and the myth is emphasized throughout "Medusa's Head." In the following passage from the second half of the essay, for example, Freud interprets the figure of Athena in the context of the primal scene:

> This symbol of horror [that is, Medusa's head] is worn upon her dress by the virgin goddess Athena. And rightly so, for thus she becomes a woman who is unapproachable and repels all sexual desires—since she displays the terrifying genitals of the mother. Since the Greeks were in the main strongly homosexual, it was inevitable that we should

find among them a *representation* of woman as a being who frightens because she is castrated.

If Medusa's head takes the place of a *representation* of the female genitals. . . . (18:273–74, my emphases)

Taken together, the first paragraph (about Athena) and the opening phrase of the second paragraph (about Medusa) perform a reversal, moving first from the myth "back" to the primal scene and then from the primal scene out to the myth (I put the word *back* in quotation marks because it is precisely the presumed priority of the primal scene that the reversal puts into question). In the first paragraph, Freud interprets the mythological figure of Athena in terms of the primal scene, as an image of a woman who frightens men because she is seen by them as castrated. His interpretation moves from the myth (that is, from the representation) to the representation's meaning: it was inevitable, he writes, that we should find among the Greeks a mythological representation of woman as a being who frightens because she is castrated. But in the opening phrase of the subsequent paragraph, when he turns his attention back to Medusa, Freud reverses the order of his exposition, moving this time from the representation's meaning (the "castrated" female genitals) to the representation (Medusa's head), instead of the other way around. Medusa's head (that is, the representation) is said *to take the place* of the female genitals (the meaning), whereas in the sentence about Athena it is the castrated woman (that is, the meaning) that takes the place of the unapproachable virgin goddess (the representation). So the dual direction of Freud's exposition (which first moves from representation to meaning and then moves from meaning to representation) underlines the bilateral and complementary nature of the relationship between the psychoanalytic register and the mythological one. It implies that the primal scene and the myth are not hierarchically related as nonfigurative meaning and figurative representation, but instead are related as one figure to another, one representation to another. This is also suggested by Freud's explicit identification of Medusa's meaning as itself a representation: Medusa's head takes the place of *a representation of the female genitals*. It is, in short, a representation that takes the place of another representation. So if Athena is a mythological representation of an unconscious idea, namely castration, what she represents is itself also a representation: the little boy's unconscious representation to himself of the female genitals as a castrated penis. The myth and its underlying meaning are both forms of representation. And Freud's commentary essentially substitutes one representation for the other and vice versa. The representation of Athena is replaced by the representation of female genitals, which in turn is replaced by the representation of Medusa's head, and so on. This loop is potentially endless because there is no nonfigurative referent, no non-representation that could ground it and thereby put a stop to the substitutions.

Freud explicitly recognizes this predicament when he concludes "Medusa's Head" by conceding the impossibility of concluding. He ends the essay, that is, by acknowledging the interpretation's lack of ground or closure: "In order seriously to substantiate [*vertreten*] this interpretation it would be necessary to investigate the origin of this isolated symbol of horror in Greek mythology as well as parallels to it in other mythologies" (18:274).[19] In a neatly symmetrical reversal of its own opening formulation ("We have not often attempted to interpret individual mythological themes, but an interpretation suggests itself easily in the case of the horrifying decapitated head of Medusa"), the essay that begins with a mythological motif to be interpreted by psychoanalysis ends up with a psychoanalytic interpretation that must be substantiated with more mythological evidence. Psychoanalysis and myth, it would seem, each depend on the other to ground it. Psychoanalytic truths like castration anxiety and the primal scene are derived from and confirmed by myths, and myths in turn are codes for underlying psychoanalytic truths. What is at stake in the mutual referencing is not only the mutual dependence of psychoanalysis and mythology, but the question of origin with which Freud's essay is so emphatically preoccupied. Freud begins the essay by situating the origin of the Medusa myth in the castration complex, and he ends by locating it in mythology, saying we must investigate the origin of the symbol in Greek mythology and other mythologies. His concluding sentence thus returns once more to the recurring question of origin but effectively only to deprive both the myth and its alleged meaning of any definitive origin. Which of the two origins Freud mentions, the reader is prompted to ask, is the true origin, the prior origin, the origin of the other origin? It appears from the symmetrical crossing of the essay's first and last sentences that while the primal scene and the myth are each cited as the origin of the other, in the end, neither is able fully to substantiate (*vertreten*) the other. So the term *origin*, which recurs frequently in the text, is deprived of its currency as referent. It effectively becomes only one more figure in the essay's repertoire of figures. And psychoanalysis and myth, like the origin each is supposed to provide for the other, are simply two figurative registers that continually substitute for one another. Psychoanalytic interpretations take the place of mythological motifs, and mythological motifs in turn substantiate those interpretations. The relay between them is potentially infinite because neither register, as Freud's final comment implies, can conclusively ground the other.[20] The German word *vertreten*, which Freud uses to describe what more mythological evidence would do for his shorthand interpretation of the Medusa myth, means to support or to substantiate, as the English translation has it, but it also means to replace or to substitute.

The continuous and ungrounded loop of substitutions has potentially destabilizing consequences for Freud's general project both in "Medusa's Head" and beyond. That project is not simply the Aristotelian "interpretation of an individual mythological theme" but the implication in the one interpretation of a general system of figurative equivalences, a tropological system. As Laurence Kahn puts this, "the [Medusa] symbol, by the simple fact that it can be translated, presupposes an undisturbed system of designations" (125, my translation). This system would extend beyond "Medusa's Head" to *The Interpretation of Dreams* and to Freud's interpretations of a wide range of symptoms, symbols, and cultural artifacts. Specific elements from the Medusa interpretation appear, among other places, in the analysis of Wilhelm Jensen's novel *Gradiva*, in which Freud interprets the protagonist Norbert's dream about his girlfriend Zoe's transformation into a marble statue as evidence of his castration fear[21]; in the essay on the "Uncanny," in which Freud notes that dreams are "fond of representing castration by a doubling or multiplication of a genital symbol" (17:235); and in the essay "The Taboo of Virginity," in which Freud interprets the decapitation of Holofernes in Christian Friedrich Hebbel's play *Judith und Holofernes* as an image of castration.[22] It seems from these examples that Freud's tropological system would provide him with a widely applicable and reliable symbolic code, a "mode of representation distinguished chiefly by the constancy of the relationship between the symbol and what it symbolises in the unconscious" (Laplanche and Pontalis, 442). Freud uses elements of the system (for example, the equation "a multiplication of penis symbols signifies castration") to interpret the Medusa myth, thereby incorporating the myth into the system's repertoire, and he concurrently uses the myth to reinforce and to confirm the overall system.[23]

The Aristotelian structure of "Medusa's Head" makes explicit that the code would not be an arbitrary one. It shows that the system's tropological equations would be supported by visible evidence and based on observations. This becomes similarly explicit in the case history of the Wolf Man, for example at the moment when Freud interprets the patient's presumed childhood observation of sexual intercourse between his parents as his seeing the "reality" of castration revealed in his mother's genitals: "What was essentially new for him in his observation of his parents' intercourse was the conviction of the reality of castration. . . . For now he saw with his own eyes the wound of which his Nanya had spoken" (17:45–46). As in the symbolic equation between seeing Medusa's head and seeing castrated female genitals, Freud would here interpret the image of parental intercourse as a castration image on the basis of a shared visibility and a shared visible property (both are frightening observations). In both "Medusa's Head" and the interpretation of the parental coitus in the Wolf Man case history, the figure and its meaning are exchanged for one another on the basis of the interpreter's vision, the figure's visibility, and the meaning's corresponding visibility. What the two examples make clear is that the underlying stake of "Medusa's Head" is not only a particular interpretation of a particular mythological theme on the basis of a particular shared property, but vision and visibility themselves, the very condition of any interpretation and any interpretative system that would be grounded in observation.

The threat that implicitly emerges in what I have called the Medusa essay's second rhetorical movement is not only that Medusa's head, petrification, decapitation, the snakes, the pubic hair, the female genitals, the mother's genitals, the castrated woman, the (present or absent) penis, the unapproachable Athena, castration, and castration fear are in the end all just figures substituting randomly for one another. More fundamentally, it is that Freud's perceptions of the symbol and of its meaning are also just figures, and that the visibilities of the symbol and of the meaning are figures. What is threatened by the figurative nature of vision and visibility is not only the Aristotelian basis of the one Medusa interpretation, but the stability of the entire tropological system, since that system would be underwritten by the evidence of actual perceptions. The following section of this chapter will demonstrate that Freud has what he himself might call a fetishistic relation to this threat, which is to say that on one hand he denies it and on the other hand he acknowledges it. He would negate the threat by means of his virtuosic Medusa interpretation, but he also personifies it in the very image of Medusa he is interpreting.

MEDUSA AS FETISH

> An investigation of fetishism is strongly recommended to anyone who still doubts the existence of the castration complex.
> —"Fetishism"

Although Freud does not actually point this out, Medusa's head is an example of a fetish, according to the definition of the fetish he offers in the 1927 essay "Fetishism." Like "Medusa's Head," "Fetishism" revisits the primal scene in which the little boy first sees female genitals and interprets them as having been castrated. It proposes that one possible response by the boy to this sight is to disavow (*verleugnen*) what he sees: to accept the truth of the traumatic observation and simultaneously to deny it. That is, the boy may accept the "truth" of the woman's castration (and therefore of his own potential castration) and also deny it. This double attitude is made possible, Freud explains, by his adoption of a fetish. A fetish is an object like fur, velvet, or shoes for which a male patient in analysis may manifest a particular sexual interest or predilection. When a fetish comes to light in the analysis, Freud claims, it can invariably be traced back to the primal scene, where it originally stood in for the female penis the boy expected to see. Insofar as the fetish symbolically takes the place of the woman's absent penis in the primal scene, it reassuringly restores that penis in the boy's unconscious, much like the snakes are said to do in the Medusa interpretation. At the same time, however, Freud maintains that the fetish also signifies the boy's unconscious recognition of the penis's absence and therefore of his own potential castration. Thus the fetish implies at the same time the recognition of castration's "reality" and the contrary belief that the woman does have a penis (a belief by which the fetishist's own penis would be saved). This split attitude is the fetishistic logic of disavowal (*Verleugnung*), a compromise formation through which the fetishist is unconsciously able to reconcile two logically incompatible positions: what he knows to be true (the woman's castration that confirms his own potential castration) and what he nevertheless believes to be true (the woman's non-castration that confirms his own non-castration).[24]

If the fetish as theorized by Freud is an object that simultaneously designates the fetishist's castration and non-castration, Medusa's head would seem to be a thoroughly fetishistic construct. Each of its details is interpreted by Freud as either a penis symbol or a castration symbol, or both at once. The snakes, for example, are reassuring phallic symbols that restore the woman's absent penis and the boy's potentially absent penis, thereby negating the "fact" of castration. On the other hand, however, they also visually reproduce the traumatic image of the "castrated" female genitals and of the surrounding pubic hair, thereby reminding the viewer of castration's "reality." Similarly, the motif of being turned to stone represents both a reassuring erection and the boy's shock in the primal scene at not seeing a penis where he expected to see one. Hence the overall figure, as Bernard Pautrat has noted, is wholly paradoxical.[25] It has two contradictory meanings, castration and non-castration, and elicits two contradictory responses, reassurance and horror, much like the fetish has two contradictory meanings and elicits contradictory feelings in the fetishist. The parallel between Medusa's head and the fetish is both thematic (each signifies both castration and non-castration) and structural (each has two opposed meanings and elicits two opposed affects).[26]

This section proposes that just as Medusa's head is a kind of fetish and the fetish is in turn a kind of Medusa's head, the interpretation of Medusa's head functions rhetorically as a fetish for Freud. If Medusa's head is a fetish for the viewer in that it signifies both his castration and his non-castration, the analysis of Medusa's head is Freud's fetish in that it signifies both an epistemological anxiety and provides a protection against that anxiety. This is to say that like the fetish for the fetishist and like Medusa's head for the viewer, the interpretation simultaneously has reassuring and terrifying implications for Freud, and that its reassuring aspect works to defend against its terrifying aspect. The terrifying aspect is the revelation by means of Freud's own exposition that his interpretation is not a unilateral movement from symbol to meaning, but merely an ungrounded and open-ended series of tropological substitutions. It is Freud's recognition of the figurativeness of all the terms he substitutes for another, the figurativeness of those terms' visibilities, and the figurativeness of his own perceptions. This predicament is what I have called Freud's blindness, because it replicates the little boy's blindness in the face of real female genitals. The reassuring aspect, meanwhile, is what in the previous section I identify as the traditional Aristotelian structure of the interpretation, in particular the interpretation's reference via the Medusa symbol to a grounding entity (castration) or event (the primal scene) that would be accessible to Freud's vision. Like castration and non-castration, these two aspects of the texts are rhetorically related to one another in a fetishistic structure of disavowal wherein the reassuring aspect covers over and protects against the threatening aspect. In its double attitude toward the stability and the visibility of its own conclusions, the text is fundamentally divided, much as the fetishist Freud describes is fundamentally divided in his attitude toward the question of his own castration. Its expository movements alternately confirm and undermine the ground and the visibility of its conclusions, rhetorically reproducing the fetishistic split, just as Freud's double interpretation of Medusa thematically reproduces that split.

Freud's fetish in "Medusa's Head" is the visual correspondence he establishes between the Medusa symbol and its meaning, the "castrated" female genitals. On one hand, this correspondence implies an epistemological threat to Freud, and on the other hand it implies a protection against that threat. The threat lies in the exposure of Freud's blindness, which is revealed in the text precisely at the moments when he insists on the Aristotelian analogies he would see between Medusa's head, the female genitals, the Medusa myth, the primal scene, and so on. The protection is due to the way that Freud's insistence on vision and visibility—that is, the very insistence through which his blindness is revealed—also covers over his blindness and his awareness of his blindness. This interplay between danger and protection makes up the fetishistic structure of Freud's text, as Freud's relation to his own blindness is similarly split as the fetishist's relation to his own potential castration.[27]

In view of the precarious balance the text strikes between a threatening blindness and a reassuring ability to see, the alleged obviousness of the interpretation assumes for Freud a fetishistic value. Freud opens his essay by asserting that "We have not often attempted to interpret individual mythological themes, but an interpretation suggests itself easily [*liegt nahe*] in the case of the horrifying decapitated head of Medusa." The German verb *naheliegen* (to suggest itself, to be obvious) literally means to lie close to something. It implies that Freud's interpretation of Medusa's head is obvious because the symbol's meaning lies in close spatial proximity to the symbol itself, so that anyone could easily see their correspondence. Laurence Kahn describes it as an interpretation "qui saute aux yeux" (120), an interpretation that stares you in the face or, more literally, that leaps up into your eyes. The interpretation's leap into Freud's eyes is reassuring to Freud because his ability to see is what is fundamentally at stake and in question in the text.[28] The visual obviousness of the interpretation that is made possible by the Medusa symbol's easy visibility would restore Freud's sight, much like the fetish would restore the fetishist's endangered penis. As Kahn puts it, "with the myth, by way of the myth, Freud sees, looks, seizes, interprets" (120, my translation). The visibilities of the myth and of the symbol would enable Freud to see and—by means of that seeing—to grasp and to interpret.[29] They would allow him to disavow his own blindness, just as the fetish would allow the fetishist to disavow his own castration. In other words, they would allow him to disavow his awareness that castration cannot literally be seen, no more than Medusa's head could be seen directly.

The paradoxical, fetishistic gesture of converting a sign of one's own weakness into a means of disavowing that weakness and asserting one's strength underlies much of Freud's Medusa interpretation, as when the viewer's petrification is revealed in an interpretative sleight of hand to be a reassuring erection. Freud explicitly addresses the gesture late in the essay, when he substantiates the interpretation by evidence he takes from anthropology and folklore. He suggests that his interpretation of the threatening Medusa's head as a means of protection is confirmed by the way displays of female and male genitals are regarded in many cultures as a form of self-defense. Like Athena's protective display of Medusa's decapitated head on her dress, he writes, the outward display of the genitals is widely considered an apotropaic gesture, meaning a gesture that has the power to turn away danger (the root of the word *apotropaic* is the Greek *apotrepein*, to avert, a compound of the prefix *apo*, away from, and *trepein*, to turn[30]):

> It may be recalled that displaying the genitals is familiar in other connections as an apotropaic act. What arouses horror in oneself will produce the same effect upon the enemy against whom one is seeking to defend oneself. We read in Rabelais of how the Devil took to flight when the woman showed him her vulva.
>
> The erect male organ also has an apotropaic effect, but thanks to another mechanism. To display the penis (or any of its surrogates) is to say: "I am not afraid of you. I defy you. I have a penis." Here, then, is another way of intimidating the Evil Spirit. (18:274)

The apotropaic "mechanism" Freud describes, at least the one pertaining to the display of the female genitals, is that what terrifies oneself will also protect and empower one when it is turned against one's enemies (who will presumably respond with the same terror as oneself). This gesture is emblematized by Athena mounting the decapitated Medusa's head on her aegis or her shield, and by the triumphant Perseus holding up the head and pointing it outward at his antagonists, as he is depicted, for example, in Benvenuto Cellini's well-known statue (Figure 4). The strength of the

FIGURE 4. Benvenuto Cellini, *Perseus*. Loggia dei Lanzi,
Florence. Photo: Alinari / Art Resource, NY.

protection from one's enemies that is afforded by the object of horror would seem to be proportional to the power the object originally had over oneself. This complementary structure is similar to the structure of fetishism, in which there is a complementary relationship between the fetish's capacity for eliciting horror (as a reminder of the fetishist's potential castration) and its reassuring capacity (as a totemic means of protection against the threat of castration).

The apotropaic display of the genitals Freud describes is to some extent the very gesture he himself makes in "Medusa's Head." Just as the displayers of genitals are confronted by enemies and evil spirits, Freud too confronts a danger in his encounter with Medusa, what in shorthand I have been calling the revelation by means of the interpretation of his blindness as an interpreter. This blindness is the enemy from whom Freud seeks to protect himself. His response to the danger reproduces the "mechanism" he associates with the display of the female genitals. That is, he makes a display of the very figures that threaten to blind him and to reveal his blindness: Medusa's head, the castrated female genitals, the Medusa myth, the primal scene, and the visual correspondences between them. He holds these figures up as something for himself and for his reader to see and to compare. In doing so, he would fetishistically convert the signs of his own weakness (that is, the signs of his inability literally to see any entities and any correspondences between them) into signs of his strength (that is, into displays, into reflexive signs of his ability to see). This conversion would transform him from Medusa's petrified, blinded victim into Perseus, Medusa's triumphant vanquisher.

If Freud's brandishing the interpretation's visual obviousness is like the display of the female genitals in that it converts a threat into a means of defense, it is moreover like the display of the penis in that it functions rhetorically as a means of intimidation and defiance. The brandish not only allows Freud to overcome the terror of being blinded, but also to make a defiant display of his ability to see, to put up an erection, as it were, in the face of his own potential castration. In erecting his apotropaic interpretation of Medusa's head, Freud is figuratively showing his penis. He is saying, as it were, "I am not afraid of you. I defy you." He would ward off the Evil Spirit and defend the Aristotelian structure of his interpretation by means of a virtuosic and explicitly visual analysis of the Medusa myth. His defiant display of the interpretation's obviousness and success is motivated by his concurrent anxiety about the stability and visibility of the interpretation's conclusions, since the epistemological stakes in "Medusa's Head," as I have shown, are especially high, given the implied exemplarity of the interpretation. So Freud must virilely defend his interpretation against its own destabilizing implications. And in accordance with the apotropaic mechanism he describes in the essay, he does so by holding up the very thing that also arouses terror in himself, the interpretation's visual basis and visual obviousness. This gesture would enable Freud to make a triumphant, fetish-istic display of his own authority as an interpreter, an authority in which the authority of his tropological system would also be implicated.

Yet the apotropaic display of the genitals Freud describes is not only an implicit analogy for his own apotropaic display of his interpretation's visual basis and visual obviousness; it concurrently poses a threat to Freud's interpretation because as a figure, it undermines that obviousness and that basis even in the very act of confirming them. When Freud makes refer-ence to the display of the female genitals and the display of the penis, it is as if he could see each of them, just as earlier he would see the "sight of Medusa's head" and the "sight of the female genitals" so as to be able to substitute one for the other. His emphasis on a display reiterates the visual nature of the object he is interpreting as well as the visual nature of the interpretation. The interpretation would link the display of the genitals in folkloric and anthropological sources to its original prototype in the pri-mal scene (the little girl's or woman's "display" of her genitals to the little boy), its mythological analogues (Athena's display of Medusa's head on her dress and Perseus's brandish of the head at his enemies), and its literary analogues (the woman's display of her vulva in Rabelais[31]), all by means of the obvious visual correspondences between each of these displays. But at the same time the interpretation also suggests that Freud is unable liter-ally to see the displays of the genitals or their correspondences. Both times that the genitals' display is referred to in the text, it is not described in the visual terms that would naturally, properly correspond to any display and that the reader would therefore expect. Instead, it is described in figurative terms that are drawn from a register wholly heterogeneous to the register of vision, namely the register of language and speech. In the first instance, Freud writes, "What arouses horror in oneself will produce [*äussern*] the same effect upon the enemy against whom one is seeking to defend oneself." And in the second instance, "To display the penis (or any of its surrogates) is to say [*sagen*]: 'I am not afraid of you. I defy you. I have a penis.'" The two times the genitals are visually displayed, they are said *to speak* to the person who looks at them. The German word *äussern* means to manifest or to produce, as it is translated here, but its more common meaning is to utter, to express, or to give a voice to. So displaying the female genitals *speaks* an effect on the enemy, while displaying the penis is synonymous with *saying* that one is not afraid. Freud's diction and imagery both reveal that he does not or cannot literally see the visual displays he describes and interprets, no more than earlier he could literally see castration or Medusa's head or the female genitals or the penis or any of the other terms he substi-tutes for one another. He can only see them and show them figuratively, in the imported, catachrestic figures of *äussern* and *sagen*. Presumably this is because like every other term his essay puts into circulation, the display of the genitals is not a literal entity accessible to Freud's vision. It is rather a figure, one that would ultimately refer, like all the other figures in the essay, to the primal scene of the castration complex. The metaphor of speaking Freud uses to describe the display is therefore not a proper metaphor in the Aristotelian sense, since there is no proper visual analogy between showing and speaking. It is rather a blind substitution for another figure, one that does not visually, naturally correspond to speaking. As such, it is much like the other blind substitutions of figures for figures in "Medusa's Head," for instance the substitution of the sight of Medusa's head for the sight of the castrated female genitals or for the "sight of something." So while ostensibly it would serve as a reflexive image of Freud's interpretative triumph, the defiant display of the genitals that "speaks" to one's enemies is one more acknowledgment by Freud's text of its own epistemological limitations. It is also one more reminder of the potential reversibility of apotropaic mechanisms, which not only transform objects of horror into reassuring shields, but conversely transform defenses back into threats, as when the reassuring multiplicity of penis symbols on Medusa's head is abruptly revealed as a castration figure.

The fetishistic relay in "Medusa's Head" between the affirmation and the denial of Freud's ability to see what he interprets is potentially infinite, like the open-ended relays between the primal scene and the Medusa myth, between castration and Medusa's head, and between a psychoanalytic register and a mythological one. At bottom, the question remains open whether Freud looks at Medusa's head to become its blinded and petrified victim, or whether he is triumphantly holding it up at his enemies, like Perseus in Cellini's statue (Figure 4) or like Agathon in Plato's *Symposium*.[32] The question, if it is understood as a choice between mutually exclusive options, is undecidable, since both things are going on simultaneously, like the concurrent affirmation and denial of castration in the fetish. It only refers Freud's reader once again to the horrifying and reassuring revelation that the interpretation of Medusa's head is itself Medusa's head.

CHAPTER TWO

A "Monstrous" Opposition

The Double Dionysus and the Double Apollo in Nietzsche's *Birth of Tragedy*

Freud's essay "Medusa's Head" and Rossetti's poem "Aspecta Medusa" not only share an interest in the Medusa theme and offer interpretations of the look at Medusa's head as a figure for an initiation into dangerous knowledge, but both set up a similar epistemological structure. In Rossetti's poem, the representation by means of what Rossetti calls shadow of a threatening revelation or object is figured as a means of protection against the threat: "Let not thine eyes know / Any forbidden thing itself . . . but be / Its shadow upon life enough for thee" (*Correspondence*, 3:557). Freud's essay makes a similar association between representation and protection. In "Medusa's Head" and in the writings on the male castration complex more generally, a frightening revelation through a visual object (specifically, the revelation of the "truth" of castration through the female genitals as seen by the little boy) is mitigated by means of its representations in the unconscious, representations like the symbolic Medusa's head and the fetish.[1] By taking the place of the original revelation or object, the representation enables its repression or disavowal, as Freud's commentaries on both Medusa and the fetish make explicit. Freud's Medusa interpretation oscillates between frightening and reassuring components of the overall Medusa image, and as Neil Hertz points out, the image is also inherently reassuring due to "the primary apotropaic power of symbolic concentration itself. The symbol of Medusa's head is reassuring not only because its elements can be read in [reassuring] ways, but because it is a symbol" (*End*, 166). As I demonstrate in the final section of the previous chapter, this apotropaic power of symbolic concentration not only protects the little boy from the traumatic recognition of his own potential castration, but protects Freud himself by means of the symbol's legibility, its obvious visual correspondence to its "meaning." It protects Freud from his insight into his interpretation's blind and arbitrary substitutions of figures for other figures (an insight that in a manner of speaking is terrifying, though not existentially, at the level of consciousness, but epistemologically, at the level of what might psychoanalytically be called the text's unconscious).

The present chapter finds a rhetorical and epistemological problematic in Nietzsche's *The Birth of Tragedy* (1872) that is both thematically and structurally similar to the problematic found in Freud's and Rossetti's texts. In the early sections of the book, Nietzsche famously introduces the idea of the Dionysian, a terrifying insight into the nature of all existence. This insight first reveals itself to the Greeks in the form of encroaching barbaric folk festivals and orgiastic revels that blend together feelings of horror and ecstasy: "The song and pantomime of such dually-minded revelers was something new and unheard-of in the Homeric-Greek world; and Dionysian *music* in particular excited awe and terror."[2] The Dionysian terrifies the Greeks because it is for them an "image of everything underlying existence that is frightful, evil, a riddle, destructive, fatal" (21).[3] Nietzsche maintains that the Greeks' insight into this frightful aspect of existence is unbearable to them to a point that they can only face it indirectly, in the tempering medium of Apollonian art and culture: "The Greek knew and felt the terror and horror of existence. That he might endure this terror at all, he had to interpose between himself and life the radiant dream-birth of the Olympians" (42). The mediation of Dionysian knowledge by Apollonian forms— for instance by the dream-like figures of the Olympian gods—has the effect of protecting the Greeks from the threat of their unmediated insight into the Dionysian horror of existence.

If the relationship of the Apollonian to the Dionysian structurally resembles both the relationship between the "forbidden thing itself" and its shadow in Rossetti's poem, and the relationship between castration and castration symbol in Freud's essay, the figure of Dionysus in Nietzsche's text is also specifically analogous to the figure of castration in Freud's text. This is because like Dionysus, the castration complex is described as a terrifying insight or foundation that underlies all existence.[4] Both what Freud calls castration and what Nietzsche calls Dionysus are identified as dangerous truths that must be faced indirectly rather than directly, and both are fundamentally privileged above their representations. As the castration complex is said to be the "original situation" of the Medusa myth, the truth at which all of Freud's interpretations arrive, and the ultimate meaning of each figure Freud interprets, so Dionysus is said to be the foundation, origin, and essence of all Apollonian forms in *The Birth of Tragedy*. And the protective representations of castration and of Dionysus (the Medusa symbol and the fetish in Freud's case, Apollonian art in Nietzsche's case) are for their part implicitly devalued in this hierarchy. In "Medusa's Head," for example, as I discuss at the end of the previous chapter's first section, the multiple and contradictory details Freud encounters in the myth are exclusively interpreted in terms of the castration complex, as unanimously and unequivocally originating out of—and referring back to—the primal scene. In *The Birth of Tragedy*, the Apollonian appearance is similarly deval-ued vis-à-vis the Dionysian essence: in each of Nietzsche's various accounts of this complex relationship, the Dionysian truth at bottom always remains the ultimate referent of the Apollonian forms to which it gave birth.

Freud of course goes on to complicate and to destabilize both this struc-ture and its underlying hierarchy, as the previous chapter demonstrates.[5] In *The Birth of Tragedy*, Nietzsche similarly puts into question the hierarchy between Apollo and Dionysus. He does so in the form of two competing metaphors and two competing narratives he tells about the Apollo/Diony-sus relationship. My aim in this chapter is to trace this movement in his text and to show that like Freud, he ends up maintaining a divided, fetishistic attitude toward his own conclusions.

* * *

In the opening sections of *The Birth of Tragedy*, Nietzsche introduces the Apollonian and Dionysian duality, first as two opposed tendencies in Greek art, then as opposed forms of art, and finally as opposed modes or prin-ciples. The contrast between the two is well known. Apollonian art is imag-istic (its exemplary form is sculpture) while Dionysian art is non-imagistic (its exemplary form is music). The Apollonian mode is associated with beauty and surface, while the Dionysian is equated with terror and depth. Nietzsche equates the Apollonian with superficial appearance or illusion (*Schein*), with the mediation of truths via symbolic figures and images, and with lucid intelligibility and understanding. His analogy for it is dreams. The Dionysian, on the other hand, is alternately defined as immediate truth and as the breakdown of logical understanding in a fundamental, original contradiction. One of Nietzsche's analogies for it is intoxication.

In the sections immediately following the first, Nietzsche uses the opposition between Apollo and Dionysus to tell a genealogical narrative about the development of Attic tragedy. He presents the Greeks' insight into their own Dionysian impulses as the origin from which the Apollo-nian work of art is engendered: "out of the original Titanic divine order of terror," he writes in section 3, "the Olympian divine order of joy gradually evolved through the Apollinian impulse towards beauty, just as roses burst from thorny bushes" (42–43). This sentence offers one version of a story Nietzsche tells again and again. In all versions of the story, the Dionysian is situated as temporally prior to its offspring, the Apollonian, just as the bushes precede and engender the roses. It is not only the starting point of Nietzsche's genealogy but also its ultimate endpoint; the second half of *The Birth of Tragedy* proclaims the rebirth of the Dionysian impulse in Wagne-rian opera and, more generally, in a new aesthetic modernity.

In certain moments in the text, Nietzsche supplements the genetic relation he describes between Dionysus and Apollo with accounts of a more
dialectical relation. Within any single work of art, he maintains, the Apollonian and Dionysian principles are always simultaneously and comple-
mentarily present to varying degrees. This is the case in Attic tragedy and
also in certain exemplary works of art, for instance in Raphael's painting
The Transfiguration: "Here we have presented, in the most sublime artistic
symbolism, that Apollinian world of beauty and its substratum, the terrible wisdom of Silenus; and intuitively we comprehend their necessary
interdependence" (45). The dialectical model as well as the genetic model
are both implicit in Nietzsche's various accounts of the Apollo/Dionysus
relationship, which move consistently from original Dionysian impulses to
Apollonian counter-impulses and then to their union in tragedy. Because
this is always a unilateral movement, the dialectical model does not at all
undermine the priority Nietzsche grants at bottom to Dionysus.[6]

In his essay "Genesis and Genealogy" from *Allegories of Reading*, Paul
de Man proposes that both the genetic and the dialectical models of the
Apollo/Dionysus relationship maintain the same ontological hierarchy.
Within either model, he claims, Dionysus represents Truth, the thing itself,
the origin, the father, the foundation, and unmediated presence, while
Apollo represents appearance and illusion, the offspring or son, symbolic
mediation, and representation.[7] De Man goes on to say that these polari-
ties also extend to a linguistic register and, more specifically, to Nietzsche's
implicit conception of the genetic relationship between Apollo and Dionysus as a relation between metaphor and meaning:

> The genetic version of the polarity Appearance/Thing is that of an
> entity that can be said to be identical with itself [Dionysus] and that
> would engender, through a process of mediation, an appearance
> [Apollo] of which it is the origin and the foundation. Such a model
> can be understood in linguistic terms as the relationship between fig-
> ural and proper meaning in a metaphor. The metaphor *is* not "really"
> the entity it literally means, but it can be understood to refer to some-
> thing in which meaning and being coincide. The meaning [Dionysus]
> engenders and determines the metaphor [Apollo] as the appearance or
> sign of this meaning.[8]

According to de Man, Dionysus is genetically related to Apollo as thing
to appearance, and rhetorically related as a metaphor's figural meaning is
related to its proper meaning and as a meaning is related to the metaphor
that refers to it. Though Nietzsche does not himself use the term *metaphor*
in *The Birth of Tragedy*, he does indicate a figurative relationship between
Apollo and Dionysus throughout the text. In section 16, for instance, he
maintains that tragic myth is a "symbolic expression" of an original, unique,

and universal Dionysian wisdom. The myth, he writes, is the offspring of Dionysian music and "expresses Dionysian knowledge in symbols" (103).[9]

In making the comparison between Dionysus and Apollo, on one hand, and meaning and metaphor, on the other, de Man notes that "the priority of the musical, nonrepresentational language of Dionysus over the representational, graphic language of Apollo is beyond dispute" (92). The assumption that such a hierarchy underlies the arguments of *The Birth of Tragedy*, he points out, has subjected Nietzsche's text to accusations of logocentrism from such critics as Philippe Lacoue-Labarthe and Sarah Kofman: "The most recent readings of *The Birth of Tragedy* are still oriented in this direction, and do not question its logocentric ontology" (89).[10] De Man goes on to suggest, however, that Nietzsche's own rhetorical praxis is not fully consistent with the kind of logocentric statements he makes in his argument.[11]

This very cursory summary of de Man's essay makes explicit that the stake of his reading of Nietzsche is the relation between Apollo and Dionysus, understood as the hierarchical relation between appearance and essence, and between metaphor and meaning. "Nietzsche was certainly right," de Man writes, "when he referred to the nature of the Dionysos/Apollo relationship as 'the capital question [*die Hauptfrage*]'" (90).[12] In the opening sections of *The Birth of Tragedy*, the present chapter proposes, Nietzsche's *Hauptfrage* takes the form of a *Medusenhaupt*, a Medusa's head. Medusa appears in these sections as one figure among others for what Nietzsche calls Dionysus, ostensibly serving to sustain the opposition between Apollo and Dionysus that would allow for their genetic and dialectical relationships and for their ontological hierarchy to be established. But the Medusa myth is also a figure in Nietzsche's text for an inextricable, non-dialectical fusion of Apollo and Dionysus; in this latter capacity, it undermines the opposition that Medusa in her first capacity establishes and supports. The second figure puts into question not only the opposition between Apollo and Dionysus but also the structure that underlies that opposition: the logocentric model privileging meaning over metaphor, truth over appearance, Dionysian music over Apollonian words, and authentic presence over representation. So the Medusa motif winds up playing a double role in Nietzsche's text, not unlike Medusa's head in Freud's essay, and the *Medusenhaupt* emblematizes for Nietzsche a double aspect of the *Hauptfrage*.

THE DOUBLE DIONYSUS

In *The Birth of Tragedy*, the Dionysian is repeatedly figured as a terrifying insight that reveals itself visually, for instance in the following passage from section 1:

> Schopenhauer has depicted for us the tremendous *terror* which seizes man when he is suddenly dumfounded by the cognitive form of

phenomena because the principle of sufficient reason, in some one of its manifestations, seems to suffer an exception. If we add to this terror the blissful ecstasy that wells from the innermost depths of man, indeed of nature, at this collapse of the *principium individuationis*, we steal a glimpse into the nature of the *Dionysian*. . . . (36)

The reader's glimpse into the terrifying and ecstatic essence of the Dionysian parallels the Dionysian man's own glimpse into that essence, a glimpse Nietzsche dramatizes in section 15:

Science, spurred by its powerful illusion, speeds irresistibly toward its limits where its optimism, concealed in the essence of logic, suffers shipwreck. For the periphery of the circle of science has an infinite number of points; and while there is no telling how this circle could ever be surveyed completely, noble and gifted men nevertheless reach . . . such boundary points on the periphery from which one gazes into what defies illumination. When they see to their horror how logic coils up at these boundaries and finally bites its own tail—suddenly the new form of insight breaks through, *tragic insight* which, merely to be endured, needs art as a protection and remedy. (97–98)[13]

Both passages associate direct insight into the Dionysian with posing a danger to the viewer. In the second passage, the interposition of art between the viewer and the unmediated Dionysus would serve as a protection and remedy, allowing the viewer to survive his recognitions and to endure his tragic insights.

Nietzsche figures the danger of Dionysian insight to the viewer specifically as immobilization or paralysis: "the Dionysian man resembles Hamlet: both have once looked truly into the essence of things, they have *gained knowledge*, and nausea inhibits action . . . true knowledge, an insight into the horrible truth, outweighs any motive for action" (60).[14] It is through the interposition of art—Apollonian art and later on in the argument also the synthesizing art of tragedy—that the insight can be endured and paralysis prevented: "We are to recognize [through the tragic artwork] that all that comes into being must be ready for a sorrowful end; we are forced to look into the terrors of the individual existence—yet we are not to become rigid with fear [*und sollen doch nicht erstarren*]" (104). The word *erstarren* (to grow stiff, to harden, to be paralyzed) establishes a link between the act of gazing (*starren*) into the Dionysian terrors of individual existence and the condition of being petrified (*erstarren*). Nietzsche also alludes to this link in the quotation from section 15, where tragic insight takes place on the periphery of science, "from which one gazes into what defies illumination [*wo er in das Unaufhellbare starrt*]." As one gazes (*er starrt*) into the Dionysian darkness, Nietzsche's diction suggests, one is simultaneously paralyzed (*erstarrt*). Nietzsche makes a similar play in the word *Schauer*, which means viewer and also awe, terror, or horror. In one of several approximations of the Dionysian he offers in section 1, Beethoven's "Ode to Joy" transformed into a painting, he tells the reader to "let your imagination conceive the multitudes bowing to the dust, awestruck [*schauervoll*]—then you will approach the Dionysian" (37). As an analogy for the experience of the Dionysian, the multitude's prostration before the painting is simultaneously an act of looking (*schauen*) and a condition of being struck with awe or horror (*schauern*).[15]

In the genetic narrative Nietzsche offers of the Apollo/Dionysus relationship, Apollonian art evolves in response to the Greeks' unmediated insights into life's Dionysian essence in order to protect and heal them from their paralyzing knowledge. By representing the Dionysian in the medium of what Nietzsche calls "naïve" art (his examples are Doric sculpture and the Homeric epic), the Apollonian safely transforms it, thereby allowing the spectator or reader to escape paralysis and to endure his Dionysian insights in the safe form of Apollonian appearances. The Apollonian representation of Dionysian truths, which Nietzsche compares specifically to mirroring and to veiling, is also figured as a victory by Apollo over Dionysus:

> Where we encounter the naïve in art, we should recognize the highest effect of Apollinian culture—which always must first overthrow an empire of Titans and slay monsters, and which must have triumphed over an abysmal and terrifying view of the world and the keenest susceptibility to suffering through recourse to the most forceful and pleasurable illusions. (43)

In this sentence, Apollonian culture is implicitly compared to an epic hero, Dionysus is compared to a monster, and the act of representing Dionysus is compared to vanquishing and killing him. Apollo's means of defeating Dionysus is his creating a transfiguring image of him: he triumphs over Dionysus "through recourse to the most forceful and pleasurable illusions [*durch kräftige Wahnvorspiegelungen und lustvolle Illusionen*]." The word *Wahnvorspiegelung*, elided in Walter Kaufmann's translation, means delusion and contains within it the words *Spiegel*, mirror, and *Spiegelung*, reflection. The figure of a transfiguring mirror appears frequently in *The Birth of Tragedy*, usually in a similar context of Apollo using a transforming reflection (that is, an image, an artwork, an illusion or appearance) to create a representation of Dionysus and thereby to protect himself from and to overcome the unmediated Dionysus.[16] In section 3, for instance, Nietzsche maintains that "the same [Apollonian] impulse which calls art into being, as the complement and consummation of existence, seducing one to a continuation of life, was also the cause of the Olympian world which the Hellenic 'will' made use of as a transfiguring mirror [*verklärenden Spiegel*]" (43). What the

Hellenic "will" transfigures by means of the mirror into something resplendent and glorious is its Dionysian recognition of the unendurable suffering of human existence: "How else could this people, so sensitive, so vehement in its desires, so singularly capable of *suffering*, have endured existence, if it had not been revealed to them in their gods, surrounded with a higher glory" (43). The glory of the Olympian world "is the sphere of beauty, in which [the Greeks] saw their mirror images [*Spiegelbilder*], the Olympians. With this mirroring of beauty [*Schönheitsspiegelung*] the Hellenic will combated its artistically correlative talent for suffering and for the wisdom of suffering" (44). As the Hellenic will here "combats" its talent for suffering by means of its own transfiguring mirror images, so the epic poet in section 5 similarly protects himself from the threat of being absorbed into a primordial Dionysian oneness by the interposition of the Apollonian images he creates, images that are figured once again as a protective mirror: the poet is said to "[live] in these images, and only in them, with joyous satisfaction. He never grows tired of contemplating lovingly even their minutest traits. Even the image of the angry Achilles is only an image to him whose angry expression he enjoys with the dreamer's pleasure in illusion. Thus, by this mirror of illusion [*Spiegel des Scheines*], he is protected against becoming one and fused with his figures" (50).[17]

In "Die dionysische Weltanschauung" [The Dionysian Weltanschauung], an 1870 preparatory text for *The Birth of Tragedy*, Nietzsche explicitly figures the danger of Dionysian existential insight as a Medusa and the Apollonian artwork as a reflection of Medusa, using much the same diction and imagery as in the passages cited earlier: "To see its existence, as it actually is, in a transfiguring mirror [*verklärenden Spiegel*] and to protect itself by means of this mirror against Medusa—that was the ingenious strategy of the Hellenic 'will' to be able to live at all" (KSA, 1:560).[18] In section 2 of the *Birth of Tragedy*, he further develops this image, comparing Apollo to Perseus, specifically to the victorious Perseus defiantly holding up the decapitated Medusa's head at his enemies. The context of the comparison is an account of the Apollonian resistance against licentious, barbaric Dionysian festivals encroaching on Greece from all sides:

> These festivals centered in extravagant sexual licentiousness, whose waves overwhelmed all family life and its venerable traditions; the most savage natural instincts were unleashed, including even that horrible mixture of sensuality and cruelty which has always seemed to me the real "witches' brew." For some time, however, the Greeks were apparently perfectly insulated and guarded against the feverish excitements of these festivals, though knowledge of them must have come to Greece on all the routes of land and sea; for the figure of Apollo, rising full of pride, held out the Gorgon's head to this grotesquely uncouth [*fratzenhaft*] Dionysian power—and really could not have countered any more

dangerous force. It is in Doric art that this majestically rejecting attitude of Apollo is immortalized. (39)

This scene of a "majestically rejecting" resistance is consistent with the overall arguments and imagery of the opening sections of *The Birth of Tragedy*.
The Dionysian is figured as a threat ("this grotesquely uncouth Dionysian
power") against which Apollo serves as a means of protection: "Apollo . . .
really could not have countered a more dangerous force." And as in the
passages cited earlier, Apollo counters the danger by creating a representation of it. In this instance, however, Apollo overcomes Dionysus not by
mirroring or veiling him, as in the earlier examples, but by petrifying him
into sculpture: "It is in Doric art that this majestically rejecting attitude
of Apollo is immortalized" (Dorian sculpture and the Homeric epic are
the exemplary forms of Apollonian art). In the battle between Apollo and
Dionysus, the implicit contrast is between the serenity of Doric art and the
frenzy of the Dionysian festivals. Apollo's turning the Dionysian onslaught
into stone implies the permanent containment of the frenzy in the fixed
form of sculpture. He transforms the Dionysian into a sculptural image
that then serves as the monument to his victory over Dionysus, much
like the safe reflection of the Dionysian in the transfiguring mirror of the
resplendent Olympian gods.[19]

Nietzsche's allusion in posing Apollo as Perseus would seem to be to
an obscure, late episode from the Perseus myth in which Perseus, now king
of Argos, battles against the satyr followers of Dionysus. In this episode,
recounted in Nonnos's *Dionysiaca* and referred to in Pausanias's *Description
of Greece*, Perseus and the citizens of Argos fight to defend the city against
the encroaching Dionysian cult.[20] The satyrs are ultimately defeated when
Perseus uses Medusa's head to turn them into stone. According to Thalia
Phillies Feldman, the episode is about the struggle between licentious and
frenetic energies, associated with the satyrs, and "the Olympian order, won
by enormous spiritual struggle" and represented by Perseus.[21] In Nietzsche's version, Apollo takes Perseus's place as the representative of culture
and the Olympian order, rising full of pride to defend Greece against the
"grotesquely uncouth Dionysian power," much as Perseus in the *Dionysiaca*
defends Argos against the threat of chaos and disintegration.

If Medusa in Nietzsche's text is a recurring figure for Dionysus, as
for example in the citation from "Die dionysische Weltanschauung," then
Apollo, when he confronts the onslaught of Dionysian festivals, is in effect
holding up Medusa's head at Medusa herself.[22] This doubling of Medusa
indicates a concurrent doubling of Dionysus: on one hand the uncontained, frenzied, *fratzenhaft* Dionysus encroaching on Greece, and on the
other hand the Dionysus who has been defeated by Apollo, figured here as
the decapitated Medusa's head which Apollo is able to wield for his purposes, and figured in the earlier examples as the Dionysus who is safely

mirrored or veiled by Apollonian art. If the overall passage is intended to dramatize Apollo's victory over Dionysus, a victory memorialized in Doric sculpture,[23] the splitting of Dionysus into two parts suggests that Apollo defeats Dionysus by his appropriation and harnessing of the very Dionysian power that threatens him, and by his use of that power as a weapon against an encroaching, uncontained Dionysus (as implied in the figure of Apollo holding up Medusa's head at Medusa herself). This is a version of the apotropaic logic Freud outlines in "Medusa's Head": "What arouses horror in oneself will produce the same effect upon the enemy against whom one is seeking to defend oneself" (18:274). In his confrontation with the Dionysian onslaught, Apollo essentially repeats the gesture of Perseus in Ovid's *Metamorphoses*, who prefaces his use of Medusa's head to petrify his rival Phineus by announcing, "Since you yourself force me to it, I shall seek the aid of my enemy" (121), except that in Nietzsche's text, Apollo seeks the aid of his enemy not against another enemy, but against that very same enemy, against Dionysus himself.[24] He is threatened and horrified by the Dionysian onslaught, and is he is able to defeat this onslaught by appropriating Dionysus's threatening and horrifying power. He successfully turns the Medusa-like Dionysus against himself, as in some versions of the Medusa myth Perseus turns Medusa to stone by mirroring her petrifying gaze back at her. The image of Apollo's petrification of Dionysus by means of Medusa's head is a figure for the transformation of the terrifying Dionysian frenzy and the terrifying Dionysian insights into the serene and protective form of Apollonian artworks, in particular Doric sculpture. And consistent with the transfer of power that is implicit in the apotropaic gesture as described by Freud, what enables Apollo to do this is the power of Dionysus himself. In other words, what makes Apollonian art so powerful, so "majestically rejecting," so petrifying a defense against Dionysus is its own Dionysian substratum: the Dionysian insights on which it is founded, which it indirectly reveals to the viewer, and which it also safely contains.

The scenario of a Perseus-like Apollo defeating a Medusa-like Dionysus fits easily into both the genetic and the dialectical models of the Apollo/Dionysus relationship as Nietzsche constructs them in the opening sections of *The Birth of Tragedy*. In the genetic model, Apollo's victory represents the apogee of a succession of confrontations between Apollo and Dionysus as two opposed principles:

> Up to this point we have simply enlarged upon the observation . . . that the Dionysian and Apollinian, in new births ever following and mutually augmenting one another, controlled the Hellenic genius; that out of the age of "bronze," with its wars of the Titans and its rigorous folk philosophy, the Homeric word developed under the sway of the Apollinian impulse to beauty; that this "naïve" splendor was again overwhelmed by the influx of the Dionysian; and that against this new

power the Apollinian rose to the austere majesty of Doric art and the
Doric view of the world. (47)

In this account of the relationship, Apollo and Dionysus mutually augment
one another by means of their periodic confrontations, a process culminat-
ing in the image of the austere, rejecting Apollo who also appears in the
Medusa passage. In terms of Nietzsche's dialectical model, meanwhile, the
scenario of Apollo holding up Medusa's head at Dionysus suggests that
the relationship between the two forces is not only oppositional but also
complementary (in that Medusa appears on both sides of the opposition,
as simultaneously Apollo's weapon and antagonist). It implies that Apollo's
power (and specifically his power over Dionysus) depends on Dionysus himself, on his appropriation of Dionysus's power. This appropriation, figured
as his holding up the decapitated Medusa's head, makes him a "majestically
rejecting" defense against Dionysus, while his veiled revelation of Dionysian truths (for example, in the Doric sculpture memorializing his victory)
is the source and the foundation of his aesthetic power.[25]

Whether the Apollo/Dionysus relationship is figured as genetic or
dialectical, however, in both cases Dionysus remains the prior, privileged
term over Apollo. Ontologically speaking, it remains that which *is* and that
which *appears* as Apollo; in de Man's rhetorical terms, it is the meaning to
which the Apollonian metaphor refers. In the scenario of Apollo holding
up Medusa's head at the Medusa-like Dionysus, for instance, the Dionysian
is that of which Doric sculpture is a mere image, and it is also the means of
creating that image (without the power of Dionysus, Nietzsche's scenario
implies, Apollo could not create forms, as he requires the petrifying power
of Medusa's head to turn Dionysus to stone). Hence the Apollonian artwork depends on the Dionysian both for its ultimate meaning and in order
to come into being in the first place, whereas by contrast, the Dionysian
meaning only depends on the Apollonian artwork in order to appear in
mitigated form.

In addition, the power of Apollonian art is said to be due entirely to its
veiled intimations of its Dionysian meaning and Dionysian origins. At one
point in the text, Nietzsche frames this hierarchical, asymmetrical relation
between the Apollonian figure and the Dionysian meaning in terms of an
existential recognition by the Greeks:

> The effects wrought by the *Dionysian* also seemed "titanic" and "bar-
> baric" to the Apollinian Greek; while at the same time he could not con-
> ceal from himself that he, too, was inwardly related to these overthrown
> Titans and heroes. Indeed, he had to recognize even more than this:
> despite all its beauty and moderation, his entire existence rested on a
> hidden substratum of suffering and of knowledge, revealed to him by the
> Dionysian. And behold: Apollo could not live without Dionysus! (46)

The Apollonian Greek's Dionysian insight here is not only into his *unheim-lich* kinship with the Dionysian. He also recognizes that his entire existence has a Dionysian foundation, and he recognizes his dependence on Dionysus in order to exist and in order to be able to recognize his existence for what it is.[26] This dependence is similar to the dependence of Doric sculpture on the Medusa-like Dionysus whom it represents and by appropriation of whose petrifying power it is able to create representations. In both examples, Dionysus is figured as the ground and the truth that (in the genetic model) precedes and postdates Apollo and that (in the dialectical model) is what fundamentally underlies Apollo. So in any dialectical "reconciliation" (*Versöhnung*) at which the two may arrive,[27] for example in the synthesizing art of tragedy, Apollo will at bottom always remain the son (*Sohn*) and Dionysus the father. And as de Man points out, "As long as the Dionysus/ Apollo relationship is referred to . . . in an imagery of parenthood, successiveness [the genetic model] and simultaneity [the dialectical model] are in fact mirror-like versions of the same ontological hierarchy" (85). The ontological hierarchy to which de Man refers is the privileging of essence over appearance, of meaning over metaphor, of Medusa over the transfiguring mirror image, of "a hidden substratum of suffering" over "beauty and moderation"—in short, of Dionysus over Apollo.

THE DOUBLE APOLLO

When Nietzsche writes, "It is in Doric art that this majestically rejecting attitude [*Haltung*] of Apollo is immortalized," the reading of this line that would be consistent with the text's overall argument and imagery is that by Doric art he refers to the Dionysus who has been petrified by Apollo holding up Medusa's head. According to this reading, the petrified Dionysus (that is, Doric sculpture) is the immortalization, the memorial, of Apollo's successful defense against the frenzied Dionysian onslaught. A more literal reading of the line, one that is inconsistent with Nietzsche's ostensible argument and with the surrounding imagery, is that it is not Dionysus but Apollo himself who has been turned to stone. What Doric art immortalizes, according to this second reading, is Apollo's bearing (*Haltung*), his "majestically rejecting" pose of holding up Medusa's head at the grotesquely uncouth Dionysian power. Doric art, the line would imply, is Apollo turned into a statue, stuck in the pose of Cellini's Perseus (Figure 4). The figure of a statuesque or petrified Apollo recurs several times in *The Birth of Tragedy*, for instance in Nietzsche's description of Apollo as *starr* (a word that means rigid, fixed, or immobile, and that also plays on gazing or staring [*starren*]): "Wherever the first Dionysian onslaught was successfully withstood, the authority and majesty of the Delphic god exhibited itself as more rigid [*starrer*] and menacing than ever" (47) and elsewhere, "against this new [Dionysian] power the Apollonian rose to the austere [*starren*] majesty of

Doric art and the Doric view of the world" (47). Another version of the petrified Apollo occurs when Homer, the exemplary Apollonian artist, is described as a "monument" to Apollo's victory over Dionysus: "With this mirroring of beauty [*Schönheitsspiegelung*] the Hellenic will combated its artistically correlative talent for suffering and for the wisdom of suffering— and, as a monument [*Denkmal*] of its victory, we have Homer, the naïve artist" (44). Like the line about the immortalization of Apollo's majestically rejecting attitude, this line can be read in two ways. To be consistent with the argument, the reference to Homer would have to be understood as a metonymy for Homer's poetry. According to that reading, the poetry is the *Schönheitsspiegelung* by means of which the Hellenic Apollo combats and defeats Dionysus and, as such, is the monument to Apollo's victory, like the Doric sculpture in the first example. A more literal reading, on the other hand, would juxtapose the account of Apollo's victory with the incongruous figure of Homer himself as a monument, the figure of Homer having been somehow turned to stone. Like Apollo in the first example, Homer is both victorious and petrified at the same time.

In the first example, in which Apollo holds up Medusa's head at the Dionysian horde, the petrified Apollo unexpectedly appears in the place where, in accordance with the logic of the text's argument, a petrified Dionysus should have appeared. Nietzsche's overall argument in *The Birth of Tragedy* maintains that Apollonian art gives plastic form to the Dionysian essence and thereby contains its threat; this is the obvious way to understand the figure of Apollo turning Dionysus into stone (that is, into Doric sculpture). The figure of the petrified Apollo implies, on the contrary, that Apollonian art does not represent or fix or contain an essential, original Dionysus. It suggests that Apollo only manages to put forth its own figures for such a Dionysus. Those Apollonian figures testify to the *aim* of representing and containing an essential Dionysus (in Apollo's gesture of holding up Medusa's head at Dionysus), but they also testify to the failure to achieve this aim (in the petrified Apollo who appears where the petrified Dionysus should have been). If the figure of a petrified Dionysus would have implied some kind of correspondence (mimetic or other) between the Apollonian artwork and its Dionysian meaning, the figure of Apollo turning not Dionysus but himself into stone implies that there is no Dionysian essence or spirit or substratum that is contained in the Apollonian artwork. There is only the Apollonian figure itself, the figure for Dionysus. And as the image of the petrified Apollo holding up Medusa's head indicates, this figure cannot be understood as a secondary representation of an original essence, or as having any kind of correspondence to an original essence. It designates only the attempt at realizing such a representation and such a correspondence, and its failure.

If Apollo's turning Dionysus to stone can be read as a figure for his successful, protective representation of an original, essential Dionysus, the turning to stone of Apollo can be read as a figure for Apollo's failure to refer to any such Dionysus. According to the second reading, what is "petrified" is Apollo's capacity to represent in any way at all (safely or unsafely, successfully or unsuccessfully) a Dionysian essence that is external and prior to him. In his commentary on *The Birth of Tragedy*, de Man proposes that this representational predicament—rather than an existential predicament—is the true Dionysian meaning of the Apollonian appearance: "the actual meaning of the Apollonian appearance is not the [Dionysian] empirical reality it represents but the Dionysian insight into the illusory quality of this reality" (92). In other words, it is not a Dionysian reality that is revealed in the Apollonian appearance; what is revealed instead is the illusoriness of the illusion that there is such a reality and that it could be somehow represented. De Man formulates the distinction between the two revelations as a distinction between what the Apollonian appearance represents and what it means, as Andrzej Warminski notes in explicating de Man's sentence: "The Apollinian representation of tragedy may *represent* all kinds of things in the empirical world—the suffering of Oedipus and his family problems, say— but what it actually *means* is the destruction of what it represents. In short, there is no Dionysus (as a deeper substratum, reality, or *Ding an sich*)—only an Apollo who is divided against himself as what he represents and what he means, and what he *means* is the destruction of what he represents."[28] What the Apollonian appearance *represents*—Dionysus, understood as deeper substratum, reality, or *Ding an sich*—is revealed by the representation to be an illusion created by that same representation, and is by means of that revelation "destroyed," as Warminski puts it. This destruction or illusoriness of what Apollo *represents* is what Apollo *means*; it is what de Man calls the Dionysian insight of the Apollonian appearance.[29] The disjunction de Man finds in Nietzsche's Apollo between what he represents and what he means emerges in the passage on Medusa's head in the split between the petrifying Apollo (that is, the one holding up the head) and the petrified Apollo. The petrifying Apollo is the one who would represent an external Dionysian reality. The petrified Apollo, for his part, is indicative of the illusoriness of such a reality and the impossibility of any such representation, as well as the recognition of that illusoriness and impossibility. As such, he would be for de Man the truly Dionysian figure in Nietzsche's text.

The two Apollos who thus emerge in *The Birth of Tragedy* are not simply two juxtaposed, coexisting figures relegated to separate spheres, two different but equally valid ways to interpret the passage on Medusa's head as a commentary on the Apollo and Dionysus relationship more generally. They each have an impact on the other, though their respective impacts are fundamentally asymmetrical, like the relation between Dionysus and Apollo in Nietzsche's dialectical model. Whereas the first Apollo is the cause of the second, the second is the destruction of the first. The petrified Apollo is a direct effect—what this book calls a Medusa effect—of the Apollonian attempt to represent Dionysus, a direct effect of the petrifying Apollo's gesture of holding up Medusa's head at Dionysus in order to turn him into sculpture. It is the gesture of trying to represent an essential, external Dionysus in an image, in other words, that reveals the absence—the illusion, as de Man puts it—of any such Dionysus in the representation. It reveals the failure of the representation to represent a Dionysian reality or essence, a failure emblematized in the figure of the petrified Apollo. If then the petrified Apollo is an effect of Apollo's attempt to represent Dionysus, the petrifying Apollo, for his part, is destroyed by the petrified Apollo who appears in his wake. In other words, the assumption that a representation could contain and reflect an external and prior essence is destroyed by the revelation that there is only the figure of that essence, and that the essence that would preexist its representation, and that would be represented by the representation, is an illusion. This revelation is emblematized in the figure of the petrified Apollo who appears in the place where a petrified Dionysus should logically have appeared.

In the figure of an Apollo who is petrified by his own attempt to turn Dionysus into a stone image, Nietzsche radically displaces the main problematic of *The Birth of Tragedy*. He shifts it away from the existential pathos associated with the name Dionysus on a purely thematic level (the horror of existence, the gruesome night, the human capacity for suffering, and so on).[30] He also shifts it away from the threat of a terrifying essence that must be safely represented by means of transfiguring mirrors, veils, or sculptures. And finally, he shifts it away from the predicament that the Apollonian appearance can only ever render the Dionysian essence inadequately and in a compromised form.[31] Even as the Apollonian artwork is said throughout *The Birth of Tragedy* to be a mere illusory image of Dionysus, the revelation that emerges in the figure of the petrified Apollo is that the Dionysian essence—the essence that would precede the Apollonian figure and that would be represented by that Apollonian figure, however inadequately—is itself the illusion. The Apollonian figure fails to represent Dionysus not because the uncontainable Dionysian essence perpetually eludes its deficient representations, but because there *is* no essential Dionysus, only the Apollonian figure for such a Dionysus. This revelation is analogous to the revelation in Freud's essay "Medusa's Head" that castration is itself always already a figure or representation, not an original essence that precedes and engenders a series of symbols and figurative substitutes.

If the Dionysian essence is an effect or illusion of the Apollonian figure, rather than the Apollonian figure being an illusory image of the Dionysian essence, the hierarchy between Apollo and Dionysus is effectively reversed: Apollo and Dionysus are no longer related as secondary and primary, but vice versa. To rephrase one of Nietzsche's own formulations cited earlier, it is Dionysus who could not live without Apollo, not the other way around. Insofar then as Dionysus is an intrinsic aspect of Apollo, rather than Apollo being the mere image of an external Dionysus, the hierarchy is not only inverted, but its underlying opposition—the opposition between Dionysus and Apollo, understood as the opposition between essence and appearance, reality and representation, meaning and metaphor, outside and inside—is destroyed. This is because Dionysus and Apollo are not opposable, at least not in the terms of the text's ostensible argument about essence and appearance. They constitute what Nietzsche calls "a tremendous [*ungeheurer*] opposition" (33). *Ungeheuer* means huge, colossal, or enormous, as the translation has it, and it also means monster or monstrous, as for instance when Euripides is said by Nietzsche to reproach Aeschylus's tragedies for having "too many tropes and monstrous expressions [*Ungeheuerlichkeiten*] to suit the plainness of the characters" (80). A monstrous, *ungeheuer* opposition is not a binary opposition, but an improper opposition, a strange or unnatural opposition, in some ways not an opposition at all. Nietzsche alludes to such an opposition in section 2 when he maintains that "we need not conjecture regarding the immense [*ungeheure*] gap which separates the *Dionysian Greek* from the Dionysian barbarian" (39). This *ungeheuer* gap between the Dionysian Greek and the Dionysian barbarian (two figures who at that particular moment in Nietzsche's exposition stand in respectively for the Apollonian and the Dionysian principle) is one that is quickly revealed not to be a gap at all: "The opposition between Apollo and Dionysus became more hazardous and even impossible, when similar [Dionysian] impulses burst forth from the deepest roots of the Hellenic nature" (39). Hence the *ungeheuer* gap is on one hand immense (as befitting the alleged opposition between Apollo and Dionysus) and on the other hand "monstrous" (which is to say not a proper gap at all). The monstrosity of the gap is due to the unexpected, *unheimlich* closeness of the two entities at either end, just as the monstrosity of the opposition is due to the affinity between the two opposed entities (that is, to the revelation that Dionysus is an intrinsic aspect of Apollo).

In *The Birth of Tragedy*, Nietzsche intermittently uses the word *ungeheuer* to characterize the Dionysian threat, a choice of words that is consistent with the alleged scope of the Dionysian and also with the recurring image of Dionysus as kind of monster. In a sentence from section 1 cited earlier, for example, he writes, "Schopenhauer has depicted for us the tremendous [*ungeheure*] terror that seizes man when . . . the principle of sufficient reason, in some one of its manifestations, seems to suffer an exception." And in the 1870 preparatory text "Die Geburt des tragischen Gedankens" [The Birth of Tragic Thought], he writes, "the recognition of the terror and absurdities of existence, of a disrupted orderliness and an irrational methodicalness, more generally of the most immense [*ungeheuersten*] suffering in all of nature, was revealed in the artfully veiled figures of the Furies, the Medusas, and the Moira" (KSA, 1:596).[32] In view of the petrified Apollo figure by means of which the paradigmatic opposition between Apollo and

Dionysus is effectively destroyed, what Nietzsche calls the Dionysian cannot exclusively be located in the text's ostensible themes, in the traumatic revelation of an *ungeheuer* terror or an *ungeheuer* suffering. It must also be located in the text's rhetorical exposition, in the opposition Nietzsche constructs between Apollo and Dionysus, the opposition that is not one, the *ungeheuer, unheimlich* opposition that displaces the text's problematic entirely away from the original opposition (and the dialectical synthesis) between Apollo and Dionysus. As de Man puts it, the recognition of the illusion of a Dionysian reality—of a reality that could be meaningfully opposed to an Apollonian appearance—is the true Dionysian insight of *The Birth of Tragedy*. It is itself the *Ungeheuer*—the monster, the Medusa, the Dionysus—in Nietzsche's exposition.

EPILOGUE: THE APOLLONIAN FETISH

What then is the relation between *this* Dionysian insight and the Dionysian insight that is explicitly described by Nietzsche, the Greeks' insight into existential terror and suffering? In "Genesis and Genealogy," de Man describes Nietzsche's text in terms of two conflicting narratives or narrators: "The narrative falls into two parts or, what amounts to the same thing, it acquires two incompatible narrators. The narrator who argues against . . . representational realism destroys the credibility of the other narrator, for whom Dionysian insight is the tragic perception of an original truth" (98). The narrator for whom Dionysian insight is the tragic perception of original truth is the one who posits a Dionysian essence and also the possibility of its representation. The narrator who argues against representational realism is the one who reveals that essence and that possibility to be an illusion. As in Warminski's account of the destructive relation between what Apollo means and what he represents, the relation between the two narrators is said to be a destruction: the first narrator "destroys the credibility" of the second. The relation is also bilateral, however, in that the second narrator in turn veils the first and thereby covers over his own destruction. Though de Man notes that "It cannot be claimed that one of the narrators is *merely* the Apollonian mask of the other" (98, my emphasis), the second narrator does partly function in just this way (even if this is not his only function, as de Man points out). In the paragraphs that follow, I propose that he functions as a fetishistic defense against the first narrator, and that fetishism (in Freud's sense of the term and also in the slightly displaced sense introduced by my reading in the previous chapter of Freud's text on Medusa) provides a useful model for tracing the relation between the two incompatible narrators. Even though Nietzsche does not himself use the terms *fetish* and *fetishism* in *The Birth of Tragedy*, there are thematic and structural parallels between his book and Freud's essay on fetishism, most obviously in the shared figure of a terrifying recognition that is veiled by its representations.

Simply at the level of Nietzsche's statements about the Apollo and Dionysus relationship, the Apollonian artwork functions as a kind of fetish against the threat of Dionysian insights. In what follows, I propose that this fetishistic function can also be extended to what de Man calls the second narrator and to his relation to the first narrator.[33]

Freud's theory of fetishism, as summarized in the previous chapter, is that the fetish covers over a traumatizing absence, the absence of the woman's (or mother's) penis that is revealed to the fetishist as a little boy in the primal scene. The fetishist has a powerful narcissistic investment in this penis because its presence would imply his own invulnerability to castration. By figuratively substituting for the absent female penis, the fetish restores this penis in the fetishist's unconscious and thus reassures him of his non-castration, even as it may also serve simultaneously as a reminder of the woman's "castration" and therefore of his own potential castration: "In very subtle instances both the disavowal and the affirmation of castration have found their way into the construction of the fetish itself" (21:156). So the fetish is by Freud's definition largely equivocal, oscillating between disavowal and affirmation, between consolation and terror, like Medusa's head as interpreted by Freud, and in some ways not unlike the Apollonian artwork described by Nietzsche.

At the level of Nietzsche's theme and argument in the opening sections of *The Birth of Tragedy*, Apollo is like Freud's fetishist, and the Apollonian artwork is like the fetish. Confronted with an existential threat, Apollo protectively posits a figure (a transfiguring reflection, a piece of sculpture, a veil) for the frightful original essence that should not be seen as such, much like the fetishist protectively substitutes the fetish for the woman's or mother's penis, an original essence that cannot be seen as such. The analogy between the two figures is not wholly symmetrical: whereas the Apollonian image of Dionysus mitigates the horror of an original essence, the fetish mitigates the horrifying *absence* of an original essence. And whereas the Apollonian image testifies to the horror of the essence, the fetish (as what Freud calls a "memorial" to the woman's lack of a penis) testifies to the horror of the essence's absence. But there is a general structural similarity within which this distinction is largely subsumed: both the fetish and the Apollonian artwork are figuratively related to an essence that is said to be nonfigurative and original, both reveal a horror that is directly related to that essence (to its absence or presence), and both serve to mitigate that horror. Moreover, in terms of the hierarchy both texts construct between the essence and its representation, the absence or presence of the essence amounts fundamentally to the same thing. In Freud's text, the essence's absence perceived by the little boy in the primal scene in no way undermines the boy's (or Freud's) assumption of an essence as such, of an essence that could empirically be present. This assumption is itself a bit of fetishism, an Apollonian gesture, on Freud's part.

As implied in my reading of Freud's essay "Medusa's Head" in the previous chapter, there is another, less literal way to understand the figurative substitution Freud calls fetishism, specifically the relation between the fetish and the absence for which it is said to substitute. What the fetish covers over in Freud's exposition, my reading suggests, is not the absence of the penis on the woman's body but rather the overall heterogeneity of the castration complex (the economy of having or not having a penis) to that body. It covers over the absence on the woman's body of a penis that could be absent as much as of a penis that could be present. It veils this absence with the fetish that is said by Freud to be a substitute for a missing penis. But the female penis that is replaced by the fetish is itself already a fetish, an imaginary penis that Freud has projected onto the woman's body only so as to be able to take it away again afterward (in the revelation of the woman's "castration"), then to restore it in the fetish or in a phallic figure like Medusa, then to take it away again ("a multiplication of penis symbols signifies castration" [18:273]), and so on. Like the rhetorical substitutions in "Medusa's Head," these removals and subsequent restorations of the woman's imaginary penis make up a potentially infinite loop. What the fetish replaces at any instance in this loop is only another fetish, not an original essence that is traumatically absent but that could be reassuringly present: empirically speaking, a woman can no more be not castrated than castrated. In making its continual substitutions, the fetish serves rhetorically as a fetish for Freud himself. It protectively covers over the absence in Freud's tropological system of an underlying essence that could be either present or absent. As a fetishistic defense against this latter absence (the recognition of which is Freud's true "Dionysian" insight, as I show in my reading of "Medusa's Head"), Freud first posits the fetish of the female penis, then takes it away, then replaces it with another fetish, then takes it away again, and so on. This continual substitution of one fetish for another (rather than for an original essence that is either present or absent) is not unlike the continual ungrounded substitution in "Medusa's Head" of castration figures for other figures rather than for an original castration entity or event. If Freud's fetish is thus understood not as per Freud's ostensible argument as a figure for an (absent) original essence, but rather as a figure for the lack of an essence that could be either present or absent, it bears a structural similarity to the petrified Apollo in *The Birth of Tragedy*. As discussed previously, the latter implies that the Apollonian image is not a representation of an original Dionysian essence. Counter to Nietzsche's ostensible claims, it reveals the impossibility or illusion of any such essence, of an essence that would precede its representations, that could be represented, and that could be contained by a representation.

If it is understood not so much in terms of what Freud literally says about it but rather as a rhetorical praxis (for example, Freud's own praxis), fetishism thus provides a model for mapping the Apollo/Dionysus relationship in each of the two incompatible narratives into which, according to de Man, *The Birth of Tragedy* is divided. What I have been calling the petrifying Apollo is a kind of fetishist who posits the Apollonian artwork as a fetish in order to protect himself against the horror of the essential Dionysus (and also to reveal that horror in the veiled form of Doric sculpture), just as the fetish adopted by Freud's fetishist ostensibly protects him against (and also reveals to him) the horror of his own potential castration. What I have been calling the petrified Apollo is for his part the kind of fetish described in the previous paragraph, the fetish that only ever takes the place of another fetish, never of an original essence. He reveals the impossibility or illusion of any Dionysus that would be essential and original, and that could be represented by an Apollonian artwork or by a fetish. This revelation, what de Man calls Apollo's Dionysian insight, is similar to the Medusa-like revelation of castration's inevitable figurativeness Freud faces in "Medusa's Head."

The petrifying and petrified Apollo are not only each a form of fetishism in, respectively, a more and less reassuring sense of the term, but have a fetishistic relation to one another. The petrified Apollo implies the destruction of the petrifying Apollo and of what he represents: an original Dionysus, and also the assumption that such an original Dionysus could be figuratively represented, however inadequately. The petrifying Apollo in turn mitigates this threat and masks his own destruction, much as in Nietzsche's genetic narrative he mitigates the threat of the existential Dionysus: by interposing as a fetish the figure of the Apollonian artwork, the shining image that would represent, veil, contain, and safely reveal an original Dionysian essence. Hence the two Apollos are related to one another as the two intrinsic aspects of the fetish Freud describes, the threatening aspect and the protective aspect. Because they are fundamentally, logically incompatible with one another, they never come to form a dialectical union or arrive at a genetic reconciliation (unlike Apollo and Dionysus in Nietzsche's argument). Nor is one of them ontologically or rhetorically privileged above the other, as Dionysus is ostensibly privileged by Nietzsche over Apollo. Instead, the one Apollo destroys the other, while the latter disavows that destruction and the recognition of it. The petrified Apollo in *The Birth of Tragedy* reveals the (Dionysian) destruction of any tenable opposition between essence and representation, while the overall doubling of Apollo is the fetishism in which that destruction and its simultaneous disavowal (by means of the petrifying Apollo) remain permanently suspended.

CHAPTER THREE

Two Impressions of Medusa

Walter Pater and A. C. Swinburne

Algernon Charles Swinburne's "Notes on Designs of the Old Masters at Florence," an 1868 review essay published in the *Fortnightly Review* several years after an 1864 trip by Swinburne to Italy, is commonly regarded by literary historians as an inaugural work of what Walter Pater comes to call aesthetic criticism, among other reasons because of its stylistic influence on Pater's 1869 essay "Leonardo da Vinci." Swinburne's text is not a coherent essay but rather a series of notes about a large, uncatalogued collection of Renaissance drawings stored in the Uffizi's basement, including works by Michelangelo, Leonardo, Botticelli, Titian, and Filippo Lippi. In his introductory remarks, Swinburne describes it as an informal documentation of his own subjective responses to the drawings:

> In these desultory notes I desire only to guide the attention to what seems worthiest of notice, without more form of order than has been given by the framers and hangers; taking men and schools as they come to hand, giving precedence and prominence only to the more precious and significant. For guide I have but my own sense of interest and admiration; so that, while making the list of things remarkable as complete and careful as I can, I have aimed at nothing further than to cast into some legible form my impression of the designs registered in so rough and rapid a fashion; and shall begin my transcript with notices of such as first caught and longest fixed my attention. (15:156)[1]

Swinburne's formulation of his critical project, in particular his wanting to call attention to "the more precious and significant" of the artists and works, and his taking as his guide his "own sense of interest and admiration," anticipates Pater's well-known definition of aesthetic criticism in the 1873 "Preface" to *The Renaissance*:

> "To see the object as in itself it really is," has been justly said to be the aim of all true criticism whatever; and in aesthetic criticism the first step towards seeing one's object as it really is, is to know one's own impression as it really is, to discriminate it, to realise it distinctly. The objects with which aesthetic criticism deals—music, poetry, artistic and accomplished forms of human life—are indeed receptacles of so many powers or forces: they possess, like the products of nature, so many virtues or qualities. What is this song or picture, this engaging personality presented in life or in a book, to *me*? What effect does it really produce on me? Does it give me pleasure? and if so, what sort or degree of pleasure? How is my nature modified by its presence, and under its influence? The answers to these questions are the original facts with which aesthetic criticism has to do; and, as in the study of light, of morals, of number, one must realise such primary data for one's self, or not at all. (xix–xx)

According to Pater, the emphasis in aesthetic criticism is not on seeing the artwork objectively, "as in itself it really is,"[2] but on the critic's realizing—in the sense of becoming aware of—his subjective impressions of the work and the sensations aroused in him by those impressions. What Pater's aesthetic critic would then realize in the work of criticism—in the sense of bringing it into being—are those impressions and sensations, rather than an objective account of the work, much as Swinburne says his aim is to "cast into some legible form my impressions of the designs registered in so rough and rapid a fashion."[3] Pater implies that the emphasis on one's own impressions is the most appropriate critical means for apprehending and analyzing the "powers or forces," the special "virtues or qualities," of the artist or artwork about whom or which one is writing.[4] His saying that the critic should aim to "realise" his impressions, and Swinburne saying that he would "cast" his impressions into "legible form," suggest that the work of aesthetic criticism is viewed by them as an artistic object in its own right, one with a considerable degree of autonomy from the artwork or artist under consideration.

In "Notes on Designs," Swinburne is particularly interested in impressions that mix together different, contradictory emotions, as for example the combined feelings of fascination, pleasure, and pain he describes himself as having while looking at a drawing by the fifteenth-century Florentine painter Filippo Lippi:

> The sketches of Filippo Lippi are exquisite and few. One above all, of Lucrezia Buti in her girlhood as the painter found her at Prato in the convent, is of a beauty so intolerable that the eyes can neither endure

nor abstain from it without a pleasure acute even to pain which compels them to cease looking, or a desire which, as it compels them to return, relapses into delight. (15:164)

Swinburne finds a similar quality of intolerableness, though a less delightful and more existentially terrifying variation, in the drawings of Michelangelo:

> Not gratitude, not delight, not sympathy, is the first sense excited in one suddenly confronted with his designs; fear rather, oppressive reverence, and well-nigh intolerable adoration. Their tragic beauty, their inexplicable strength and wealth of thought, their terrible and exquisite significance, all the powers they unveil and all the mysteries they reserve, all their suggestions and all their suppressions, are at first adorable merely. Delightful beyond words they become in time, as the subtler and weightier work of Aeschylus or Shakespeare; but like these they first fill and exalt the mind with a strange and violent pleasure which is the highest mood of worship; reverence intensified to the last endurable degree. The mind, if then it enjoys at all or wonders at all, knows little of its own wonder or its own enjoyment; the air and light about it is too fine and pure to breathe or bear. (15:157–58)

The diverse catalogue of emotions Swinburne claims one feels when looking at Michelangelo's drawings includes gratitude, sympathy, fear, oppressive and unendurable reverence, intolerable adoration, unspeakable delight, and strange and violent pleasure. He suggests that these responses are at least partially caused by the drawings' intimation and revelation to the viewer of powerful and mysterious truths: "all the powers they unveil and all the mysteries they reserve, all their suggestions and suppressions." The experience of the drawings, it seems from Swinburne's description, is as much cognitive as aesthetic; he notes "their *inexplicable* strength and *wealth of thought*" as much as he does "their tragic *beauty*" and "their terrible and *exquisite* significance." And even the aesthetic experience of the drawings is said by Swinburne to pose a challenge to the viewer's cognitive and reflexive capacities: "The mind, if then it enjoys at all or wonders at all, knows little of its own wonder or its own enjoyment."

Swinburne elaborates on the drawings' powerful "suggestions and suppressions" in a passage immediately following, which extends the comparison between Michelangelo, Aeschylus, and Shakespeare:

> All mysteries of good and evil, all wonders of life and death, lie in their hands or at their feet. They have known the causes of things, and are not too happy. The fatal labour of the world, the clamour and hunger of the open-mouthed all-summoning grave, all fears and hopes of

ephemeral men, are indeed made subject to them, and trodden by them
underfoot; but the sorrow and the strangeness of things are not lessened
because to one or two their secret springs have been laid bare and the
courses of their tides made known; refluent evil and good, alternate
grief and joy, life inextricable from death, change inevitable and insuperable fate. (15:158)[5]

Swinburne explicitly associates Michelangelo, Aeschylus, and Shakespeare
with having knowledge of secret forces (the mysteries of good and evil, the
wonders of life and death, the causes of things), and he associates the power
of their art with the subjugation and revelation of those forces. Yet there is
nothing Apollonian about these revelations; the artists and artworks evidently do not mitigate in any way the horror of the insights they expose
to the viewer or reader: "the sorrow and the strangeness of things *are not
lessened* because to one or two their secret springs have been laid bare and
the courses of their tides made known." It is unclear from Swinburne's syntax and punctuation just how the list of forces that concludes the passage
(refluent evil and good, alternate grief and joy, life inextricable from death,
change inevitable, and insuperable fate) is supposed to fit grammatically
into the sentence in which it appears, but what is explicit is that the viewer
or reader is not protected from these forces by means of Aeschylus's, Shakespeare's, and Michelangelo's art, as the Greeks for example are protected in
The Birth of Tragedy by the power of the Apollonian artwork from insights
into their own Dionysian nature, or as the addressee in Rossetti's poem
"Aspecta Medusa" is said to be protected by visual art or poetic language
from any direct insight into the "forbidden thing itself." On the contrary,
it seems that for Swinburne, powerful works of art like those of Aeschylus,
Shakespeare, and Michelangelo subject their viewers or readers to certain
dangers by exposing them to the revelation of frightening, mysterious existential forces. In making his inventory of Michelangelo's drawings, Swinburne at one point distinguishes among them between the horrifying and
the "merely terrible" (15:162), he remarks that a particular drawing "strikes
upon" the viewer's sight and memory (15:162), and he insists that lesser artists "cover their faces" (15:157) when confronted with Michelangelo's work
(the point of this gesture is presumably to show that they are put to shame
by Michelangelo's greatness as an artist, but there is also the implication
that Michelangelo's art is somehow dangerous to look at).

    In "Leonardo da Vinci," an essay avowedly influenced by "Notes on
Designs,"[6] Pater is similarly interested in mixed impressions, specifically in
the extreme and varying emotions he claims that Leonardo's art elicits in
its viewer. He describes the art in some of the same terms Swinburne uses
to describe Michelangelo's drawings, for example as an "interfusion of the
extremes of beauty and terror" (82).[7] And as Swinburne does in the case
of Michelangelo, he attributes the extremity and diversity of the viewer's

responses to suggestions he finds throughout Leonardo's work of Leonardo possessing and revealing a secret knowledge:

> It is still by a certain mystery in his work, and something enigmatical beyond the usual measure of great men, that he fascinates, or perhaps half repels. . . . His type of beauty is so exotic that it fascinates a larger number than it delights, and seems more than that of any other artist to reflect ideas and views and some scheme of the world within; so that he seemed to his contemporaries to be the possessor of some unsanctified and secret wisdom; as to Michelet and others to have anticipated modern ideas. (77–78)[8]

The fascination, delight, and partial repulsion that Leonardo's strange type of beauty elicits, Pater specifies, is due to its reflection of ideas, of an inner scheme, of an "unsanctified and secret wisdom." In a similar formulation elsewhere in the essay, he writes, "Out of the secret places of a unique temperament [Leonardo] brought strange blossoms and fruits hitherto unknown; and for him, the novel impression conveyed, the exquisite effect woven, counted as an end in itself" (92). Just as Swinburne links the powerful effects of Michelangelo's drawings to the disturbing existential insights they provide, Pater implies a connection between the "fruits hitherto unknown" that Leonardo brings forth in his art and the "novel impression" that this art makes on the spectator.[9]

Throughout the essay, Pater also equates the exposure to Leonardo's art and secrets with danger. In an episode he recounts about Leonardo's boyhood apprenticeship in Verrocchio's workshop, for example, Verrocchio is said to "[turn] away as one stunned" when he sees an angel painted by Leonardo and realizes that he has been surpassed by his young pupil in his own artistic purpose, "a larger knowledge and insight into things" (80). In another, chronologically much later episode, Leonardo's pupils are said to "efface their own individuality" when they are initiated by Leonardo "into his secret" (92). And like Verrocchio and Leonardo's pupils, Pater suggests, we too are potentially subjected to this dangerous force when we are exposed to Leonardo's art. In describing the subjects of Leonardo's drawings, for example, he writes,

> Nervous, electric, faint always with some inexplicable faintness, these people seem to be subject to exceptional conditions, to feel powers at work in the common air unfelt by others, to become, as it were, the receptacle of them, and pass them on to us in a chain of secret influences. (91)

According to this sentence, the people depicted in Leonardo's drawings are visibly subjected to exceptional conditions and powers, conditions and powers of which they become vessels and which they also "pass on to us."

They pass them on to us by subjecting us to the power of the drawings in which they appear, drawings that influence us much as the unseen powers at work in the enveloping air influence them.

Although neither Swinburne nor Pater says this explicitly, the implication in both "Notes on Designs" and "Leonardo da Vinci" is that if powerful works of art like Michelangelo's and Leonardo's pose a potential danger to the viewer, then writing about the works would be a way of mastering their danger and overcoming their power.[10] It would be a way of mitigating the fascination by analyzing the work and by establishing correspondences between elements of the viewer's complex impression and formal elements in the work itself. In the "Preface" to *The Renaissance*, Pater prescribes the analysis of an artist's or artwork's "virtue"—and of the relation between this virtue and the impression made by the artist or work on the viewer or reader—as an important imperative for the aesthetic critic:

> The function of the aesthetic critic is to distinguish, to analyse, and separate from its adjuncts, the virtue by which a picture, a landscape, a fair personality in life or in a book, produces this special impression of beauty or pleasure, to indicate what the source of that impression is, and under what conditions it is experienced. His end is reached when he has disengaged that virtue, and noted it, as a chemist notes some natural element, for himself and others; and the rule for those who would reach this end is stated with great exactness in the words of a recent critic of Sainte-Beuve:—*De se borner à connaître de près les belles choses, et à s'en nourrir en exquis amateurs, en humanistes accomplis.* (xx–xxi)

Pater ostensibly advocates this approach as a means for deepening and varying the critic's susceptibility to impressions. But the method he describes assumes more of a defensive function when placed into a context like that of the Leonardo essay, one in which works of art are said to pose a potential danger to the viewer and the critic. In such a context, distinguishing and analyzing the special virtues by which a personality or art object makes its impression is not a self-nourishing form of connoisseurship, nor an objective scientific curiosity like that of the chemist noting the elements that make up a compound substance, but a means of protecting oneself from that personality or object by making sense of it and its powers. If Michelangelo's and Leonardo's art is indeed a kind of Medusa, as both Swinburne's and Pater's formulations variously suggest, the task of "disengaging" its virtue and "separating" it from its adjuncts puts the critic into the role of the decapitating Perseus.[11]

PATER'S MEDUSA

In "Leonardo da Vinci," Pater's catalogue includes a painting in the Uffizi entitled *Head of Medusa* (Figure 5), a work attributed for most of the

FIGURE 5. Anonymous, *Head of Medusa*. Uffizi, Florence. Photo: Scala / Art Resource, NY.

nineteenth century to Leonardo and which art historians have since generally attributed to an unknown seventeenth-century Flemish artist.[12] The discussion of the painting occurs late in the section of the essay documenting Leonardo's early years in Florence. Pater analyzes Leonardo's art during this period as an "interfusion of the extremes of beauty and terror," a combination of "curious beauty" and grotesquery, and of an outer stylistic perfection and an inner "seed of discontent" (81–82). The analysis culminates in the account of the Medusa painting, which to Pater best exemplifies this mixed aesthetic:

> All these swarming fancies unite in the *Medusa* of the Uffizii. . . . The subject has been treated in various ways; Leonardo alone cuts to its centre; he alone realises it as the head of a corpse, exercising its powers through all the circumstances of death. (83)

From Pater's point of view, Leonardo's unique and original insight into his subject matter is that for the purposes of producing a powerful effect on the viewer, the motif of Medusa's decapitated head must be understood and rendered by the artist as itself a kind of Medusa's head: many artists have variously treated the subject, but Leonardo "alone realises it as the head of a corpse, exercising its powers through all the circumstances of death." The power of Leonardo's painting, as Pater sees it, lies in its unprecedented realization (in both senses) of its subject as an actual corpse's head and in its appropriation—through that realization—of its subject's original power, the power to fascinate and figuratively to petrify the viewer (which parallels the literal petrifying power of Medusa's head in the myth). The appropriation by the painting of its subject's power is indicated in the pronoun "it" in the phrase "exercising its powers through all the circumstances of death," which refers both to the Medusa subject and also to the subject's realization in the painting. The double reference—and the analogy between subject and painting it implies—is confirmed by the immediately following sentence in Pater's description, "What may be called the fascination of corruption penetrates in every touch its exquisitely finished beauty" (83). In that sentence, the pronoun "it" unequivocally refers to the painting, not the subject, given that the beauty in question is said to be "exquisitely *finished*." Thus Pater inscribes a slippage between Leonardo's subject and his painting, and it is the painting—as much as the painting's subject—that exercises its powers on the viewer through all the circumstances of death.

The Medusa painting's tangible appropriation of its subject's Medusa-like powers confirms Pater's more general association of Leonardo's art with danger. It also confirms Pater's allusions throughout the Leonardo essay to Medusa—for instance in the phrase "interfusion of the extremes of beauty and terror"—as a metaphor for that art, and to Medusa's effect on the viewer—for instance in the phrase "fascinates, or perhaps half repels"—as a metaphor for its effect on the people who look at it. The word *fascinate* is Pater's paradigmatic term for describing the effect of Leonardo's work, as in the phrase "it fascinates a larger number than it delights." Derived from *fascinum*, a Latin word for witchcraft, it suggests that the viewer might be transfixed or spellbound by the irresistible power of Leonardo's art, much as Leonardo's pupils are said to be deprived of their individuality by it. As such, it complements various diction and imagery used throughout Pater's essay to characterize the effect of Leonardo's work in similar terms. Megan Becker-Leckrone has noted, for example, that the words Pater uses at two different moments in the essay to describe two different viewer reactions— one by Leonardo's father and one by Verrocchio—to paintings by Leonardo, "astonishment" and "stunned," "share an etymological connection to the Old French root 'estoner,' which specifically calls up the power Medusa's severed head has to turn men to stone" (361n22).

In describing the realization of the Medusa subject in the Medusa-like painting, Pater makes an implicit analogy between Leonardo, who "alone cuts to [his subject's] centre," and Perseus. Just as Perseus defeats Medusa where lesser heroes have failed, he suggests, Leonardo vanquishes the daunting subject of Medusa's head where lesser artists have failed: "the subject has been treated in various ways; Leonardo alone cuts to its centre."[13] Alongside this parallel between Leonardo and Perseus, the passage on the Medusa painting introduces a concurrent but more muted parallel between Leonardo and Pater himself. If Leonardo's unique strength as an artist lies in recognizing the true nature of his subject's power and in so doing transferring that power to his painting, Pater's unique strength as a critic in turn lies in recognizing the Medusa-like power of Leonardo's art and in so doing transferring some of that power to his prose. Pater indeed not only recognizes Leonardo's art as a kind of Medusa, but Leonardo himself, as suggested by some of the details in his subsequent description of the Medusa painting:

> What may be called the fascination of corruption penetrates in every touch its exquisitely finished beauty. . . . The delicate snakes seem literally strangling each other in terrified struggle to escape from the Medusa brain. The hue which violent death always brings with it is in the features; features singularly massive and grand, as we catch them inverted, in a dexterous foreshortening, crown foremost, like a great calm stone against which the wave of serpents breaks. (83)

The word *fascination*, here associated with the painting's peculiar beauty, occurs frequently in Pater's descriptions of Leonardo's art, as noted in the previous paragraph, and it also occurs in accounts of his appearance and personality, for instance in sentences like "Leonardo's nature had a kind of spell in it. Fascination is always the word descriptive of him" (85) and "We see him in his boyhood fascinating all men by his beauty" (79). In addition, the image of the "delicate snakes" and the "wave of serpents" struggling to escape "from the Medusa brain" echoes an image Pater gives of Leonardo himself, from whose "overwrought and labouring brain" are delivered "intricate devices of line and colour" and "swarming fancies" (82–83). Pater suggests through these analogies that he alone among critics has seen and "realised" both the famously enigmatic Leonardo and his famously enigmatic work for what they truly are, a kind of Medusa, just as Leonardo alone among artists has successfully realized his difficult subject-matter for what it is: an image of violent death. This recognition of Leonardo as a Medusa would distinguish Pater from the mass of critics who have written about Leonardo, to several of whom he makes reference in the essay,[14] just as Leonardo's Medusa painting distinguishes Leonardo from the many other artists who have treated the same subject. And if Leonardo's recognition of his subject's power transfers that power over to his painting, as Pater's text makes explicit, then by virtue of the analogy Pater's recognition of Leonardo's power would implicitly endow his prose with a kind of power similar to the one he finds in Leonardo's Medusa-like art and personality. It suggests that he too might have the strength to cut to his subject's center and to carry it beyond the range of its traditional associations.[15]

The analogy between Pater and Leonardo implies that like Leonardo's power as an artist, Pater's power as a critic manifests itself in the particular way he realizes his subject. He associates his subject, Leonardo's art, with posing a threat to the viewer, as the comparison of the Medusa painting to a Medusa's head makes explicit. His account of the painting would acknowledge this threat and also mitigate it by "analyzing" it, by "disengaging" it, by "distinguishing" it, by "noting" it, and by "separating it from its adjuncts," to use some of the paradigmatic terms from the "Preface" to *The Renaissance*. By writing about the painting, Pater would escape being petrified by it and by Leonardo's Medusa-like art more generally. He would escape being "stunned" by it, like Verrocchio, or being "astonished" by it, like Leonardo's father.

As Pater sees it, the threat of the Medusa painting—and of Leonardo's art more generally—has two aspects. For one thing, it threatens to overwhelm and confound the critic in its mixing together of disparate aesthetic categories such as beauty and terror or beauty and grotesquery. Pater describes Leonardo's art as an "interfusion of the extremes of beauty and terror," and as a "curious," "remote," or "refined" type of beauty "mingled inextricably" with elements of mockery, caricature, and grotesquery (82). He calls it a swarm of diverse "fancies" and identifies the Medusa painting (in which beauty and corruption are said to be inextricably linked) as its most representative image: "all these swarming fancies unite in the *Medusa* of the *Uffizii*." If the painting is indeed a convoluted knot of different styles and qualities, and if its beauty is indeed permeated in every touch by corruption, it would seem to be difficult or impossible for the critic to analyze it in the way Pater prescribes in the "Preface" to *The Renaissance*. It would be difficult to untangle and "disengage" its beauty and corruption from one another, just as it would be difficult to separate out and distinguish beauty, terror, grotesquery, and mockery in the confusing swarm of fancies as which Pater sees both the painting and Leonardo's art more generally.

Yet Pater's description of the painting does precisely this: even as it explicitly recognizes the interfusion of beauty and terror in the painting—and celebrates this combination as an unprecedented type of beauty Leonardo has brought into being[16]—its exposition also works rhetorically to separate beauty and terror by outlining where one ends and the other begins, and by attributing beauty to certain details and terror to others. In examining Medusa's features, for example, Pater juxtaposes the cheek's "dainty lines" with its death-like coloring ("the hue which violent death always brings with it") and with the nearby figure of a bat.[17] In another sentence, he similarly juxtaposes the "delicate" snakes with their "terrified struggle to escape from the Medusa brain." So while in the painting beauty and terror are inextricably linked, in Pater's description beauty is specifically attributed to Leonardo's rendering of the individual snakes and to the lines of the cheek, while terror is attributed to the bat, the knotting together of the snakes, and the cadaverous hue of Medusa's features.

This kind of analysis, to use Pater's word, has a dual purpose. It protects the critic from Leonardo's swarming fancies, from his willful confounding of traditional aesthetic styles and categories, by restoring to the work a reassuring legibility. Even though as a critic Pater is not invested in traditional styles and categories as such, and even though he appreciates Leonardo's mixed aesthetic for itself, he does have an investment in making sense of the painting when he writes about it. Consistent with what he says about the method of aesthetic criticism in the "Preface," he wants to analyze its "virtue" by breaking it down into distinct constitutive elements. In the description of the Medusa painting, the analysis takes the form of distinguishing and juxtaposing elements of beauty and elements of terror. This allows him to see and to present the picture not as an inextricable knot or confusing swarm of different aesthetic styles and effects (as which, he suggests, it strikes most viewers), but as a legible, mappable dialectical tension between two clearly delineated styles and effects: the terrifying and the beautiful. Such a presentation of Leonardo's painting would affirm his power as a critic, much like Leonardo's presentation of Medusa's head is said to affirm his power as an artist. And it also has a second protective function, as it concurrently mitigates an existential threat Pater finds in the Medusa painting, one that is similar to the threat Swinburne finds in Michelangelo's drawings.

For Pater, the Medusa painting is disconcerting not only in its blending of disparate aesthetic styles and effects, but also as an image of human death.[18] He attributes the painting's power to its naturalism: "the hue which violent death always brings with it is in the features." Realizing the particular quality of the horror it reveals to the viewer ("the head of a corpse"), he opens his discussion of the painting with the remark, "It was not in play that [Leonardo] painted that other Medusa" (83). For Pater, part of the strength of his own criticism lies in this realization, which to him implicitly parallels Leonardo's strength in seeing and rendering—that is, in realizing—the motif of Medusa's head in a naturalistic way. Yet at the same time Pater tempers his appreciation of the painting's horror with a concurrent appreciation of its beautiful elements. The purpose of the juxtaposition is not only to make the painting legible in dialectical terms, as discussed in the previous paragraph, but is existential, since the beauty to which Pater calls attention works rhetorically to balance and mitigate the horror of his having seen—and his having to show his reader—a corpse's head. Pater maintains about the painting that "corruption penetrates in every touch its exquisitely finished beauty," and in his description of the painting, this penetration also works in reverse: beauty tangibly penetrates each of the painting's "corrupt" elements, thereby working to distill their horror. Medusa's death-like hue and the image of the bat are offset by the "dainty lines" of Medusa's cheek, for example, and the image of the snakes "literally strangling each other in terrified struggle to escape from the Medusa brain" is palliated by Pater's characterization of the snakes as delicate and by the description of Medusa's features as a "great calm stone against which the wave of serpents breaks." Just as the stone acts as a restraining barrier against the breaking wave of serpents, Pater suggests, so the beautiful elements act to mitigate and contain the terrifying elements. This kind of mitigation occurs not only in the passage on Medusa's head but in other descriptions of Leonardo's works as well, in which a given work's terrifying aspect is tempered by the abrupt revelation of an element of beauty located within or juxtaposed against that horror. In describing a preparatory sketch for Leonardo's lost painting *The Battle of Anghiari*, for example, Pater writes, "we may discern some lust of terrible things in it, so that even the horses tore each other with their teeth. And yet one fragment of it, in a drawing of his at Florence, is far different—a waving field of lovely armour, the chased edgings running like lines of sunlight from side to side" (100). The movement performed in these two sentences from "some lust of terrible things" and "horses [tearing] each other with their teeth" to "a waving field of lovely armour" and "lines of sunlight" is the same movement Pater makes in the description of the Medusa painting.[19] Given the general identification of Leonardo's art as threatening to the viewer, it would counteract the threat at the level of the commentary.

Pater balances and tempers the Medusa painting's horror not only by pointing to individual elements of beauty, but also by referring to the painting as a whole and to its details in explicitly compositional terms. He describes the painting in two ways: as a naturalistic image of human death and as a crafted formal composition. And like the elements of beauty he juxtaposes with the elements of terror, the formal elements implicitly work to alleviate the existential threat posed by the elements of terror and by the painting as a whole. For example, Pater refers to the "*hue* which violent death always brings with it," the "dainty *lines* of the cheek [about which] the bat flits unheeded," and the "exquisitely *finished* beauty" that is permeated at every touch by the fascination of corruption. These lines seem at first glance to attribute an Apollonian function to the painting itself, implying it is Leonardo's "exquisitely finished" presentation of the subject (as the lines and hues of a painting) that protectively coats the subject's horror. But it is in fact Pater's text that performs the Apollonian function in the way that it notes and thereby disengages from one another the terrifying elements, the beautiful elements, and the compositional elements. It is Pater's prose, and not necessarily Leonardo's painting, that demonstrably moves between terror and beauty, and between emotional responses and formal analysis. The mitigation of the painting's horror by means of its beauty or by means of its formal composition is therefore more a rhetorical effect of Pater's description of the painting than an aesthetic effect of the painting itself.

Pater's affirmation of his own powers as a critic, which is implied in the analogy between Leonardo's and Pater's realization of their respective subjects, manifests itself in the passage on the Medusa painting in his defense against the painting's Medusa-like effects. The passage suggests that by writing about the painting, Pater is able to mitigate the effect the painting has on him. His text enables him to become the Apollonian Greek in *The Birth of Tragedy*, seeing and showing the painting's terrors in a securely veiled form, or to become the chemist in the "Preface" to *The Renaissance*, disengaging the painting's elements—terrifying elements, beautiful elements, and compositional elements—from one another and noting them for himself and for his readers. Pater's distinguishing of these virtues by means of his incisive analysis is not only a defense against the painting, however, but also his Perseus-like victory over his subject, his cutting to his subject's center. If the Medusa painting is for Leonardo both a means of protection against his Medusa-like subject and a form of artistic empowerment, writing about the painting is for Pater both a protection against Leonardo's Medusa-like art and a brandish of his power as a critic.

SWINBURNE'S MEDUSA

In "Notes on Designs," Swinburne encounters his own version of Medusa in a series of three female portraits by Michelangelo (Figure 6):

> But in one separate head there is more tragic attraction than in these [previously discussed drawings]: a woman's, three times studied, with divine and subtle care; sketched and re-sketched in youth and age, beautiful always beyond desire and cruel beyond words; fairer than heaven and more terrible than hell; pale with pride and weary with wrongdoing; a silent anger against God and man burns, white and repressed, through her clear features. In one drawing she wears a head-dress of eastern fashion rather than western, but in effect made out of the artist's mind only; plaited in the likeness of closely-welded scales as of a chrysalid serpent, raised and waved and rounded in the likeness of a sea-shell. In some inexplicable way all her ornaments seem to partake of her fatal nature, to bear upon them her brand of beauty fresh from hell; and this through no vulgar machinery of symbolism, no serpentine or otherwise bestial emblem: the bracelets and rings are innocent enough in shape and workmanship; but in touching her flesh they have become infected with deadly and malignant meaning. Broad bracelets divide the shapely splendour of her arms; over the nakedness of her firm and luminous breasts, just below the neck, there is passed a band as of metal. Her eyes are full of proud and passionless lust after gold and blood; her hair, close and curled, seems ready to shudder in sunder and divide into snakes. Her throat, full and fresh, round and hard to the eye as her bosom and arms, is erect and stately, the head set firm on it without any droop or lift of the chin; her mouth crueller than a tiger's, colder than a snake's, and beautiful beyond a woman's. (15:159–60)[20]

FIGURE 6. Michelangelo, *Bust of a Woman*. Uffizi, Florence. Photo: Scala / Ministero per i Beni e le Attività culturali / Art Resource, NY.

FIGURE 7. Michelangelo, *Head of a Woman*. British Museum, London. © British Museum / Art Resource, NY.

While less muted in its imagery and more extravagant in its claims, this passage has obvious parallels with Pater's statements about Leonardo. Like the decapitated Medusa's head in the Leonardo painting, for instance, the woman depicted in the three Michelangelo portraits is said to pose a threat: "a silent anger against God and man burns, white and repressed, through her clear features. . . . Her eyes are full of proud and passionless lust after gold and blood." And like the viewer of Leonardo's art, the viewer of the portraits is said to experience a dangerous fascination, a "tragic attraction."

Unlike Pater, however, Swinburne frames the threat he finds in the Michelangelo portraits specifically in sexual terms. The danger he claims to see takes the form of a woman, and more specifically of an image of feminine evil that is at once archetypal and conventionally nineteenth-century, the figure of the so-called Fatal Woman. In the passage itself, Swinburne alludes to Medusa ("her hair, close and curled, seems ready to . . . divide into snakes") and he ascribes to the woman depicted in the three portraits a series of traditional attributes of the Fatal Woman: a "cold" gaze, a "cruel" mouth, a hieratic posture, a fusion of beauty and cruelty, and so on. Further on in his description, he maintains about the woman that "many names might be found for her" (15:160) and identifies her with Venus, Lamia, Amestris, Cleopatra, and Jezebel, all common nineteenth-century exemplars of the Fatal Woman (15:160–61).[21] By explicitly figuring the threat of Michelangelo's subject in terms of femininity and in terms of the Fatal Woman, he implicitly defines the viewer of the drawings as the woman's male victim, one who is subjected both to the woman's bloodlust and to the drawings' dangerous allure (there is an implicit identification in Swinburne's text between the drawings and the woman they depict, in part because Swinburne uses the same imagery and diction to describe the woman as he uses earlier in the essay to describe Michelangelo's drawings in general[22]). Swinburne suggests that the viewer is subjected to the power of the drawings and of their lurid subject matter much as imperiled male protagonists like Tannhäuser, Marc Antony, and Ahab are subjected to the powers of Venus, Cleopatra, and Jezebel, their Fatal Woman antagonists.

As does Pater's description of Leonardo's Medusa painting, Swinburne's account of Michelangelo's female portraits implies that by writing about the drawings, Swinburne could somehow protect himself from the threat they pose. The passage adheres to a similar Apollonian assumption as Pater's essay on Leonardo: the assumption that the verbal, rhetorical exposition of a dangerous work of visual art would somehow mitigate the powerful effect of that work itself. In Swinburne's text, the mitigation takes the form of unveiling the woman depicted in the drawings, of removing her obscuring ornaments (her bracelets, rings, and headdress) and exposing her body. This unveiling is implied by Swinburne's repeated claims that the woman's evil is revealed to the viewer not in her ornaments, but in her various body parts. For example, Swinburne specifies that the woman's "fatal nature" becomes visible in her features, her eyes, her hair, and her mouth: "Her eyes are full of proud and passionless lust after gold and blood; her hair, close and curled, seems ready to shudder in sunder and divide into snakes." The description opens with the claim that "a silent anger against God and man burns . . . through her features" and concludes with a reference to "her mouth crueller than a tiger's, colder than a snake's, and beautiful beyond a woman's." It would seem from these statements that it is the drawings themselves that reveal the woman's evil through various parts of her body, but this is a projection on Swinburne's part. It is his exposition of the drawings, not necessarily the drawings themselves, that locates the evil in the woman's features, eyes, mouth, and hair. The hair turning into snakes, for example, is a rhetorical figure in Swinburne's text, not something that can be seen in the actual drawing.

The unveiling performed by Swinburne's description has a mitigating effect because it attributes a reassuring visibility to the existential threat Swinburne claims to find in the portraits. However frightening that threat may be to a viewer, it is reassuringly exposed by Swinburne's description, and moreover is exposed in the reassuring form of a woman's body. Swinburne's use of a woman's body as a vehicle for conveying the threat is reassuring on several levels. It partially provides reassurance through the misogynist scenario staged in the passage: a male critic figuratively stripping away a woman's ornaments so as to reveal to his male readers her body (and the evil that is said to be clearly intelligible through that body). And it also provides reassurance through the identification of that evil with a figure that is thoroughly marked in all of its details as an other to both Swinburne himself and his reader (because of the definitive gendering of this other as female, the reader of the passage is implicitly constructed as male). This woman in the portraits may well pose all kinds of threats to the man who looks at her, but because Swinburne's description of her defines her as wholly remote and foreign to the (male) reader, because this "woman" is figured as man's abject other (rather than, say, as his relation), the description is fundamentally reassuring.[23]

So as to be able clearly to see the woman's body—and to see her "fatal nature" reassuringly revealed through that body—Swinburne has to be able to distinguish her body from her numerous ornaments. He has to be able to strip away the ornaments, so to speak, and to expose the various parts of her body as exclusive indices of her evil. Thus the ornaments are like the veil that his description must lift in order for the underlying truth to become visible. Swinburne associates this process of unveiling with some difficulty, as apparently there is in the drawings a lack of a clearly visible distinction between the body and the ornaments: "In some inexplicable way all her ornaments seem to partake of her fatal nature, to bear upon them her brand of beauty fresh from hell. . . . The bracelets and rings are innocent enough in shape and workmanship; but in touching her flesh they become infected with deadly and malignant meaning." It seems that the ornaments take on qualities of the flesh they touch, and so it is difficult for the viewer of the drawings to see exactly where one leaves off and the other begins. Due to this "infection" of the ornaments with the woman's "fatal nature," they become virtually inseparable from the body, much as the beauty of Leonardo's Medusa painting is for Pater inextricable from its corruption and grotesquery. The viewer's inability to separate the ornaments from the body is on one hand indicative of the decadent quality Swinburne appreciates in Michelangelo's drawings: their perverse fusion of the organic and the artificial, and of innocence and corruption. But it also poses a potential impediment for Swinburne's rhetorical purpose, his would-be reassuring revelation of the woman's evil exclusively and unequivocally through the parts of her body.

Swinburne derives the conceit of ornaments that are inseparable from the body they decorate from Flaubert's 1862 novel *Salammbo*, a text to which he explicitly makes reference in "Notes on Designs."[24] In chapter 11 of the novel, the disguised Carthaginian priestess Salammbo secretly comes into the Barbarian army's camp in order to retrieve from their leader Mâtho the return of the zaïmph, a sacred veil he had earlier stolen from the Temple of the moon goddess Tanit in Carthage. When she first appears in the camp and asks to be taken to Mâtho's tent, "she had over her face a yellow veil with black flowers and so many draperies round her body that it was impossible to guess anything about her. From the top of the terrace, [Mâtho] considered this vague form rising like a ghost from the shadows of the night" (181). This initial description sets up a pattern for the ensuing tent scene, a pattern in which Mâtho's inquisitive gazes at Salammbo are repeatedly confounded by the fusion of her veils and ornaments with her body. Once in his tent, Salammbo removes the veil from her face and demands the return of the zaïmph, but Mâtho, so overwhelmed by his own desire and curiosity, "did not hear; he gazed at her and for him her clothes were fused [*se confondaient*] with her body. The shimmer of the material, like the splendour of her skin, was something special and peculiar to her. Her eyes and her diamonds flashed; her polished nails were a continuation of the fine jewels on her fingers" (183). In these lines, Flaubert indicates both Salammbo's mysteriousness (as Mâtho sees it) and Mâtho's disconcertion in the fusion of Salammbo's body with her clothes and ornaments. The continuity he describes between her clothes and her skin, her diamonds and her eyes, and her jewels and her nails, is like the continuity Swinburne finds between the woman's body and her ornaments in the Michelangelo drawings. In both texts, a male viewer gazes at a woman with a desire that is as much interpretative as sexual: "Irrepressible curiosity overcame him," Flaubert writes about Mâtho, "like a child stretching out its hand to an unknown fruit" (183). And in both texts, the male viewer's comprehension of the woman at whom he gazes is confounded or potentially confounded by his inability to see her body as such, to penetrate past her veils and ornaments. The verb *se confondre*, translated here as to fuse, also means to become confused or to get mixed up. It suggests that not only do Salammbo's body, clothes, and ornaments fuse together in Mâtho's gaze, but that Mâtho is visually disoriented by Salammbo's appearance because he cannot tell the difference between her body and her veils. Mâtho alludes to this confusion when he and Salammbo look at the moon together through an opening in the tent: "'Oh, how many nights have I spent gazing at it! It looked like a veil hiding your face; you looked through at me; your memory was mingled with its rays; I could no longer distinguish between the two of you!'" (187). In Mâtho's inability to distinguish between Salammbo and her veil, the tent scene dramatizes the failure of the kind of unveiling Swinburne aims to perform in the passage on the Michelangelo portraits; the denouement of Flaubert's plot reiterates this failure in that all of Mâtho's subsequent attempts to possess and to understand Salammbo are frustrated.[25]

In remarking on the blending of body and ornament in the Michelangelo portraits, Swinburne's exposition alludes to the kind of interpretative predicament into which Mâtho falls when faced with Salammbo's body and ornaments, and also works rhetorically to resolve it. It does this by insisting on a fundamental distinction: the woman's evil manifests itself through her body, while the ornaments only "*seem* to partake of her fatal nature." The ornaments, Swinburne claims, are in themselves "innocent enough in shape and workmanship." They only become "contaminated" with evil if they happen to touch the woman's body: "in touching her flesh they have become infected with her deadly and malignant meaning." Rhetorically speaking, one might say they are metonymies for the woman's evil, associations by mere contiguity. The distinction Swinburne establishes between the "innocent" ornament and the "corrupt" body would serve to stabilize the unveiling performed by his exposition of the drawings: the stripping away of the ornaments and the exposure of the woman's "fatal nature" through various parts of her body. Even if the ornaments and the body do seem to blend in with one another, the distinction between the innocence of the one and the corruption of the other would enable Swinburne to separate them by giving him a tenable criterion for such a separation.

Swinburne's paradigmatic figure for the woman's body is the serpent. The woman's hair is described as "ready to . . . divide into snakes," and her mouth is said to be "colder than a snake's." In the third of the three portraits, her "serpentine hair is drawn up into a tuft at the crown with two ringlets hanging, heavy and deadly as small tired snakes" (15:161). And in describing a fourth drawing by Michelangelo, a study of Cleopatra that is said to reproduce the design of the first three portraits (Figure 8), Swinburne calls attention to the hair "shaping itself into a snake's likeness as it unwinds, right against a living snake held to the breast and throat" (15:161). In his commentary on the drawing, he develops the implied analogy between Cleopatra and the snake, comparing the Cleopatra portrait to the "mystic marriage . . . painted in the loveliest passage of 'Salammbô,' between the maiden body and the scaly coils of the serpent and the priestess alike made sacred to the moon" (15:161). The "marriage" between Salammbo's body and the serpent's scaly coils (the reference is to Salammbo's dance with the snake in chapter 10) parallels the pairing of Cleopatra and

FIGURE 8. Michelangelo, *Head of Cleopatra*. Casa Buonarroti, Florence. Photo: Scala / Art Resource, NY.

the snake in Michelangelo's drawing, and Swinburne's formulation identifies Salammbo's body with the snake's body just as Michelangelo is said to identify Cleopatra with her snake in the way he sketches her hair as serpentine. Because Swinburne's chiasmic syntax ("between the maiden body and the scaly coils of the serpent and the priestess") reverses the proper order of the second two terms in the parallelism, the sentence can be read either as attributing a "maiden body" and "scaly coils" to both the priestess and the serpent, or as attributing the scaly coils to the priestess and the maiden body to the serpent.

Images like the serpentine female body and the serpentine hair not only function in Swinburne's text as revelations of "feminine evil," but also work rhetorically to secure the opposition between the "corrupt" body and the "innocent" ornament on which those revelations depend. In describing the ornaments, Swinburne maintains that they might seem to the viewer to partake of the woman's fatal nature and to bear upon them her type of hellish beauty, but he insists that they do so "through no vulgar machinery of symbolism, no serpentine or otherwise bestial emblem." This qualification can be understood simply to mean that none of the ornaments is vulgarly symbolic, and that none of them is shaped like a snake or another animal. But it also reiterates Swinburne's point that rhetorically speaking, the ornaments are only metonymies for the woman's evil and that their relation to it is thus purely contiguous ("in touching her flesh they become infected with deadly and malignant meaning"). By contrast with the metonymic ornament, the woman's serpentine body and serpentine hair are said to be symbols or "serpentine emblems" of her evil. (Unlike Freud in "Medusa's Head," Swinburne does not have a consistent or rigorous concept of the term *symbol* in "Notes on Designs," as suggested by the fact that he uses it synonymously with the word *emblem*. But for him too, as for Freud, it would seem to imply a less contiguous and a more organic relationship between the two entities or ideas being substituted for one another.)

Even as Swinburne insists that the ornaments are expressly not serpentine emblems or symbols, however, he describes the headdress the woman is wearing in one of the three drawings as snake-like: "In one drawing she wears a head-dress . . . plaited in the likeness of closely welded scales as of a chrysalid serpent." This description directly contradicts his assertion that the ornaments partake in the woman's evil "through no . . . serpentine or otherwise bestial emblem." The contradiction is not simply a matter of an inconsistency in the statements he makes about the drawings, but has wider implications. The introduction of the serpentine headdress into the description of the drawings collapses the description's underlying oppositions between ornament and body, between innocence and evil, and between metonymy and symbol or emblem, the very oppositions on which the success of Swinburne's exposition structurally depends. This is because the serpent is not merely one image among others in Swinburne's description, but functions in that description as a paradigmatic, defining figure on three levels: it is a privileged figure for the body (as opposed to the ornament), a figure for the evil that manifests itself through that body (as opposed to the innocence of the ornaments), and, as indicated in the phrase "serpentine emblem," a figure for a symbolic or emblematic (as opposed to metonymic) figuring of that evil. For Swinburne to describe one of the ornaments as snake-like is therefore not merely a minor inconsistency or contradiction. It splits the headdress into being both an ornament and also a version of the body (since the woman's body is by definition serpentine), and it taints the headdress's metonymic innocence (qua ornament) with a simultaneous "serpentine emblematic" or symbolic quality. Insofar then as the headdress is effectively both an ornament and also a variant of the body, and both a metonymy and a serpentine emblem or symbol, it collapses the binary oppositions between those four terms. It deprives the ornament of its defining innocence and it conversely deprives the body of its defining association with evil, implying that the woman's evil is as much revealed by her ornaments as by her body.

If the serpentine headdress is a variant of the woman's body, the body that is revealed in Swinburne's exposition is in turn a variant of the headdress. When Swinburne maintains that the woman's "hair, close and curled, seems ready to shudder in sunder and divide into snakes," for example, his statement can be read in two ways. On one hand, it designates the revelation through an element of the woman's body of something frightening, indicated in the figure of the woman's imminent transformation into Medusa. Such a reading would be consistent with the majority of Swinburne's statements in the passage. On the other hand, however, the description of the woman's hair as "close and curled" and "ready to . . . divide into snakes" can also be read as a reference to—or even a loose quotation of—the description of the headdress "plaited in the likeness of closely-welded scales as of a chrysalid serpent, raised and waved and rounded." At the level of this second reading, the Medusa-like hair is an approximation of the headdress. In that sense, it is as much an ornament, a variation of the headdress, as it is an element of the body. And the headdress is in turn as much an element of the body, an uncanny variant of the serpentine hair, as it is an innocent ornament. This mutual doubling of the hair and the headdress into both body and ornament is even more explicit in Swinburne's description of the Cleopatra portrait: "Here also the electric hair, which looks as though it would hiss and glitter with sparks if once touched, is wound up to a tuft with serpentine plaits and involutions" (15:161). On one hand, the hair described in this line is a "serpentine emblem" of feminine evil. On the other hand, however, its serpentine plaits and involutions are also a direct citation of the phrase "plaited in the likeness of closely-welded scales as of a chrysalid serpent, raised and waved and rounded" that is used to describe the headdress. Hence the plaits are as much a variation of the headdress, and therefore an ornament, as they are a part of the body. And the headdress is in turn a variation or quotation of Cleopatra's serpentine plaits and involutions. So here too Swinburne's paradigmatic opposition between the ornament (explicitly defined as *not* serpentine) and the body (explicitly defined as serpentine) effectively breaks down. And what also breaks down is the implied hierarchy between the corrupt body and the merely contiguous ornament, because the serpentine hair in Swinburne's text is as much a variation on or citation of the serpentine headdress as vice versa. From the perspective of an exposition that would decisively unveil a corrupt body underneath an innocent ornament, the monstrosity of these figures lies neither in their Medusa-like hair or serpentine bodies, nor in their bizarre and exotic ornaments,[26] but rather in their perverse fusion of terms that according to the logic of the argument should not come together, opposed terms like body and ornament, corruption and innocence, and symbol or emblem and metonymy.

Because it does not consistently sustain the oppositions that would ground its argument, Swinburne's exposition of the drawings ultimately fails at what it attempts to do. It does not reassuringly expose the woman's body underneath her ornaments, and does not definitively reveal her evil through her body as distinct from those ornaments. In attempting to establish a tenable, fundamental distinction between ornament and body, it falls instead into a state of confusion. This confusion is like that of Mâtho, who is unable to tell Salammbo apart from her clothes and jewels, and like that of the viewer of Michelangelo's drawings, who is said to be disoriented by the drawings' blending of the woman's ornaments with her flesh. It is the very predicament that Swinburne's exposition would rhetorically obviate by carefully laying out the paradigmatic opposition between ornament and body and all of its attendant oppositions. From the tangible collapse of those oppositions in the text, however, it would seem that the exposition only produces disconcertion itself, rather than mastering the disconcertion produced by Michelangelo's drawings.

* * *

In "Notes on Designs" and "Leonardo da Vinci," Swinburne and Pater construct scenarios that are remarkably similar: both critics introduce artworks they say are unusually compelling and potentially dangerous. Both then suggest that this danger could be mitigated by the critic's description and exposition of the work or works in question. The danger is explicitly associated with death (the Fatal Woman in one case, the head of a corpse in the other) and explicitly or implicitly associated with the figure of a woman[27] (while sex and sexuality are obviously important in Swinburne's account of Michelangelo's female portraits, Pater never as much as mentions Medusa's sex is his description of the Leonardo painting). It is also associated with a paralyzing fascination of the viewer by means of contradictory elements that have been fused together in the work: beauty "mingled inextricably" with terror, corruption, and grotesquery in the Medusa painting, and the "infection" of the ornaments by the flesh in the Michelangelo drawings. In view of this fusing, the protection promised by the critical exposition of the painting or drawings takes the form of separating out these elements: the separation of beauty from corruption and from terror, of ornament from body, and of innocence from evil. Such a separation would restore a natural order (the distinction between organic and artificial, for example) and would make the image reassuringly legible: Pater could juxtapose clearly delineated terrifying elements in the Medusa painting with clearly delineated elements of beauty, and thereby temper the former by means of the latter, while Swinburne could penetrate past the obscuring ornaments and reveal both the woman's body and an evil emblematized by that body (this revelation would be in itself reassuring, no matter how existentially or sexually terrifying the evil that is revealed). Pater's exposition ostensibly succeeds in its endeavor, which accounts for the protective and empowering effects he associates with his own criticism by means of the analogy to Leonardo's art. Swinburne, on the other hand, demonstrably fails in his analysis to separate out the elements that Michelangelo has fused together in the drawings and that become similarly fused in his text. So while he alludes as much as Pater does to the potential protection that would be afforded by the exposition of a dangerous artwork, he ultimately does not realize this protective effect in the same way as Pater.[28]

In spite of the parallels between the two texts and their contexts, there is a significant dissymmetry between Pater's success and Swinburne's failure. While Pater's commentary implicitly presents itself as triumphant over the Medusa-like Medusa painting and Leonardo's Medusa-like art and personality more generally, Swinburne is for his part not overcome by the Medusa-like Michelangelo drawings, however disorienting they might be to look at, but by his own use of figurative language. His exposition fails not because he has been paralyzed by a Medusa-like visual object that proves too powerful for him. It fails, rather, because of a blending of opposites that takes place in the analysis of the drawings, not in the drawings themselves: a blending that is demonstrable and legible in the text rather than visible in the drawings, for example in the mechanical repetition of words like *plait* and *serpentine*, and of images like the snake, the plait, and the involution, on both sides of the opposition that structures the argument. The confusion that manifests itself in Swinburne's text is therefore not an effect of the drawings, but is rather a rhetorical effect—a Medusa effect—of the commentary on the drawings. What Swinburne is unable to master, it suggests, is less the drawings themselves than his own tropes for those drawings. Even as his text presents itself as a form of protective representation that would make a frightening and disconcerting image reassuringly legible, it becomes itself a source of confusion and even danger. This danger is not external (like the danger of the drawings and of their Fatal Woman subject, which would be safely contained by the representation) but internal, one that lies within the representation itself, namely Swinburne's inability to control it.

Swinburne's inability to control fully his own exposition of the Michelangelo drawings is indicative of the autonomy of his text. According to literary historians, the idea that the work of criticism should be somehow autonomous is a central conceit of aesthetic criticism. This is the argument of Oscar Wilde's essay "The Critic as Artist," for example, which proposes that the highest kind of criticism "treats the work of art simply as a starting-point for a new creation" (1029). Swinburne alludes to this kind of autonomy when he announces that his essay on the Uffizi drawings will "cast" his impressions of the drawings "into legible form," implying that the essay will constitute its own sculpture-like work of art. Pater makes a similar allusion in the "Preface" to *The Renaissance* when he exhorts the aesthetic critic to "realise" his impressions "distinctly."[29] The autonomy of the work of aesthetic criticism would generally be from the original artwork or artist under consideration, and from the task of having to account for its subject matter objectively, "as in itself it really is"; hence it would liberate and empower the critic, as exemplified in Pater's essay on Leonardo, or in Wilde's remark in "The Critic as Artist" that "To the critic the work of art is simply a suggestion for a new work of his own, that need not necessarily bear any obvious resemblance to the thing it criticizes" (1030).

Yet the kind of autonomy that becomes legible in Swinburne's passage on the Michelangelo portraits is neither self-empowering nor liberating. Unlike the conscious attempt to transform the work of criticism into an autonomous work of art, it is not an effect of a critical method, a particular style of writing, or an intention to be autonomous. It is not due to Swinburne's poetic imagination, his unique sensibility and taste, or, as Pater might put it, his "engaging personality." It is instead a more threatening, more radical, and less subjective kind of autonomy, an autonomy of the text not only from the artwork and from any mimetic obligation to the artwork, but from Swinburne himself, from Swinburne as a self, from Swinburne as a would-be controlling agent behind the writing. It is an autonomy that manifests itself in the text's own agency, its continuous, seemingly uncontrollable citations of itself in phrases like "plaited in the likeness of closely-welded scales as of a chrysalid serpent," "serpentine hair," and "serpentine plaits and involutions." This agency is heterogeneous to any agency on Swinburne's part (as a writer, as a perceiving aesthetic critic, or as a consciousness) and in "Notes on Designs" it runs wholly counter to the logic of Swinburne's argument, as suggested in the breakdown by the text's metaphors of the opposition between body and ornament.

One final example of this self-citing, self-generating quality is the following excerpt from an inventory of motifs in the drawings of Antonio del Pollaiolo: "a lady lightly *veiled* and sharply smiling, with *ringlets* on the neck and the main mass of *hair plaited* up behind; groups of saints and virtues, chief among them Justice and Prudence with *serpents emblematic* of wisdom" (15:177, my emphases). This description does not indicate the autonomy of Swinburne's impressions from the actual drawings as much as it indicates his text's autonomy from even those impressions. This is because it is less a record of uniquely subjective impressions and perceptions than an almost mechanical citation by the text of its own imagery and diction, the imagery and diction of the earlier passage on the Michelangelo portraits. The motif of the plait which here appears in the lady's hair ("the main mass of hair plaited up behind") also appears of course in the description of the Michelangelo headdress, "plaited in the likeness of closely-welded scales as of a chrysalid serpent." In the latter phrase, the plait is not literal, as in the case of Pollaiolo's lady, but is a metaphor for the shape of the headdress. It is possible to read this metaphor as a reference to the plaits Swinburne sees in various drawings, for example the plaited hair of the woman in the Pollaiolo drawing. Such a metaphor would presumably be based on a visible resemblance between the headdress and the literal plaits seen in the drawings. On the other hand, however, it is equally possible to read the "plaited" headdress not as a reference to any actual plaits, but as a citation by Swinburne's text of itself. The headdress could be read, for example, as a reference to the phrase "serpentine plaits and involutions" Swinburne uses to describe the hair in the Cleopatra portrait. Both readings are legitimate, but what adds support to the latter is one of the two additional metaphors Swinburne appends to the original metaphor of the plait: "in the likeness of closely-welded scales as of a chrysalid serpent." The metaphor of the chrysalid serpent would indicate that the original plait is a reference to the phrase "serpentine plaits and involutions" in the text, rather than a reference to any actual plaits visible in the drawings. As such, it implies not only the plait's autonomy from the plaits depicted in the drawings, but the text's autonomy more generally from both the drawings and Swinburne's perceptions of them.

My reading of "Notes on Designs" proposes that Swinburne more or less consciously and more or less explicitly recognizes the autonomous quality of his own text. The recognition takes place in his failed unveiling of the Michelangelo Fatal Woman, an unveiling that fails not on account of the ambiguity of Michelangelo's drawings but because his own text generates too many figures that run counter to the exposition's logic. The text's autonomy undermines not only the unveiling but the Apollonian assumption—which is also Pater's assumption—from which the unveiling departs, that the representation of a dangerous image could serve as a transforming shield against the terrifying revelations afforded by that image. Swinburne's recognition of this representational predicament—which Nietzsche might call a Dionysian recognition—is the Medusa he encounters in his own text, more so than Michelangelo's Medusa-like drawings and Medusa-like Fatal Woman.

CHAPTER FOUR

Sympathy and Telepathy

The Problem of Ethics in
George Eliot's *The Lifted Veil*

Presentiments are strange things! and so are sympathies; and so are signs.
— Charlotte Brontë, *Jane Eyre*

SYMPATHY AND ANTIPATHY

If art does not enlarge men's sympathies, it does nothing morally.
— George Eliot, Letter to Charles Bray

I have never been encouraged to trust much in the sympathy of my fellow men.
— Latimer, in *The Lifted Veil*

Pater's injunction in *The Renaissance* that the aesthetic critic must "realise
such primary data for one's self, or not at all" (xx) is indicative, as I suggest
in the previous chapter, not only of aesthetic criticism's subjective methodology but of its self-confirming, self-empowering agenda. Perhaps it is
this emphasis on the self as the means and ends of criticism that accounts
for George Eliot's "strong aversion" to Pater himself and to *The Renaissance*
in particular.[1] In her own work as a critic and as a novelist, Eliot turns in
an almost opposite direction as Pater, a direction away from the self and
toward the other. In her essays and in her first full-length novel, *Adam
Bede*, she elaborates an altruistic ethics of art and aesthetics, specifically of
realist art. This ethics is founded on emotional responses, what she calls

sympathy and compassion, by which she means a person's ability to feel and to suffer with another person. Her theory insists that art should give a reader or viewer access to the experiences, thoughts, and feelings of a great variety of different characters. It proposes that our insights into the minds and experiences of these characters "extend" our sympathy for other people and for humanity in general, thereby producing an ethical response in us. In her 1856 essay "The Natural History of German Life," Eliot writes, "The greatest benefit we owe to the artist, whether painter, poet, or novelist, is the extension of our sympathies. . . . Art is the nearest thing to life; it is a mode of amplifying experience and extending our contact with our fellow-men beyond the bounds of our personal lot" (*Essays*, 270–71).[2] And in an early letter to her editor, John Blackwood, composed around the time of *Scenes of Clerical Life*, she writes, "My artistic bent is not at all the presentation of eminently irreproachable characters, but to the presentation of mixed human beings in such a way as to call forth tolerant judgment, pity, and sympathy."[3] So whereas Pater describes the experience of art as a retraction into the self ("What is this song or picture, this engaging personality presented in life or in a book, to *me*?"), Eliot describes it as an extension beyond the limitations of the self, as a coming up against some form of otherness.[4]

Although Eliot's gothic novella *The Lifted Veil* is not a work of realism, and although it has until recently been treated by critics as a marginal anomaly in Eliot's oeuvre, its themes are in several respects central to Eliot's work overall and to Eliot's ethics in particular. Most recent scholars working on *The Lifted Veil* have noted in passing that the relation between art and ethics is implicitly taken up in the novella, but their analyses have largely sidestepped this issue and concentrated instead on contextualizing elements from the plot within such Victorian scientific theories and practices as mesmerism and animal magnetism, phrenology, clairvoyance, vivisection, blood transfusions, and physiological psychology.[5] In this chapter, I bring critical attention to the ethical dilemma that is implicitly and explicitly raised in *The Lifted Veil*. I focus in particular on the central conceit of telepathic power and on its equivocal relation to the moral value Eliot calls sympathy.

The Lifted Veil is told retrospectively in the form of a confessional manuscript written by an overly sensitive aesthete and misanthrope named Latimer. As a young man, Latimer discovers that he is intermittently and involuntarily subjected to two kinds of clairvoyant powers: he has prescient visions of future events and telepathic access to the thoughts and feelings of those around him. His insights into what he describes as the pettiness, stupidity, and egotism of other people alienate him from all society. He eventually meets Bertha Grant, a beautiful young woman who soon after becomes engaged to marry his half-brother Alfred. He falls in love with Bertha, in part because "she made the only exception, among all the human beings about me, to my unhappy gift of insight."[6] He has a prescient vision of an older Bertha as his wife, which reveals to him her cruelty and hatred of him, but he nevertheless continues to love and desire her. Following Alfred's death in an accident, Latimer and Bertha are married and eventually come to live together in the state of mutual alienation anticipated in Latimer's vision. A visit from Latimer's childhood friend Meunier, now a renowned scientist, is the occasion for a gothic reanimation scene in which a recently deceased maid is momentarily restored to life to accuse Bertha of plotting to poison Latimer. In this climactic scene, Bertha is revealed to Latimer as a Fatal Woman whose outer beauty has veiled her inner monstrosity. After the couple's final separation following this incident, the story ends with Latimer finishing his account and awaiting, in the narrative present, his own death predicted at the novella's outset.[7]

Following a suggestive essay by Charles Swann, I propose that *The Lifted Veil* implicitly tests the premises of Eliot's ethics of sympathy through the conceit of Latimer's telepathic "participation in other people's consciousness" (LV 17). Latimer's clairvoyance can be read as a figure for realist art as Eliot defines it because it gives him access to the thoughts and feelings of a large number of different people. Latimer is in this sense a stand-in for the reader or viewer, and also, in another sense, a stand-in for Eliot herself and for the artist in general. As Swann puts it, "Latimer *knows* the pains and joys of others. . . . [His] position is strikingly analogous to that of the reader of a George Eliot novel" (47). Latimer himself characterizes his telepathic powers as

> the obtrusion in my mind of the mental process going forward in first one person, and then another, with whom I happened to be in contact: the vagrant, frivolous ideas and emotions of some uninteresting acquaintance . . . would force themselves on my consciousness like an importunate, ill-played musical instrument, or the loud activity of an imprisoned insect. (LV 13)

Latimer's reference to an obtrusion of frivolous emotions, and his metaphors of the importunate instrument and the imprisoned insect, suggest the potential failure of Eliot's ethical theory of art. This is because while Latimer has access to the thoughts and feelings of others, he does not respond according to Eliot's prescription; he feels neither sympathy nor affection. Rather than eliciting pity and compassion, Latimer's telepathic insights elicit in him only boredom and contempt. To have involuntary access to the minds of his neighbors, he complains, is at best "wearying and annoying," at worst "an intense pain and grief" (LV 13–14). Thus Latimer's experiences would seem to contradict Eliot's theory that art can and should enlarge our sympathy simply by granting us access to the thoughts and feelings of those around us. Latimer in fact makes reference to this theory, but only to dismiss it as a wishful illusion:

> This is one of the vain thoughts with which we men flatter ourselves. We try to believe that the egotism within us would have easily been melted, and that it was only the narrowness of our knowledge which hemmed in our generosity, our awe, our human piety, and hindered them from submerging our hard indifference to the sensations and emotions of our fellow. (LV 21–22)

Latimer briefly considers the possibility that an expansion of our insight into others might lead us to feel pity and generosity for them. But his final assessment is that this is only "one of the vain thoughts with which we men flatter ourselves."[8]

Through Latimer's "hard indifference" to the sensations and emotions of the people around him, *The Lifted Veil* dramatizes a crisis for Eliot's ethics of sympathy.[9] Latimer's misanthropic responses to other people suggest a less stable relation between art and ethics than the one presumed and necessitated by Eliot's theory. Eliot herself alludes to this more unstable relation in a line she wrote to her friend Charles Bray at the time of the novella's composition: "If art does not enlarge men's sympathies, it does nothing morally" (L 3:111). There are at least two ways to read this sentence, and the ambiguity compactly condenses the ethical predicament in *The Lifted Veil*. On one hand, Eliot maintains that art can be morally effective by enlarging our sympathies. On the other hand, her use of the double negative suggests that art is morally inefficient because it does *not* enlarge our sympathy, a more pessimistic assessment that Latimer's clairvoyant experiences would seem to confirm.[10] I propose that Eliot both acknowledges and resolves this predicament at the level of the plot. In order to defend her ethical theory against the implications of Latimer's narcissism, she stages a conversion narrative in which Latimer makes an unexpected transition from antipathy to sympathy. She then projects Latimer's antipathy onto another character, Bertha Grant. This projection allows her to delineate the antipathy more distinctively (using the convenient scapegoat figure of a transgressive woman) and ultimately to expel it.

The initial step in the expulsion of antipathy is the moral conversion Latimer undergoes on the evening of his father's death. The father's dying from an illness becomes the first occasion for Latimer to feel sympathy for another human being: "As I saw into the desolation of my father's heart, I felt a movement of deep pity towards him, which was the beginning of a new affection . . . the first deep compassion I had ever felt" (LV 28). This feeling of compassion initiates Latimer into a sense of community with the father and with humanity in general, much as Eliot's ethical theory prescribes:

> Perhaps it was the first day since the beginning of my passion for [Bertha], in which that passion was completely neutralised by the presence

of an absorbing feeling of another kind. I had been watching by my father's deathbed: I had been witnessing the last fitful yearning glance his soul had cast back on the spent inheritance of life—the last faint consciousness of love he had *gathered* from the pressure of my hand. What are all *our* personal loves when *we* have been *sharing* in that supreme agony? In the first moments when *we* come away from the presence of death, every other relation to the living is *merged*, to *our* feeling, *in the great relation of a common nature and a common destiny.* (LV 31, my emphases)

Latimer's telepathic witnessing of his dying father's consciousness is a conversion moment because it elicits his sympathy rather than his habitual contempt or indifference, and also because it marks the first time in the novella that Latimer does not feel completely isolated from the people around him. He claims a connection with his father by way of their shared mortality. The word *sympathy* derives from the Greek *sympathes* (having common feelings), and the feeling of sympathy is evoked in Latimer's emphasis on community ("the great relation of a common nature and a common destiny"). Through his communion with the father and through his sense of their common nature and destiny, Latimer is also able to claim a connection with humanity in general, as indicated by the telling shift in the passage from the first person singular to the first person plural, and by his uncharacteristic use of words like *gather, merge*, and *share*.[11]

Latimer's conversion to sympathy at his father's death leads directly to his first clairvoyant insight into Bertha's mind. Up until this point in the narrative, Bertha has remained a "fascinating secret" (LV 20) and an "oasis of mystery" (LV 18) to him, and for this reason an object of intense speculations and desires. But immediately following his communion with his dying father, Latimer experiences a "terrible moment of complete illumination," which directly reveals to him Bertha's "scheming selfishness" and her "repulsion and antipathy harden[ing] into cruel hatred" (LV 32). He explicitly depicts this illumination as a direct effect of the bond he has just shared with his father:

In that state of mind I joined Bertha in her private sitting-room. . . . I remember, as I closed the door behind me, a cold tremulousness seizing me, and a vague sense of being hated and lonely—vague and strong, like a presentiment. I know how I looked at that moment, for I saw myself in Bertha's thought as she lifted her cutting grey eyes, and looked at me: a miserable ghost-seer, surrounded by phantoms in the noon-day, trembling under a breeze when the leaves were still, without appetite for the common objects of human desire, but pining after the moonbeams. We were front to front with each other, and judged each other. The terrible moment of complete illumination had come. (LV 31–32)

Among other things, this scene is explicitly a moment of moral recognition: "We were front to front with each other, and judged each other." In the exchange of looks between the two characters, the function of Bertha's gaze is to appropriate Latimer's earlier antipathy. What Latimer sees when he looks at Bertha is *the way in which she sees him*: "I saw myself in Bertha's thought as she lifted her cutting grey eyes, and looked at me: a miserable ghost-seer, surrounded by phantoms in the noon-day, trembling under a breeze when the leaves were still, without appetite for the common objects of human desire." Bertha's perception of Latimer, as revealed here by Latimer's clairvoyance, closely resembles Latimer's earlier perceptions of the people around him, people whom he would see as miserable, pitiful, and isolated from one another. At the same time, her antipathy towards him stands in explicit contrast to his sympathizing communion with his dying father in the scene just before, suggesting that Eliot has simply projected Latimer's misanthropy and contempt onto Bertha. In the way that she looks at Latimer, Bertha is unveiled as Latimer's uncanny double.[12]

The recognition scene between Latimer and Bertha moves from revealing Bertha's antipathy for Latimer specifically to revealing her inner nature as a Fatal Woman: "I saw all round the narrow room of this woman's soul— saw . . . the systematic coquetry, the scheming selfishness, of the woman— saw repulsion and antipathy harden into cruel hatred, giving pain only for the sake of wreaking itself" (LV 32). Throughout the text, Bertha is associated with the standard attributes of the Fatal Woman type. For example, Latimer's telepathic vision of Bertha's inner self elicits in him a "chill shudder of repulsion" (LV 32), just as an earlier prescient vision of Bertha causes him to feel a "chill of horror" (LV 26). Like the woman in the Michelangelo portraits described by Swinburne in "Notes on Design," Bertha is associated with the figure of the snake ("I saw the great emerald brooch on her bosom, a studded serpent with diamond eyes" [LV 19]) and with the figure of Cleopatra (LV 19, 34). She is compared to Lucrezia Borgia (LV 18–19), a Siren (LV 26), and a Water-Nixie ("this pale, fatal-eyed woman . . . looked like a birth from some cold, sedgy stream, the daughter of an aged river" [LV 12]). Her hair is described as "great rich coils" (LV 32) and as "arranged in cunning braids and folds" (LV 11). In one clairvoyant vision, she appears to Latimer "with her cruel contemptuous eyes fixed on me, and the glittering serpent, like a familiar demon, on her breast" (LV 34), while in another scene "she looked like a cruel immortal, finding her spiritual feast in the agonies of a dying race" (LV 41).[13] This is generally not the kind of language or imagery a reader associates with George Eliot, and even if one allows for the fact that it comes from the narrating character Latimer, not from the familiar George Eliot narrator of the novels, one nevertheless has to ask what it is doing here.

I would argue that Eliot's purpose in exposing Bertha as both Latimer's misanthropic double and as a prototypical Fatal Woman is to protect her ethics of sympathy from the implications of Latimer's antipathy. Like the Medusa figures discussed in the previous chapters, Bertha functions on a fundamental level as an apotropaic device. By demonstrably taking on Latimer's antipathy, she leaves Latimer free to convert to sympathy. The moral redemption of Latimer in the plot signals the concurrent redemption of Eliot's literary ethics and the successful warding off of an implicit threat by means of the projection. The protective effect of the projection lies in Bertha's much more unequivocal and unadulterated embodiment of antipathy. While Latimer's misanthropy is explained and exonerated in the plot by the oedipal and social pressures to which he is continually subjected by his family and neighbors, and while it is ultimately (though only partially) transformed into sympathy for the dying father and for humanity in general, Bertha is an image of antipathy as pure, absolute evil. Eliot uses the standard conventions of the Fatal Woman (the cruel eyes, the coiled hair, the serpentine ornament, and so on) to make this antipathy intelligible, suggesting a direct correspondence between Bertha's moral character and her sex, an association readily available in Victorian culture.[14] The Fatal Woman provides Eliot with a stock personification of antipathy, an antipathy that can easily be exposed, indicted, and exorcized, much as the character Bertha is expelled from Latimer's life once her secret plan to poison him is unveiled. The public sacrifice of Bertha, the story's exotic and transgressive scapegoat, eliminates the threat of an antipathy closer to home, and redeems both Latimer specifically and Eliot's ethics of sympathy more generally.[15]

The redemption of the latter is suggested specifically in the frame narrative of *The Lifted Veil*, in which Latimer, announcing he is about to die, appeals to his reader for a kind of sympathy akin to the sympathy he has shown his dying father:

> Before that time [of death] comes, I wish to use my last hours of ease and strength in telling the strange story of my experience. I have never fully unbosomed myself to any human being; I have never been encouraged to trust much in the sympathy of my fellow-men. But we have all a chance of meeting with some pity, some tenderness, some charity, when we are dead. . . . I have no near relatives who will make up, by weeping over my grave, for the wounds they inflicted on me when I was among them. It is only the story of my life that will perhaps win a little more sympathy from strangers when I am dead than I ever believed it would obtain from my friends while I was living. (LV 4)

Unlike his dying father, Latimer has no relatives who will show him pity, tenderness, and charity now that he is dying and once he is dead. But he suggests that the story he will tell of his life "will perhaps win a little . . . sympathy from strangers." This claim signals his conversion to Eliot's theory that art can produce ethical effects, since it grants to his story an affective power he reserves otherwise only for death: the power to move one's fellow-men to pity, charity, and tenderness. He considers the possibility that his story could elicit sympathy, even as he remains skeptical about trusting in the feelings of others and unsure about the effect his story will have on its readers. He recognizes that any kind of sympathy and compassion he does receive will depend on the story he is going to tell, and on his willingness to enter into a reciprocal relationship with the reader.[16]

SYMPATHY AND METAPHOR

> All of us, grave or light, get our thoughts entangled in metaphors and act fatally on the strength of them.
> —*Middlemarch*, chapter 10

The structure outlined at the end of the previous section is what Neil Hertz has identified as "a structure common in Eliot's novels, of double surroga-tion, in which the author's investment in her characters is split into 'good' and 'bad' versions, and the valued imaginative activity of the 'good' surro-gate is purchased by the exiling of the 'bad'" (*End*, 224). In *The Lifted Veil*, Latimer transforms into Eliot's good surrogate, while Bertha assumes the role of the bad surrogate. In his reading of *Middlemarch*, Hertz considers the overcoming of the threat posed by the bad surrogate a protective displace-ment of a different threat, one which Eliot cannot overcome as easily. He identifies the second threat as an "open and indeterminate self-dispersion associated with a plurality of signs or with the plurality of interpretations that writing can provoke" (*End*, 85). For Hertz, the danger displaced by the moral conflict in *Middlemarch* between good and bad authorial surrogates is a categorical threat to the self as such, to its ability to conceive of itself as a unified and coherent entity. My reading of *The Lifted Veil* follows Hertz in identifying an opposition between a good and a bad surrogate for Eliot and in suggesting that the entire double surrogation structure is a displacement of a different threat altogether. But unlike Hertz, I identify the latter not as an extra-moral threat to the self's ability to constitute itself, but as another moral threat. I argue that this second threat is ethically more troubling to Eliot than either Latimer's egotism or Bertha's evil. I specifically locate this threat not in any one character's disposition toward another character but in the visual metaphors through which Latimer's moral insights are formu-lated. Insofar as these insights take the form of metaphors, they are based on principles of similarity, analogy, and commonality. Such principles are fundamentally at odds with Eliot's notion of what a genuine ethics should be, namely an attentiveness to what is irreducibly different or apart from oneself. Ultimately the more disturbing ethical conflict in *The Lifted Veil* is not between antipathy and sympathy but between an ethics based on similarity and one based on difference.

As its title suggests, *The Lifted Veil* has an interest in the commonplace Victorian theme of knowledge and, more specifically, in the play between knowledge and ignorance, veiling and unveiling, secrecy and initiation. The privileged object of knowledge for Eliot's novels in general and for *The Lifted Veil* in particular is the consciousness of other people, what the narrator of *Middlemarch* calls "the difficult task of knowing another soul" (147). In *The Lifted Veil*, the theme of Latimer's telepathy demonstrates Eliot's preoccupation with the idea of gaining access to someone else's mind. For Eliot, the appreciation of another person's consciousness that is made possible by art is the first step toward moral agency, which is for her the aim of all great art and criticism. Thus any understanding one may gain of another person's thoughts and feelings is never a neutral kind of knowledge but always has a strong moral dimension; in *The Lifted Veil*, for instance, Latimer's sympathetic witnessing of his dying father's thoughts, and the revelation to him of Bertha's antipathy, are distinctly moral insights.

As its title also suggests, *The Lifted Veil* portrays the initiation into moral knowledge in specifically visual terms. Here, for example, is Latimer's experience of his grieving father's consciousness: "As I *saw* into the desolation of my father's heart, I felt a movement of deep pity towards him, which was the beginning of a new affection" (my emphasis). And here is Latimer's telepathic insight into Bertha's mind, partially quoted earlier: "I *saw* myself in Bertha's thought as she lifted her cutting grey eyes, and looked at me: a miserable ghost-seer. . . . The terrible moment of *complete illumination* had come to me, and I *saw* the *darkness* had hidden no landscape from me, but only a blank prosaic wall" (LV 32, my emphases). Latimer's conversion to sympathy and the revelation of Bertha's antipathy are both represented visually: Latimer sees into his father's desolate heart, he sees into Bertha's mind, and he sees himself in Bertha's thought. Both moments demonstrate the extent to which Eliot frames morality and immorality in visual terms and the extent to which she makes moral conclusions intelligible through visual metaphors such as clairvoyance, darkness, and illumination. These kinds of metaphors traditionally imply an epistemological reliability, as they do, for example, in Freud's perceptually based interpretation of Medusa's head, and they would thus serve to strengthen the authority of Latimer's insights.

The "blank *prosaic* wall" as which Bertha is revealed to Latimer in the second quotation indicates a second metaphorical strand in *The Lifted Veil* that is intertwined with the visual metaphors (clairvoyance, illumination, darkness, and so on), namely a series of metaphorical references to prose: to writing, reading, texts, and to language. Rather than comparing Bertha to a visual object, the latter metaphors compare her to a text that must be deciphered or read. Latimer compares Bertha to an epigram (LV 26), her glances to "feminine nothings which could never be quoted against her" (LV 16), and his recollections of her to "an oriental alphabet" (LV

35). Like the visual metaphors, these metaphors concentrate around Bertha in scenes of considerable epistemological stress. But unlike the visual metaphors, they designate her inaccessibility, rather than her accessibility, to Latimer's clairvoyant powers: "Bertha's inward self remained shrouded from me, and I still read her thoughts only through the language of her lips and demeanour" (LV 31). In this line, Latimer associates vision with certainty, and reading with uncertainty and tentativeness.

Several of the examples I have cited join together the two metaphorical strands in which Bertha is entwined: the visual metaphors (which compare her to a visual object) and the textual metaphors (which compare her to a piece of writing). For instance, the "blank prosaic wall" simultaneously compares her to a physical object and to a piece of prose. Yet even as the two metaphorical strands sometimes overlap, they each designate their referent, Bertha, in very distinct terms: the one in terms of the senses ("seeing" her) and the other in textual terms ("reading" her). Reading and seeing are not wholly analogous, and thus the two strands sometimes come to interfere with one another and to comment on one another. J. Hillis Miller has noted about the relation between different metaphorical strands in *Middlemarch* that "the interpretation of one metaphor by another metaphor is characteristic of Eliot's use of figure" ("Optic," 102). In *The Lifted Veil*, the textual metaphors "interpret" the visual metaphors, revealing them to be mere metaphors, not empirical events or entities. In doing so, they undermine the authority of the visual metaphors. This is because simply by their pointed juxtaposition with the visual metaphors, the textual metaphors call attention to the metaphorical nature of the visual metaphors. The combination of the two strands, for instance in the phrase "blank prosaic wall," emphasizes that the "illumination" and "unveiling" of Bertha's inner self are also only metaphors, just as the comparisons of Bertha to an oriental alphabet or an epigram are metaphors. However, because the unveiling and the illumination evoke the sensual experience of seeing an object with one's eyes (rather than the experience of reading a text), they veil their own metaphorical nature in a way that the textual metaphors arguably do not. By veiling their status as figures, the visual metaphors imply a revelation by means of the senses; this revelation would be decisive and absolute insofar as it would not be mediated by means of language and tropological figures. The claim to a sensory (rather than a linguistic) access to a character's inner self underwrites the moral conclusions of the novella; I have shown this in my reading of moral truths becoming visually intelligible in Latimer's visions of his father's desolate soul and Bertha's misanthropic consciousness. My claim now is that the juxtaposition of Latimer's insights with the textual metaphors brings out the metaphorical nature of those insights. That metaphorical nature in turn implies the insights' potential arbitrariness and unreliability.

The comparisons of Bertha to a piece of writing suggest that rather than being an object Latimer can see, Bertha is a kind of impenetrable text that has to be read or deciphered. The metaphor of a text designates the otherness of Bertha from Latimer; Eliot makes this explicit insofar as she repeatedly associates versions of this figure with opacity, as in the image of the oriental alphabet. If the other is a kind of obscure text, Eliot suggests, it is open to something like numerous, potentially contradictory interpretations, but not to something like clear, unequivocal vision. As only one possible interpretation (out of many) of the text as which Bertha becomes intelligible, then, Latimer's visual exposure of Bertha's moral character is not an absolute revelation of truth. It is rather the revelation of a truth that is more arbitrary and subjective, one that potentially says more about Latimer than about Bertha. Hence even at the moment of her alleged unveiling, Bertha "remain[s] virtually unknown" to Latimer and to us; she is "known merely as a cluster of signs for [her] neighbours' false suppositions."[17] Latimer's recognition of her inner selfishness is only one supposition made on the basis of the cluster of signs as which she is intelligible to him. His insight into her consciousness, and by extension any insight into it, is only one interpretation of "the language of her lips and demeanour," of that obscure language which (figuratively) indicates her difference from him and from us.

To some extent, the possibility that Latimer is interpreting Bertha, rather than directly seeing into her, is covered over, so to speak, by the veil of the visual metaphor, by the veil of Bertha's visual unveiling. Eliot covers it over because she wants to protect the authority of Latimer's moral insights; once we realize that those insights are only metaphors and interpretations, their authority would be compromised due to the potential arbitrariness of metaphors and interpretations, an arbitrariness that Eliot acknowledges not only here but throughout her writings, as for instance in *The Mill on the Floss*: "It is astonishing what a different result one gets by changing the metaphor!" (208). At the same time that she protects Latimer's insights, however, Eliot also uses the textual metaphors implicitly to undermine the authority of those insights. She does this by showing that Bertha is Latimer's other, and that his insights into her are only his own approximations of that otherness via metaphor. Figuratively speaking, she suggests, those insights are like interpretations of a text and thus subject to the same kind of uncertainty and capriciousness to which any interpretation is subject.[18] If Bertha is like a text, in other words, Latimer cannot literally see into her. She could not literally be unveiled, only metaphorically. Thus Eliot calls the epistemological authority of Latimer's visions into question. In the concluding section of this chapter, I consider how she calls the moral authority of those visions into question as well.

As a first step in that direction, I should like to offer an example of how Latimer's use of figurative language destabilizes the moral insights made possible by Bertha's visual unveiling. In the climactic scene of *The Lifted Veil*, Bertha's recently deceased maid, Mrs. Archer, is temporarily brought back to life to reveal Bertha's secret plot to poison Latimer:

> The dead woman's eyes were wide open, and met [Bertha's eyes] in full recognition—the recognition of hate. With a sudden strong effort, the hand that Bertha had thought for ever still was pointed towards her, and the haggard face moved. The gasping eager voice said—"You mean to poison your husband." (LV 41–42)

Like Latimer's insights into the consciousnesses of his father and Bertha, Mrs. Archer's exposure of Bertha is pointedly visual; it takes the form of her eyes meeting Bertha's eyes. The scene is crucial to the plot because it provides empirical evidence for Bertha's exposure and indictment as a Fatal Woman, adding to Latimer's earlier clairvoyant evidence. And it is also crucial to the double surrogation structure because it provides empirical evidence for the indictment of Bertha as Eliot's bad surrogate. In the passage, the good surrogate, Latimer, explicitly equates Mrs. Archer's "full recognition" of Bertha with "the recognition of hate," the kind of hate of which Eliot wishes to purge him by projecting it onto Bertha.

Yet the moral authority of Bertha's decisive exposure ("we all felt that the dark veil had completely fallen" [LV 41]) is undermined by a suggestion that the evidence in question is as much metaphorical as empirical. Bertha's plan to poison Latimer is not only a secret plot unveiled by Mrs. Archer but also a reference to one of Latimer's recurring analogues for Bertha, the figure of Lucrezia Borgia. Earlier in the story, Latimer and Bertha are in Vienna, visiting a picture gallery:

> I had been looking at Giorgione's picture of the cruel-eyed woman, said to be a likeness of Lucrezia Borgia. I had stood long alone before it, fascinated by the terrible reality of that cunning, relentless face, till I felt a strange *poisoned* sensation, as if I had long been inhaling a fatal odour, and was just beginning to be conscious of its effects. (LV 18–19, my emphasis)

Latimer's choice of the word *poisoned* to describe the strange sensation he feels while looking at the portrait would seem to be derived from the subject matter of the painting itself. At the same time, the epithet "cruel-eyed" indicates an affinity between the woman in the portrait and Bertha, an affinity that is confirmed in a scene immediately following. As Bertha takes Latimer's arm, he relates that "a strange intoxicating numbness passed over me, like the continuance or climax of the sensation I was still feeling from the gaze of Lucrezia Borgia" (LV 19). The identification of Bertha with Lucrezia Borgia raises the possibility that the poisoning plot that is later revealed by

Mrs. Archer is merely Latimer's taking his metaphor for Bertha to its logical conclusion. If Bertha is (like) Lucrezia Borgia, it follows that she would attempt to eliminate her enemy by poison. The literal poison intended for Latimer is in this sense just a variant of the "poisoned sensation" Latimer claims to feel in the presence of the Lucrezia Borgia portrait.[19]

The poison metaphor appears elsewhere in the novella as well. For example, Latimer refers to the scene just described as "that hideous vision which poisoned the passion it could not destroy" (LV 21) and he justifies his ongoing infatuation with Bertha by claiming, "The fear of poison is feeble against the sense of thirst" (LV 20). Given this recurring metaphor, one has to be just a little suspicious when Bertha's plan to poison Latimer is finally revealed. At best, Mrs. Archer's exposure of Bertha's plan leaves us unable to choose between taking this moment as a revelation of an empirical truth and taking it as one more recurrence of the Lucrezia Borgia metaphor. The status of the revelation is ultimately undecidable because Eliot provides us with no means by which to know for sure. Certainly the unveiling of Bertha's secret plot is crucial to the novella's resolution, but its truth is not empirically (that is to say, non-metaphorically) verifiable. This is not because Latimer may be an unreliable narrator, as Terry Eagleton has argued, but because the poisoning plot is at the same time simply a reference to a metaphor taken from a series of metaphors that leads back to the woman in the portrait, "said to be *a likeness* of Lucrezia Borgia" (LV 18–19, my emphasis).[20]

Faced with this predicament, we should not try to verify whether the scene is "really" a moment of truth or "just" a citation of a metaphor. Eliot's point—insofar as she does not make an intelligible distinction between a genuine insight and a metaphor—is that it is both at once. This is the epistemological predicament personified by the figure of Bertha. The many textual metaphors for Bertha imply that any revelation of her inner self, including this one, is already a metaphor, whether that metaphor is drawn from the sensual realm ("seeing" into her mind) or the linguistic realm ("reading" her) or from elsewhere. To put it another way, the unveiling of Bertha's character is one interpretation (among many possible interpretations) of the text as which she is intelligible to Latimer and to us. This general point about the constitutive relation between the other and metaphor is merely reconfirmed in the revivification scene by the uncanny coincidence of a frequently recurring metaphor and an allegedly decisive revelation of a character's inner nature.

Eliot's recognition of metaphor's constitutive role in our insights into other people has fundamental consequences for her understanding of moral judgments, as she acknowledges in a comment made by her good surrogate, Latimer. At a point late in the narrative, Latimer explicitly interrogates the validity of any judgment of another person that is mediated through one's own verbal representation of that person's experience. He concludes an assessment of his and Bertha's unhappy marriage by questioning the moral authority of such assessments:

> That course of our life which I have indicated in a few sentences filled the space of years. So much misery—so slow and hideous a growth of hatred and sin, may be compressed into a sentence! And men judge of each other's lives through this summary medium. They epitomise the experience of their fellow-mortal, and pronounce judgment on him in neat syntax, and feel themselves wise and virtuous—conquerors over the temptations they define in well-selected predicates. (LV 34)

Latimer insists here on a distinction between years of misery and the compression of those years into a single sentence, between actual experience and the epitome of that experience (an epitome is a brief verbal summary). In light of this distinction, what men judge when they judge one another is never the other's actual experience but always only its epitome. These judgments, Latimer points out, allow the judges to "feel themselves wise and virtuous—conquerors over the temptations they define in well-selected predicates." At the same time, he calls this kind of morality into question because it is based on one's own definition of the other's temptations and on one's own summations of the other's experience, rather than on an appreciation of the other's experience itself, of that experience in its otherness.

Latimer's reflections on the ways our judgments of one another are verbally mediated substantiate my earlier claim that Eliot's epistemological emphasis on the metaphorical bases of moral insights puts not only the reliability but the morality of those insights into question. The epistemological problem is that metaphors are arbitrary and subjective, which in turn subjects one's insights to a potential arbitrariness. The moral problem is that these metaphors are always *one's own* figures for the other; as such, they ultimately refer back to oneself, not to the other. Metaphors are based on analogy and similarity, not on difference. They establish a relation between the other and something that is already familiar to oneself in order to make the other more familiar. In the *Rhetoric,* Aristotle identifies familiarization as both the means and the aim of metaphors: "in using metaphors to give names to nameless things, we must draw them not from remote but from kindred and similar things, so that the kinship is clearly perceived as soon as the words are said" (1405a 170).[21] The kinship to be perceived is not only between the metaphor and the nameless thing but also between us and the thing. The ethical problem here is the implicit emphasis on the other's kinship to oneself. Latimer suggests in the passage quoted in the previous paragraph that a more just ethics would be an appreciation of the other as other: an appreciation of the other's actual

experience, not of one's definition of that experience. His point complements similar points Eliot makes throughout her writings. In her essay
"The Natural History of German Life," for instance, she argues that great
art "surprises even the trivial and the selfish into that attention to *what is
apart from themselves*, which may be called the raw material of moral sentiment" (*Essays*, 270).[22] Elsewhere, in a letter to Charles Bray from which I
quoted earlier, she writes, "the only effect I ardently long to produce by my
writings is that those who read them should be better able to *imagine* and
to *feel* the pains and joys of those who differ from themselves" (L 3:111).
And in *Middlemarch*, her narrator condemns the egotistic Rosamond for
her inability or unwillingness to engage with Lydgate as someone autonomous from herself: "Rosamond, in fact, was entirely occupied not exactly
with Tertius Lydgate as he was in himself, but with *his relation to her*"
(196, my emphasis). So Eliot explicitly defines the ethics of art and of
interpersonal relations as an attention to what is apart or different from
oneself. This appeal to our awareness of the other's difference from us,
rather than its similarity to us, has been largely overlooked by critics working on Eliot's ethics, critics who primarily define those ethics in terms of a
fellowship or sympathy between the self and the other.[23] Eliot derives the
imperative to acknowledge the other's otherness from the work of Ludwig
Feuerbach, a writer with whom she claimed a great affinity (L 2:153), and
especially from Feuerbach's *Essence of Christianity*, a text she translated in
1854. "The consciousness of the moral law, of right, of propriety, of truth
itself," Feuerbach writes in Marian Evans's translation, "is indissolubly
connected with my consciousness of another than myself" (268).

Eliot's appeal to a consciousness of the other's difference from ourselves
would seem to be at odds with her own attention to Bertha, which ultimately does not acknowledge and respect Bertha's otherness, even though
Bertha is the novella's exemplar of otherness by virtue of her gender (she is
the only significant female character in the story) and by virtue of her opacity. Eliot ultimately exposes Bertha as a "bad" double of Latimer and, by
implicit extension, of herself, not as someone truly apart from Latimer or
herself. As Rosamond is with Lydgate, she is preoccupied not with Bertha
as she actually is, but with Bertha's relation to herself. This preoccupation
with Bertha as her own bad double ultimately allows her to resolve her ethical dilemma and to bring her narrative to a close, but the ethics of that closure are simultaneously called into question by her own insistence that the
other must be appreciated as other, not as a (negative or positive) reflection
of the self. In the final section of this chapter, I argue that this discrepancy
between an ethics based on difference and an ethics based on similarity
points to an ethical dilemma in *The Lifted Veil* that is itself radically different from the sympathy/antipathy problem on which the novella and Eliot's
work in general ostensibly concentrate. The latter problem, I propose, is a
protective displacement of the former.

SYMPATHY AND TELEPATHY

The moral is plain enough . . . the one-sided knowing of
things in relation to the self.

—George Henry Lewes, on *The Lifted Veil*

In *The Lifted Veil*, the truly ethical attention to the other as "apart from
oneself" would seem to be exemplified by the conceit of Latimer's telepathy.[24] Etymologically, the word *telepathy* implies distance (*tele*) and apart-
ness; literally, it means to feel something from a distance. Telepathy is
usually defined as extrasensory impressions of something or someone far
away and separate from oneself. Thus it designates an appreciation of the
other from a distance, a relation to the other that is absolutely unmediated
by one's own senses or language. In accordance with Eliot's injunction to
respect the difference between oneself and the other, it would seem to be
a figure for a purely ethical relation. It is a figure for gaining access to the
actual person rather than to an epitome of the person. Yet Eliot is tellingly
unable to represent Latimer's telepathy except through sensory metaphors
like "microscopic vision" (LV 14) and "a preternaturally heightened sense
of hearing" (LV 18). These metaphors indicate the extent to which Eliot
is forced to represent the radical alterity of telepathic experience in familiar analogues. Something that is by definition extrasensory is rendered in
images of heightened sensory experiences. Telepathy, it would seem, can
only be represented metaphorically, which is to say it cannot be represented
as such; thus the representation of telepathy as heightened senses paradoxically points to the impossibility of representing telepathy. Along a similar
vein, Eliot represents the thoughts and feelings of other people to which
Latimer gains clairvoyant access not as an irreducible otherness but in familiar (though admittedly opaque) similes like "a ringing in the ears not to be
got rid of" (LV 18), "a sensation of grating metal" (LV 14), an "ill-played
musical instrument" (LV 13), "the loud activity of an imprisoned insect"
(LV 13), and "a roar of sound where others find perfect stillness" (LV 18).
These metaphors for the otherness of other people's consciousnesses ostensibly designate the epistemological problem outlined in the previous section:
the recognition that the other necessarily becomes intelligible through one's
own appropriating metaphors for it.[25] For Eliot, this epistemological problem has profound and explicit ethical repercussions.

I would maintain that the novella's failure to represent Latimer's telepathy is indicative of its true ethical dilemma: the inability to face the other
as other, despite Eliot's injunction that we must do precisely that, and the
inevitable recourse to framing the other in terms of oneself. This recourse
to one's own terms is a recourse to metaphor, to a framing of the relation
to the other as a similarity, not as irreducibly differential. Eliot's failure to
write "telepathically" about Latimer's telepathic experiences suggests that

the kinds of verbal summations and judgments we make of each other's experiences are inevitable. This is because the person doing the judging could never have access to the other's experiences as such, could never, that is, have telepathic access to the other. Through this failure, Eliot insists that as soon as one enters into a relationship with the other, a relation of ethically judging, say, this relationship is never telepathic but always mediated through one's own metaphors and interpretations. This is the argument of the narrator in *Middlemarch* when he states that people remain *virtually* unknown to one another, and can be known only as clusters of signs for their neighbors' false suppositions. Latimer, for instance, comes to condemn Bertha through such clusters of signs as the blank prosaic wall, the cold gaze, the secret plot to poison him, and so on, but he does not ever know her virtually, telepathically, as someone completely and irreducibly apart from himself. So despite the novella's title, Bertha's veil is never truly lifted at all.[26]

Through her failure to represent Latimer's telepathy as such, Eliot suggests that an ethics based on difference may be impossible to realize. In attempting to stake out a moral position, her only recourse is sympathy, an ethics based on commonality, on what she calls the fellowship of all human beings.[27] The word *sympathy*, derived from the Greek *syn* (with, together with) and *pathos* (feeling), would seem to be opposed to telepathy, a word derived from *tele* (distant) and *pathos*. The difference is between understanding and relating to the other in terms of its similarity to oneself, and understanding it in terms of its irreducible distance from oneself. In *The Lifted Veil*, Eliot can only understand or represent the other in terms of similarity, which is to say in terms of metaphors (the ill-played musical instrument, the imprisoned insect, the narrow room, and so on). The other is not known as "apart from oneself," even though the conceit of telepathy is a reminder of the (failed) imperative to know it in just such a way. It is known only in terms of an analogy to the self, in terms of what Latimer at his father's deathbed calls "the great relation of a common nature and a common destiny." Latimer's implicit interpretation of his father's mortality as a figure for his own mortality is indicative of this ethics of sympathy. It is indicative of the necessary recourse to metaphor in the relation to the other (for Latimer, the dying father is fundamentally a figure for himself, and the father's death is a figure for his own death). Latimer's conversion to sympathy is in this sense also a figure for the failure of telepathy, for the impossibility of facing the other as other.[28]

Eliot's turn from telepathy to sympathy is not only an epistemological necessity but a compensatory move aimed at restoring the possibility of any ethical agency at all.[29] To put it in terms of Freud's essay "Fetishism," it is an apotropaic belief in similarity (here, the fellowship between oneself and the other) that indicates and simultaneously covers over an awareness of difference (here, the other's difference from oneself, and the difference between an ethics based on difference and an ethics based on similarity). Sympathy is in Eliot's text a kind of Freudian fetish, designating both the presence and the absence of something deemed valuable, something whose loss would be traumatic (in Eliot's case not the maternal phallus but an ethical relation to the other). It enables Eliot and her reader to be moral agents, but it also subverts that morality through its uncanny similarity, at a fundamental level, to antipathy, its alleged opposite.

Insofar as sympathy is based on a presumed commonality between the other and oneself, it effectively collapses the distinction between itself and egotism. That distinction is the fundamental opposition within which critics have traditionally located the defining ethical conflict in Eliot's work. The distinction collapses, Eliot implies in *The Lifted Veil*, because both sympathy and egotism similarly relate the other back to the self, either in terms of its similarity or dissimilarity to the self. In the end, the two kinds of relationships come back to the same thing, the self, and neither meets Eliot's ethical criterion of appreciating what is "apart from oneself" (in other words, neither is telepathic). This is true no matter how good or bad one's intentions, or how compassionate or misanthropic one's language. Both positions are fundamentally metaphorical, since any relationship to the other, whether friendly or hostile, is based on a (positive or negative) comparison of the other to oneself. This implicit comparison is what such diverse metaphors as the blank prosaic wall, the great relation of a common destiny, and the ill-played musical instrument have in common. Eliot's failure to represent the radical alterity of Latimer's telepathy suggests that this recourse to metaphor is inevitable; it implies that we can only ever face the other as some kind of metaphor. Eliot uses the figure of obscure writing to designate her awareness of Bertha's irreducible otherness, but it too is just a metaphor.

If the recourse to sympathy and thus to metaphor is epistemologically unavoidable, however, Eliot also indicts it as ethically deficient. Sympathy is in one crucial respect not a fully ethical position for her because it does not attend to the other as such, but is rather, in George Henry Lewes's words, a "one-sided knowing of things in relation to the self."[30] It is a unilateral relation not only insofar as it relates the other back to the self via the assumption of a fellowship, but insofar as it empowers and inflates the self by means of this relation. In *The Lifted Veil*, Eliot suggests that there is a kind of narcissism implicit in sympathy, since sympathy, not unlike antipathy, ultimately refers the other back to the self in order to confirm and nourish the self. As Latimer puts this in a phrase cited earlier, the assumption of a sympathetic bond between ourselves and our neighbors "is one of the vain thoughts with which we men flatter ourselves." His critique of sympathy here is twofold. On one hand, he argues that sympathy is simply impossible, due to our "hard indifference to the sensations and emotions of our fellow." This is his misanthropic critique of sympathy, against which a defense of sympathy could meaningfully be opposed. On the other hand, and much more problematically for Eliot, he states that sympathy and the very idea of sympathy are essentially narcissistic. According to this latter critique, we are not indifferent to the other at all, but use the other (and our relation to the other) as a means of flattering ourselves.[31] In the sense of such an underlying narcissism, Latimer's "good" sympathy for his father is not fundamentally distinct from his "bad" condemnations of his neighbors' pettiness and stupidity. Neither is Latimer's antipathy fundamentally distinct from his ostensibly moral recognition of Bertha's selfishness and shallowness, or from Eliot's indictment of Bertha as her bad authorial surrogate. These are all not only self-referential but self-serving, self-confirming relationships; as Latimer puts it, they are relations that make people "feel wise and virtuous—conquerors over the temptations they define in well-selected predicates." To use the words of the *Middlemarch* narrator, they are a taking of the world as an udder to feed the supreme self.[32] In *Middlemarch*, Eliot equates our feeding on the external world with infantilism and moral stupidity. The danger she allows herself to dramatize in *The Lifted Veil* is the possibility that we can never outgrow this infantile, narcissistic relation to what is outside of us, even by means of a transition from immature egotism to mature sympathy. The collapse in *The Lifted Veil* of any tenable distinction between sympathy and egotism is an indictment of sympathy as implicitly narcissistic. Eliot not only asks whether sympathy is possible without narcissism, without seeing the other in terms of its "great relation of a common nature" to oneself. She suggests that compassion and sympathy are disguised forms of narcissism and, as such, not fundamentally different from the kinds of character traits (selfishness, misanthropy) she and her good surrogates routinely condemn.[33]

The Lifted Veil suggests Eliot's awareness of this ethical dilemma in the problematic figure of Bertha, the privileged object of the text's epistemological, moral, and sexual energies. It is this figure that implies a true moral threat to Eliot.[34] The threat is not Bertha's revelation as a Fatal Woman, nor is it her role as Eliot's "bad" surrogate. Those threats can be (and are) visually exposed and then reassuringly expelled from the text, so they pose no real danger. The Fatal Woman is openly unveiled as such and then exiled from the novella's community, while the bad surrogate is replaced by the good surrogate, Latimer. Insofar as they pose threats that can demonstrably be overcome, they play a fundamentally apotropaic role, much like Freud's Medusa or the dangerous images Pater and Swinburne write about. The revelation of Bertha as the bad surrogate, for instance, allows Latimer to be realized more fully as Eliot's good surrogate, thereby helping to redeem Eliot's ethics of sympathy. At the same time, however, Eliot's injunction to face the other as other implies that there is something unethical and narcissistic in the revealing of Bertha as Latimer's and Eliot's bad double. This implication hints at a second ethical threat in *The Lifted Veil*, one that is only partially veiled by the more visible threat of Bertha's antipathy. This latter threat takes the form not of antipathy but of sympathy, a relation to the other that is fundamentally metaphorical (and therefore unethical insofar as it is not telepathic).[35]

Bertha is the face of both aspects of Eliot's ethical project and ethical dilemma. On one hand, she is the text's exemplary figure for otherness and for the awareness of otherness: "she made the only exception, among all the human beings about me, to my unhappy gift of insight. About Bertha I was always in a state of uncertainty" (LV 15). At various points in the novella, Latimer compares Bertha to a piece of writing, often a piece of writing he cannot read or comprehend, in order to designate her inaccessibility. The illegible or incomprehensible writing to which Bertha is compared is a figure for the other's irreducible otherness, just as Latimer's telepathy is a figure for the appreciation of that otherness as such. On the other hand, Latimer repeatedly compares Bertha to a visual object when he wants to designate her accessibility. In claiming that he "saw all around the narrow room of this woman's soul," he defines Bertha's accessibility in terms of visibility and his own telepathy in sensory terms, as clairvoyance. In light of the traditional Aristotelian association between perception and the use of metaphor, Latimer's visions into Bertha's inner self are figures for a relation to the other that is based on metaphorical principles of similarity and analogy. The complementary images of Bertha's visibility and Latimer's sight are reflexive figures for the way the other becomes intelligible through our own metaphors for it. They are indicative of how the other becomes intelligible to us through its (visual) similarity and dissimilarity to ourselves. In *The Lifted Veil*, Latimer tellingly gains clairvoyant access to Bertha's mind at the moment when he looks at her in terms of himself, or, more specifically, in terms of her dissimilarity to himself. He contrasts her antipathy for him with his own sympathy for his dying father, thereby transforming her into his bad double. At that moment, he also tellingly stops thinking of her as radically other to himself, as an oriental alphabet he cannot read or decipher. The revelation of Bertha as Latimer's double makes possible the narrative's moral resolution. But it also functions apotropaically to cover over the ethical obligation that is neutralized (as Eliot might say) by this resolution: the imperative to know the other's otherness, the otherness for which the oriental alphabet is a metaphor or, more precisely, a catachresis. Eliot's dilemma in the novella (and perhaps in her novels and criticism more generally) is that her sympathetic ethics succeeds only at the expense of a telepathic relation, what she calls our obligatory "reverence before the secrets of each other's souls" (L 3:164).

Conclusion

The motif of dangerous and horrifying insights is a commonplace in nine-teenth-century European literature, in particular in those writings that in one or another way fall in the gothic, romantic, and decadent traditions. Depending on the work in question, the danger or horror is framed in social, political, or economic terms, in sexual or racial terms, in moral or existential terms, or in aesthetic terms, as for instance in the various lit-erary and philosophical discourses on monstrosity or the sublime. It is a critical commonplace that the anxieties that are thematized in a given work of literature relate in some way to the dominant popular anxieties of the corresponding place and time period: according to scholars, in Victorian England and in nineteenth-century northern and central Europe more generally, such anxieties are often about the emergence of feminism and the "woman question," about increasingly mechanized and industrialized social organization, about the emergence of modern cities, about unchecked forms of entrepreneurial capitalism and social Darwinism, about the eco-nomic disempowerment of the traditional gentry and the perceived loss of rural values, about the emergence of the urban and rural working classes as a social and political force, about political revolutions on the Continent and political reform movements in England, about colonialism and the encoun-ter at home and abroad with the colonized "other," about sex and sexuality (two topics of prolific discursive attention in Victorian culture, as Michel Foucault famously demonstrates in volume I of the *History of Sexuality*), and so on.

The texts I discuss in this book certainly partake in this tradition. They belong to a strand of Victorian literature (if we define *Victorian* and *literature* in such a way as to include the texts of Freud and Nietzsche) preoccupied with the depiction of revelations that are variously terrifying or danger-ous, in particular sexual and existential revelations. Nietzsche, for instance, finds "the terror and horror of existence" (*Birth of Tragedy*, 42) revealed in what he calls the Dionysian and the Apollonian, while Swinburne finds "the sorrow and strangeness of things" (15:158) revealed in Michelangelo's drawings. Eliot's protagonist Latimer clairvoyantly intuits the feelings and thoughts of the people around him as a "struggling chaos of puerilities, meanness, vague capricious memories, and indolent make-shift thoughts," a revelation he experiences as "an intense pain and grief" (*The Lifted Veil*, 13–14). Freud's terrified little boy recognizes his own potential castration in the "castrated" genitals of the girl or woman he looks at, Swinburne finds a dangerous female sexuality in Michelangelo's female portraits, Pater finds a wholly corrupted kind of beauty in Leonardo's Medusa painting, and Latimer describes himself as both attracted and threatened by Bertha's indifference and contempt.

What this book and its various examples demonstrate is that in addition to a recurring preoccupation with the theme of terrifying revelations, Victorian texts reflect critically on the ways those revelations are represented. Among other things, they reflect on the very representations they themselves perform. Freud is explicitly interested in the figurative means by which taboo ideas, wishes, and insights are represented in the unconscious—means such as symbolization, condensation, displacement, and fetishism—and he also implicitly reflects on the stability of his own interpretations of those representations, as demonstrated in my reading of "Medusa's Head." Nietzsche, Swinburne, and Pater write about terrifying insights that are specifically provided by works of art, and Swinburne and Pater suggest moreover that their own commentary on the artworks in question may defend against the terror of those insights. For her part, George Eliot considers the metaphors by which other people's consciousnesses become intelligible to her protagonist and to herself, and the epistemological and ethical implications of those metaphors.

As anticipated in Rossetti's poem "Aspecta Medusa," the argument that these authors explicitly or implicitly make is that representations are somehow protective. More specifically, it is that representations protect a given subject from its traumatic encounter with some kind of horrifying external object, event, or insight—an object, event, or insight that has destabilizing or fatal consequences for the subject: for instance, the primal scene and the recognition by the little boy of his potential castration, Dionysus and the disconcerting recognition by the Greeks of their Dionysian nature, the violent and disorienting artworks of Michelangelo and Leonardo, the existential insights those artworks are said to prompt in the viewer, and, in Eliot's case, the recognition that the other's consciousness remains in itself unknown and inaccessible, a recognition that has troubling ethical implications for Eliot. To somehow protect against these traumatic kinds of recognitions and encounters is the function that is shared by Freud's fetishes and castration symbols, by Nietzsche's Apollonian artwork, by Swinburne's and Pater's works of criticism, and by Latimer's and Eliot's metaphorical approximations of the other's consciousness, approximations that reassuringly cover up their problematic inability to have an unmediated access—what chapter 4 calls telepathic access—to that consciousness.

What this book and its examples also demonstrate is that Victorian literature and aesthetics regard representation not only as a means of protection against threats that impinge on an author, narrator, or character from outside of himself or herself, but as itself somehow threatening. This latter threat is one that inheres within representation, rather than in an object or event that is external and prior to representation. Rossetti, for example, suggests in "Aspecta Medusa" that a potential danger of representation lies in its deceptiveness, illusoriness, or secondariness. The poem is founded on a Platonic scheme in which the representations it prescribes, what Rossetti calls shadows of the thing, are implicitly devalued vis-à-vis that which they represent, what Rossetti calls the forbidden thing itself. Some readers of *The Birth of Tragedy*, for instance Sarah Kofman in her book *Nietzsche and Metaphor*, have found in it a scheme that similarly devalues Apollonian appearances (*Schein*) as a deficient and compromised representation of Dionysian truths. (Kofman critiques Nietzsche on this point for what she takes to be his logocentrism, a critique that in turn becomes a point of departure for Paul de Man's reading.) Taking a somewhat different approach to the potential danger that inheres within representation, Latimer in *The Lifted Veil* criticizes language on the basis that words do not adequately correspond to the experiences and entities they would designate: "That course of our life which I have indicated in a few sentences filled the space of years. So much misery—so slow and hideous a growth of hatred and sin, may be compressed into a sentence! And men judge each other's lives through this summary medium" (34). As the narrator of Eliot's novel *Daniel Deronda* similarly puts this point, "The word of all work Love will no more express the myriad modes of mutual attraction, than the word Thought can inform you what is passing through your neighbour's mind" (301). In both statements, words are said to fall short of what they represent, a deficiency that according to Latimer may lead to unjust consequences: he implies that any judgment made via the "summary medium" of language is ethically suspect.

The readings performed in the preceding chapters demonstrate that the threat that inheres within representation, as it is conceived by the texts and authors under discussion, does not lie in representation's deceptiveness or in its inadequacy vis-à-vis the thing it represents. It lies, rather, in the repeated breakdown of the fundamental opposition between the representation and what it represents, a breakdown that is effected by means of the representation itself (and more specifically, by means of its rhetorical tropes and figures). In order to make the particular argument that it does, each text or set of texts establishes a fundamental distinction between a thing and its representation: Freud makes a distinction between the castration complex's primal scene and its symbolic representations, Nietzsche distinguishes between an original Dionysian essence and a secondary Apollonian artwork that represents it, Swinburne draws a distinction between the Michelangelo woman's body and the ornaments that uncannily resemble and thus "represent" this body, and Eliot distinguishes between the other's consciousness and its various metaphorical approximations. Yet as each constructs a version of this opposition in order to make its specific (hermeneutic, genealogical, expository, or ethical) argument, the tropes and figures through which it does so also work simultaneously to break down the opposition. In *The Birth of Tragedy*, what Nietzsche calls the Dionysian essence is revealed to be only ever one or another Apollonian figure for such an essence, never an original entity or event that actually precedes and engenders the various Apollonian figures for it. Eliot similarly finds that the other's consciousness is inseparable from her various metaphors for it. (There is a difference between the way this inseparability is figured in her text and the way it is figured in Nietzsche's text, but the epistemological problem both writers confront is, from a structural point of view, similar.) In Freud's essays, castration, the would-be referent of a series of symbolic representations, is revealed to be as much a representation, a figure, as the symbols that represent it. Like Dionysus in *The Birth of Tragedy* and like the other's consciousness in *The Lifted Veil*, it does not exist in a nonfigurative form. In "Medusa's Head," for instance, castration and the primal scene demonstrably refer as much to the castration symbol, Medusa's head, as the symbol in turn refers to them, thus creating an open-ended circuit of bilateral references in which neither the primal scene nor the myth of the petrifying head has ultimate priority or finality. For its part, Swinburne's commentary on the Michelangelo female portraits conflates the woman's body and ornaments into an impossible, monstrous combination in which each of the two opposed terms effectively becomes an extension of the other. These various breakdowns of the opposition between thing and representation take place in the very figures and tropes through which each text or set of texts constructs its version of the opposition in the first place: the metaphor of Lucrezia Borgia in *The Lifted Veil*, for instance, the figure of the plaited headdress in "Notes on Designs," or the figure of the rigid Apollo defiantly holding up Medusa's head at Dionysus in *The Birth of Tragedy*.

These breakdowns pose an inherent threat because the success of each given project—Freud's psychoanalytic interpretation, Nietzsche's genealogical narrative, Swinburne's explication of Michelangelo's art, Eliot's ethics—depends on the validity and stability of its structuring opposition, and on the presumption of some kind of entity that would be distinct from its representations. Freud, for example, posits a primal scenario that would be distinct from its symbolic representations, while Eliot posits a consciousness that would be distinct from her own metaphorical approximations of it. Nietzsche's genetic account of the Dionysus/Apollo relationship posits Dionysus as a distinct point of origin of the Apollonian artwork and also of any artwork in which the two principles are fused, while his dialectical account of the relationship similarly posits Dionysus as the underlying foundation of any such fusion. The protective capacity of Swinburne's commentary on Michelangelo's powerful drawings depends on its ability to bestow a reassuring legibility onto the images, a legibility that in the case of the female portraits would be premised on a tenable distinction in Swinburne's exposition (as opposed to in the drawings themselves) between a "corrupt" body and an "innocent" ornament. In the case of Rossetti's poem, meanwhile, the moral depends on the assumption that there exists a distinct "forbidden thing" that could be apprehended directly and that, as per the argument, should only be apprehended in the form of its shadows and reflections. By repeatedly breaking down various versions of this recurring, foundational distinction, the representations performed in each text or set of texts call into question not so much the potential success as the very premise of each given project. This is the case even as they are also the rhetorical means by which each project is realized: each project performs figurative representations in making its argument, and each structurally requires a devalued and secondary term, the representation, against which to juxtapose a privileged and primary term, the thing itself. Each requires these two terms and their opposition to one another in order to be meaningful according to its own specific definition of meaningfulness (meaningful in the sense of grounded, for instance, as in a genealogical narrative or hermeneutic interpretation that is grounded in a decidable origin and endpoint). However, that meaningfulness, insofar as it is premised on a structure that is destabilized by the text's tropes and metaphors, is also simultaneously jeopardized.

As I discuss in the final sections of the chapters on Freud, Nietzsche, and Eliot, this threat is one to which the texts I examine have what Freud would call a fetishistic relation: they simultaneously recognize and disavow it. They recognize it by means of their capacity to reflect critically on themselves, a capacity for which I hope to have made a case in my individual readings. And they disavow it by foregrounding a different threat, namely the more obvious threat on which they ostensibly and anxiously concentrate: the threat of castration fear, of existential horror, of human narcissism and antipathy, of the Fatal Woman, of the "forbidden thing," and so on. Following Freud's structure of fetishism, I have argued that these external, highly visible threats ultimately serve an apotropaic function,[1] covering over the more fundamental threat that inheres in the given text's inadvertent breakdown of the very concepts and distinctions on which its meaning and meaningfulness are premised. The coinciding of the two threats, which sometimes occurs in the shared figure of Medusa, and the use of the second threat to veil the first, is the structure I call the Medusa effect.

My readings in this book find in a thematically linked series of Victorian texts a critical, epistemological reflection on—and ambivalence about—representation, in particular the representations that they themselves perform.

On one hand, representation is held up in the texts I examine as a defensive, protective mechanism against a series of perceived external threats. This is an explicit or implicit argument in the texts themselves, and similar arguments have been made by critics like Neil Hertz, W. J. T. Mitchell, and James Heffernan about other nineteenth-century texts that are thematically and structurally complementary to the ones discussed in this book.[2] On the other hand, representation—in particular verbal representation—is also seen to pose a threat of its own insofar as its tropes and figures are tangibly, repeatedly insubordinate to the logic of argument. The resulting ambivalence suggests that Victorian literature and aesthetics have a more complex and less stable view of the act and the mechanisms of mimetic representation than has been assumed by many of their commentators. Judging on the basis of the examples discussed in this book, it would seem they regard representation not only as a mirror of Perseus but also as a Medusa's head.

Notes

INTRODUCTION.

1. Rossetti, *Correspondence*, 3:590. All further references in this chapter to Rossetti's correspondence are identified parenthetically as C and followed by volume and page numbers. In a review essay on the 1868 Royal Academy Exhibition, A. C. Swinburne, writing about the exhibit of one of Rossetti's preparatory sketches for the painting, specifically identifies the source of the reflection motif as a Pompeian picture (15:215). On the origins of the motif in a Pompeian fresco, and its significant differences from Rossetti's version, see Roussillon, 5, 8–10.

2. Quoted in Macleod, 263–64n142.

3. Rossetti's assurances notwithstanding, Matthews refused to change his mind about the Medusa motif and encouraged Rossetti to propose a different subject. Ultimately, he and Rossetti could not come to an agreement on a mutually suitable subject and price, and the commission was cancelled. Only one of Rossetti's preparatory studies for the painting is known still to exist (Figure 1), along with several sketches of Andromeda's head (Figure 2), a motif to which Oscar Wilde makes reference in "The Decay of Lying." See Surtees, I: no. 183, and II: pl. 270. On the biographical circumstances surrounding the commission and its ultimate failure, see Marsh, 328 and 335–36, and Patterson, 114–15. See also Macleod, 242–43, who discusses the episode in the context of historically changing relations between Victorian artists and middle-class art patrons.

4. On these motifs in the Perseus myth, and their evocative relation to visual art, see Derrida, *Memoirs*, 73–87.

5. On the double work of art in Rossetti's oeuvre, see Ainsworth.

6. Yet at the same time, the poem's added subtitle "For a Drawing" cannot and should not be overvalued or taken too literally. According to Rossetti's brother, William Michael, the poem was written in 1865, two years before Matthews commissioned the painting. See Rossetti, *Works*, xxviii. This was the same year Rossetti first began making studies for the painting. So it is impossible to know for sure which in fact came first chronologically, the poem or the idea for the painting. And even if it were possible to establish a reliable chronology, this would in no way establish a definite hierarchical relation between the two works.

As J. Hillis Miller has noted about the two works making up the double work of art, "Either [work] may be taken as the 'original' of which the other is the 'illustration' or the explanatory poetic 'superscription,' writing on top of another graphic form. This relation does not depend, of course, on the chronology of Rossetti's actual creation of the two works in question" ("Mirror's Secret," 336). So the picture is as much drawn for the poem as the poem is written for the picture, the implications of which I consider in this chapter.

7. On "Aspecta Medusa" as an allegory about artistic representation, see Patterson, 113–15. Patterson contrasts Rossetti's view of art as a purifying and idealizing medium with Shelley's view of it as a suggestive and revealing medium, a view which Patterson finds expressed in a poem that is also about a painting of Medusa, the fragmentary "On the Medusa of Leonardo da Vinci in the Florentine Gallery."

8. Caravaggio himself alludes to the explicit parallel between the painting and the reflection of Medusa's head in Perseus's mirror shield (Figure 3). He paints the image on a round surface and in such a way as to suggest the convex curvature of that surface. In the painting, Medusa is depicted at the moment of her decapitation, as indicated by the blood coming out of her neck. And her gaze is directed off to the side, making it impossible for the viewer of the painting to meet her eyes.

For a complex and thoughtful reading of Caravaggio's painting as a commentary on representation, see Louis Marin, *To Destroy Painting*, Part II.

9. On the mirror in Rossetti's work more generally, and its reflection from within that body of work on the mirror in the Western tradition overall, see Miller, "The Mirror's Secret."

10. Going against Rossetti's own recommendations in the poem, critics have predictably attempted to remove the "forbidden thing itself" from the shadows and to bring it into the light. Jerome McGann interprets it as the revelation of a terrifying and previously undiscovered aspect of oneself ("Beauty," 21–22). David Riede takes it more literally, as the revelation of the mysteries of death ("Aestheticism," 145), and elsewhere expands his interpretation to include also "the fatal appeal of female sexuality" (*Dante Gabriel Rossetti Revisited*, 91–92). Laurence Roussillon (10–12), Bram Dijkstra (137–38), Martin Danahay (48–49), and Richard Dellamora (138–39) all identify it as the revelation of a threatening form of sexuality.

11. At least two readers of the poem, Laurence Roussillon and Richard Dellamora, have noted the close juxtaposition of life and death. For Roussillon, it marks the contrast between Andromeda and Medusa (6), whereas for Dellamora, it suggests an affinity between Andromeda and Perseus (139).

12. See Shelley, *Major Works*, 210–11 and 740. Both Jerome McGann (*Dante Gabriel Rossetti: Collected Poetry and Prose*, 384) and David Riede ("Aestheticism," 145) hear allusions to Shelley's poem in "Aspecta Medusa."

"The Lady of Shalott," an episode from which Rossetti illustrated for an 1857 edition of Tennyson's poems, and Plato's Allegory of the Cave would also seem to be significant intertextual references for Rossetti's poem. On the Pre-Raphaelites' adoptions of various motifs from "The Lady of Shalott," see Poulson, who specifically considers the topics of female sexuality and female curiosity that several readers have also found addressed in "Aspecta Medusa."

13. On Rossetti's "deconstruction" of Plato's metaphysics, see Shaw, *The Lucid Veil*, 168–74. What Shaw calls a deconstruction is simply an inversion of Plato's hierarchy, an alleged privileging by Rossetti of form over content, of the sensual over the supersensual, of the visible world over the invisible world of ideal forms, and so on.

14. For a generous sampling of such clichés, see Shaw, *The Lucid Veil*, 168–74.

15. Unlike the other works included in the series, *The Lifted Veil* is a work of fiction and is not explicitly about art and aesthetics in the way Nietzsche's, Pater's, and Swinburne's texts are. But both visual art and aesthetic experience are important motifs in the novella. Moreover, like many of its commentators, I read *The Lifted Veil* as an allegorical reflection by Eliot on the process of writing fiction and, more specifically, on the poetics and ethics of realism.

16. See, for example, Levine, Anger, Rauch, and Shaw, *Victorians and Mystery*.

17. See, for example, Neil Hertz, "Medusa's Head: Male Hysteria under Political Pressure," in *End*, 160–93.

18. For helpful summaries of the various classical literary accounts of Medusa's story, see Suther (163–67) and Woodward (3–23).

19. On the "head-viewing" motif in classical visual arts, see Phinney (460–63) and Schauenburg (55–82).

20. For a psychoanalytic interpretation of Burne-Jones's painting and of the entire Perseus cycle, see Kestner (98–106).

21. The connection between Medusa and dangerous or impossible knowledge is not only implied by the conceit of a monster that is dangerous or impossible to see, but is somewhat of a commonplace. According to Tobin Siebers, for example, "The remarkable ability of the head of Medusa to represent what cannot be represented or what should not be represented constantly surfaces in the history of thought. Medusa's head frequently signifies those aspects of philosophy that are . . . simply unthinkable" (8).

22. Although Medusa is consistently identified in the classical sources as female, the explicit equation of her horrifying and petrifying powers with her femininity only goes back to romanticism and the early nineteenth century. On the classical interpretations of Medusa's power, see Feldman, "Origin" and "Gorgo." Feldman does maintain that one aspect of Medusa's threat lies in her femininity, which "renders a man frigid as stone and unmans him" ("Origin," 221). But this claim is avowedly speculative and seems to be more Feldman's own post-Freudian interpretation than a classical Greek one. See "Origin," 220–21, and "Gorgo," 491–93. On the nineteenth-century Medusa as a version of the romantic (and later decadent) Fatal Woman, see Praz, chapters 1 and 4.

In the twentieth century, Freud explicitly analyzes Medusa's petrifying power as the threat of potential castration that the image of female genitals "reveals" to man. I discuss this interpretation in detail in chapter 1. Many contemporary feminist critics have followed Freud in interpreting Medusa's gaze as indicating male fears about the power of women (for instance, their procreative power), often framing their discussion as gynocentric revisions of Freud's phallocentric theories. I make reference to some of these revisions in the endnotes for chapter 1. Perhaps the most well-known example is Hélène Cixous's essay

"The Laugh of the Medusa." While the equation of Medusa's horror with her femininity is a Freudian innovation, although arguably one that is anticipated in nineteenth-century romantic and decadent literature, critics have retroactively interpreted earlier Medusas in terms of this association. Besides Feldman ("Gorgo," 492–93, and "Origin," 220–21), Bowers (220–22) and duBois (87–92) discuss classical images of Medusa in terms of sexuality and gender. Garber (96–123) and Vickers (109–12) address the topics of sex and gender in Renaissance images of Medusa.

23. The relevant passages are *Odyssey* 11, 632 ff., and *Iliad* 5, 738 ff. and 11, 36. According to Vernant, the *Iliad* evokes the tradition of seeing the Gorgon as an emblem of the warrior's battle fury (116–17), while the *Odyssey* evokes her canonical association with death (121).

24. According to Tobin Siebers, Medusa "simultaneously expels and embodies a nefarious ideal. [She] literally contains evil mixtures and confuses the sacred and profane, law and taboo, pure and impure [and] the opposing yet similar elements of contagion and cure" (9). On Medusa's protective and healing power, see Siebers (1–11), Feldman ("Gorgo," 488–89, and "Origin," 212–15), and Belfiore (9–30).

25. Helpful surveys of the Medusa image in nineteenth-century British and European literature include McGann ("Beauty"), Patterson, and Suther (170–73).

CHAPTER ONE. APOTROPAIC READING

1. On the evocation of the absent body by the decapitated Medusa's head, see Thalia Phillies Feldman ("Origin," 215–16).

2. On decapitation as a castration symbol, see Freud's essay "The Taboo of Virginity," in which Freud interprets Judith's decapitation of Holofernes in Hebbel's tragedy *Judith und Holofernes* as castration (11:207–08). On the Judith theme and Freud's essay, see Sarah Kofman's *Freud and Fiction* (54–82). See also Kofman's "'It's Only the First Step'" (116–17) for other examples of this symbolic equation, taken from *The Interpretation of Dreams*.

3. This version of the boy's entry into the castration complex represents Freud's first extensive articulation of the male castration complex, which occurs in his 1908 essay "On the Sexual Theories of Children." In that essay, Freud uses the phrase "threat of castration" for the first time. The material Freud presents on the castration complex is usually attributed to his findings in the analysis of the case of Little Hans ("Analysis of a Phobia in a Five-Year-Old Boy," 10:5–149). That case history, though published a year after "On the Sexual Theories of Children," was being written during the same time Freud was writing the latter.

In 1915, Freud appended a brief summary of the material from "On the Sexual Theories of Children," including the material on the boy's castration complex, to his *Three Essays on the Theory of Sexuality* (originally published in 1905). He then returned to the topic of the castration complex during the 1920s in a remarkable series of essays identifying the castration complex as a universal reality, not as merely one complex among many others. The version of the complex anticipated in "On the Sexual Theories of Children" is elaborated in such later essays as "The Infantile Genital Organization" (19:139–45), "Some Psychical Consequences of the Anatomical Distinction Between the Sexes" (19:248–58), and the 1938 fragment "Splitting of the Ego in the Defensive Process" (23:273–78).

4. On this version of the boy's castration complex, see, besides "The Dissolution of the Oedipus Complex," Freud's lecture "The Sexual Life of Human Beings" from the *Introductory Lectures on Psychoanalysis* (16:303–19), and "Femininity" from the *New Introductory Lectures* (22:112–35). See also, of course, "Medusa's Head."

For a lucid and helpful general account of the boy's castration complex in Freud's writings, see Laplanche (44–75).

5. Cf. Laplanche and Pontalis: "Empirically, there are two concrete facts which have a part to play in the genesis of the castration complex as described by Freud. The emergence of the complex depends entirely upon the child's *discovery* of the anatomical distinction between the sexes. This discovery actualises and validates a *threat* of castration which may have been real or phantasied" (57).

On these two "ingredients" of the castration complex, see also Laplanche, *Problématiques* (65–68). Laplanche points out that the sequence of these two events may be interchangeable, and that the effect on the boy will be, at bottom, the same (68).

6. Freud's most complex exposition of the castration complex's structure of deferred action is in the case history of the Wolf Man. See *From the History of an Infantile Neurosis*, especially chapter 4.

7. This equation is one of several places where Freud's Medusa interpretation quickly comes up against its own limitations. Because Freud interprets the Medusa myth exclusively in terms of the male castration complex, he does not (and cannot) account for the scenario depicted in Rossetti's "Aspecta Medusa": the eventuality that a woman, such as Andromeda, would look at Medusa's head.

8. Barbara Creed proposes an alternative interpretation of the snakes as an image of potential male castration. She focuses on the "vaginal significance" of the snakes, an aspect she rightly claims Freud overlooks. Her interpretation is that the snakes are not only symbols of the woman's present or absent penis, as Freud maintains, but that they represent the mother's vagina. She dwells on the "symbolic meaning of the snake's open mouth and pointed fangs" (111), identifying the snakes as a version of the *vagina dentata*, the devouring or castrating vagina. She also claims that this vaginal significance of Medusa's head is terrifying to Freud, a terror that Freud's reassuring interpretation of the snakes as penis symbols is trying to mask. While I concur with her point about Freud's hesitancy to acknowledge the vagina, it should be pointed out that Creed's interpretation displaces the castrating significance of the snakes to someplace entirely outside the bounds of the Freudian castration complex. Her point may be perfectly valid in itself (as an alternative interpretation of the Medusa image), but it seems to me that it does not help much if one's aim is to read and make sense of Freud's text on its own terms.

9. Every detail mentioned by Freud in "Medusa's Head" appears only insofar as it has already been interpreted by Freud, which is to say already linked back to the castration complex. No detail Freud brings up remains unaccounted for, though he also leaves out telling details from the source material, details for which his interpretation may be less able to account. These include the motif of Andromeda looking at the decapitated head, mentioned earlier, and those

versions of the myth in which it is Medusa's own gaze that petrifies, not the spectator's gaze at her.

10. For a critique of the Freudian logic that reduces multiple, various instances of a figure or symptom to the singularity of Castration with a capital C, see Deleuze and Guattari's essay "1914: One or Several Wolves?" in *A Thousand Plateaus* (26–38). The title of the essay refers to the case history of the Wolf Man and to Freud's reduction of the six or seven wolves in the famous wolf dream into one single wolf (the castrated and castrating Father).

11. On the longstanding association in the Western philosophical tradition between perception and the use of metaphor, see Jacques Derrida, "White Mythology" (*Margins*, 207–71).

12. The figural meaning is what the metaphor stands for, while the proper meaning is the property the metaphor (in its literal sense) and the figural meaning have in common and can therefore exchange. One way to understand what Freud and Aristotle call similarity is as the shared proper meaning that in Freud's text, for example, would link the dream-picture (that is, the metaphor) and its truth (that is, the metaphor's figural meaning). On this tripartite structure of metaphor, see de Man (65–66).

13. In his important essay "Two Aspects of Language and Two Types of Aphasic Disturbances," Roman Jakobson famously proposes that Freudian dream symbols can be understood linguistically, in terms of what he calls the metaphorical and metonymic poles of language. He maintains that Freud's symbols can be read metaphorically as an association by similarity, or metonymically as an association by contiguity: "in an inquiry into the structure of dreams, the decisive question is whether the symbols and the temporal sequences used are based on contiguity (Freud's metonymic 'displacement' and synecdochic 'condensation') or on similarity (Freud's 'identification and symbolism')" (113).

Jean Laplanche has applied Jakobson's argument to "Medusa's Head," stating that Medusa's head "recalls" the problem of castration in both metaphorical and metonymic ways (171).

14. Freud does not actually say this in so many words in the original German text, and the injunction to the reader to "observe" is an addition of the translator, James Strachey. Yet this does not significantly detract from the point I want to make. Strachey is tapping into the spirit of the interpretation, if not into its letter. He is being sensitive to the repeated insistence in Freud's text on the connection between seeing and interpreting.

15. Throughout "Medusa's Head," Freud emphasizes the visual nature of his object, as when his opening sentence refers to Medusa's head as a *Gebilde*. Strachey translates this word as theme, but the German also has embedded within it the word *Bild* (image or picture). In the paragraph on the snakes, Freud notes, "The hair upon Medusa's head is frequently represented [*gebildet*] in works of art in the form of snakes." According to Klaus Heinrich, Freud was looking at a reproduction (*Abbildung*) of a sixth-century BC Gorgon antefix from the Portonaccio temple of Apollo at Veii while writing his notes on Medusa's head (343).

16. On the girl's perception of her genitals as lacking a penis, see "Some Psychological Consequences," "Femininity," and "Female Sexuality" (21:221–43).

17. According to Barbara Spackman, "Freud's infantile theorist does not ever see 'castration' but rather 'sees' an interpretation of an earlier perception" (*Fascist Virilities*, 95).

In "Medusa's Head," the interpretative nature of the boy's perception is made explicit in Freud's description of the female genitals the boy sees as "probably those of an adult, surrounded by hair, *and essentially those of his mother*" (18:273, my emphasis). The boy does not as a rule literally see his mother's genitals but rather makes an oedipal interpretation when he sees the female genitals he looks at as being "essentially" those of his mother. This is similar to the interpretation he makes when he sees them as "essentially" a castrated penis. On the relation between the Oedipus complex and the castration complex, see "The Dissolution of the Oedipus Complex."

Freud notes in the essay "The Infantile Genital Organization" that his contribution to Ferenczi's earlier Medusa interpretation is the point that "what is indicated in the myth is the *mother's* genitals" (19:144n3). On Medusa and the mother, see Sarah Kofman, "'It's Only the First Step'" (115) and *The Enigma of Woman* (82–83).

18. Rhetorically speaking, the symbol of Medusa's head is not an Aristotelian metaphor for the "castrated" female genitals, but is what Paul de Man calls a "blind metonymy" (102), a figure that blindly substitutes for its referent because it does not properly see that referent.

Andrzej Warminski explicates de Man's phrase as follows: "'metonymy' because it is a substitution by contiguity, mere juxtaposition, mere 'putting next to'; 'blind' because it does not know anything about what it substitutes for, does not even know whether there is anything there to put something next to it" (*Readings*, l).

The blind metonymy does not know anything about what it substitutes for because it cannot see it. The implication is that the metonymy is an arbitrary substitution on two levels: because it is a metonymy (that is, related to its referent by mere juxtaposition) and because it is blind. Thus there is neither a natural correspondence nor a visible similarity between the trope and that for which it substitutes. The latter is not accessible to vision nor to any kind of cognitive orientation: the trope substituting for it "does not even know whether there is anything there to put something next to it." "There" is only another trope, something that can be seen and apprehended figuratively, but not literally.

For a detailed commentary on blind metonymy and its destabilizing implications for the canonical distinctions between figurative and literal, and between seeing and not seeing, see Warminski's thoughtful discussion of the rhetorical figure of catachresis in *Readings in Interpretation* (xlix–lxi).

19. Sarah Kofman reads this disclaimer as a disavowal of the essay's seriousness. She proposes that Freud wrote the text as a form of speculative amusement and therefore did not want to publish it. See "'It's Only the First Step,'" 115. My own reading of the disclaimer in this paragraph identifies the lack of seriousness Freud (playfully) alleges with the demonstrable lack of any definite substantiation or grounding of the interpretation.

20. A comprehensive discussion of the complex relationship between psychoanalysis and mythology in Freud's work is beyond the scope of this chapter and of this book. However, "Medusa's Head" does condense some of Freud's

frequently revisited points about this relation: for instance, that myths like Medusa's head are psychoanalytic interpretations *avant la lettre*, and also that psychoanalysis can be read as a kind of mythology.

A suggestive commentary on the relation between myth and psychoanalysis, with specific reference to Medusa's head, is Laurence Kahn's fine essay "Le monde serein des dieux d'Homère," which takes up the question about which of the two discourses is the origin, ground, or foundation of the other. See also Jean Starobinski, "Hamlet and Oedipus," in *The Living Eye*, 166–67. On Freud's writings about femininity, female castration, and the castration complex as a kind of mythologization, see Renate Schlesier, *Konstruktionen der Weiblichkeit bei Sigmund Freud.*

21. See Sarah Kofman's *Freud and Fiction* for a link between this interpretation and "Medusa's Head" (106).

22. Other examples of the latter two equations can also be found in *The Interpretation of Dreams.*

23. In the lecture entitled "Revision of the Theory of Dreams" from the *New Introductory Lectures on Psychoanalysis*, for example, Freud inquires of his audience, "You know, perhaps, that the mythological creation, Medusa's head, can be traced back to the . . . *motif* of fright of castration" (22:24). Here it is as if the link between Medusa and castration is a matter of common knowledge.

24. See "Fetishism" (21:149–57). On the logic of disavowal, see also Freud's text "The Splitting of the Ego in the Defensive Process."

Freud's categorical interpretation of the fetish as a stand-in for the woman's or girl's penis in the primal scene does not allow for any possibility of female fetishism or a female fetishist, just as his interpretation of Medusa's head as a figure for male castration anxiety does not allow for the possibility that a woman would look at the head.

25. According to Pautrat, "Medusa's head is entirely paradoxical, being at once an image of castration (open-mouthed, eyes bulging) and a multiple image of the threatened penis. . . . This seems a very paradoxical figuration, since Medusa's face conveys *castration and its denial at the same time*" (168–69).

According to Ferenczi, Medusa's bulging eyes signify an erection, not castration (69). Within Freud's overall tropological system, however, the difference amounts to little or nothing. In the end, interpreting the eyes as an erection or as castration comes back to one and the same thing, namely the castration complex. Freud makes this explicit in "Medusa's Head" when he says that the erection has "the same origin from the castration complex" as the viewer's petrification.

26. On Medusa's head as a fetish, and on parallels between "Medusa's Head" and "Fetishism," see Pautrat (168–69), Hertz (*End*, 161–68), Kofman (*Enigma*, 82–89), Creed (110–11, 115–17), and Spackman (*Decadent*, 201–03).

27. The figurative relationship I am establishing between a sexual threat to the fetishist and an epistemological threat to Freud himself is confirmed by the categorical symbolic equation Freud draws between castration and blindness. In the essay on the "Uncanny," for example, he writes, "A study of dreams, phantasies, and myths has taught us that anxiety about one's eyes, the fear of going blind, is often enough a substitute for the dread of being castrated" (17:231). This substitution can, of course, also function in reverse, as I suggest it does in "Medusa's Head."

28. Louis Marin (145) and Sarah Kofman ("'It's Only the First Step,'" 115) also note the interpretation's alleged obviousness, but unlike Kahn they don't comment specifically on the obviousness as a distinctly visual and visible obviousness.

29. Neil Hertz comments on the visibility of the Medusa symbol as such and suggests that this visibility is reassuring as much to Freud the interpreter as to the viewer in the myth: "The symbol of the Medusa's head is reassuring not only because its elements can be read in [reassuring] ways, but because it is a symbol" (*End*, 166). If Medusa's head is reassuring to the fetishistic viewer because some of its elements can be read in ways that assure him that he is not castrated, the symbol is reassuring as such to Freud simply because it can be read (or seen . . .) at all, and because it would therefore be accessible to an interpretation.

30. Marjorie Garber notes, "the word 'apotropaic,' so frequently associated with the power of the severed Medusa head, means 'turning away' or 'warding off,' and derives from the same root as 'trope'" (120). The word's etymology would therefore support my reading in this chapter of apotropaic gestures in rhetorical and, more specifically, tropological terms.

31. As in Freud's theories of female penis envy and the female castration complex, in this example too the woman is shown to be herself fully complicit in Freud's phallocentrism and gynophobia. Here, the woman's showing her vulva to the devil and thereby putting him to flight is said to be an illustration of the principle, "What arouses horror in oneself will produce the same effect upon the enemy against whom one is seeking to defend oneself."

32. After Agathon's speech in the *Symposium*, Socrates maintains that "his speech reminded me so strongly of that master of rhetoric, Gorgias, that I couldn't help thinking of Odysseus, and his fear that Medusa would rise from the lower world among the ghosts, and I was afraid that when Agathon got near the end he would arm his speech against mine with the Gorgon's head of Gorgias' eloquence, and strike me dumb as a stone" (198b-c 550).

CHAPTER TWO. A "MONSTROUS" OPPOSITION

1. The Freudian fetish can be called a representation of the missing female penis and of the attendant idea of castration, even though it is not a mimetic representation, one based on the metaphorical principle of a visual analogy, like Medusa's head. It is rather a representation based on the metonymic principle of contiguity: "the Freudian fetish may, in the patient's experience, be determined by metonymy, the last thing seen before the 'revelation' being a likely choice" (Spackman, *Decadent*, 191–92). Freud himself identifies the fetish as a form of representation when he calls it a "substitute" for the female penis and a "memorial" to the fetishist's horror of castration (21:154).

2. *The Birth of Tragedy*, 40. Unless otherwise noted, all citations of Nietzsche in this chapter are from *The Birth of Tragedy*, with page references given parenthetically.

3. This remark is taken from the preface Nietzsche appended to the book's 1886 edition, entitled "Attempt at a Self-Criticism."

4. Over the course of Freud's writings, the castration complex comes increasingly to be described not as one complex among many, but as a universal

phenomenon, a universal fear (among men) or loathing (among women) of one's own castration. According to Laplanche and Pontalis, "the castration complex is encountered in every single analysis" (57).

Of course there are numerous qualitative differences between what Freud calls castration and what Nietzsche calls Dionysus. For example, the recognition of castration as a universal condition lacks the elements of ecstasy and abandonment Nietzsche associates with insight into the Dionysian. However, what I would establish is a structural parallel between two scenarios: in each case, the juxtaposition of a terrifying existential insight and its protective representation.

5. Rossetti's poem does so as well, as the second and third moves of my reading of the poem, given in the Introduction's first section, attempt to demonstrate.

6. The dialectical relationship between Apollo and Dionysus in *The Birth of Tragedy* may account partially for Nietzsche's well-known remark in *Ecce Homo* that the book "smells offensively Hegelian" (270).

7. This distribution of roles helps to explain why I structurally align Dionysus with castration in Freud's texts and with "the forbidden thing itself" in Rossetti's poem, just as I align Apollo with the castration symbol and the fetish in Freud's texts and with the "shadow upon life" in Rossetti's poem.

8. *Allegories of Reading*, 90. In this chapter, all further references to de Man are to this essay, "Genesis and Genealogy," with page numbers indicated parenthetically.

9. The actual word in the quotation is *Gleichnisse* (parables), not *symbols*. Throughout *The Birth of Tragedy*, Nietzsche is preoccupied with figurative relationships and with the topic of figurative language. His text introduces a diverse and sometimes confusing (because inconsistently applied) set of terms designating figurative relationships, including *Gleichnis, Symbol, Gestalt, Analogon, Bild*, and *Exempel*.

On rhetoric and Nietzsche's use of rhetorical terminology in *The Birth of Tragedy*, see Lacoue-Labarthe (14–36).

10. Sarah Kofman's *Nietzsche and Metaphor*, for example, makes the argument that *The Birth of Tragedy*, unlike Nietzsche's later work, privileges an authentic Dionysian essence over Apollonian metaphor (13–17). For a critique of Kofman's reading, see Warminski (*Readings*, xli–xlix).

11. See *Allegories of Reading*, 83–93.

De Man locates Nietzsche's questioning of his own apparent logocentrism in, on one hand, "metalinguistic statements about the rhetorical nature of language, and, on the other hand, a rhetorical praxis that puts these statements into question" (98). For example, the logic of Nietzsche's exposition demands that he provide a description of pure, non-representational Dionysian music, so as to be able to distinguish it from an imitative, verbal Apollonian realism. But in providing a verbal account of allegedly unrepresentable, literally intolerable music, he undermines his claim that music is original truth, that it cannot be mediated, and that it falls outside the entire literal/representational distinction in the first place. Nietzsche's text, de Man writes, consequently "acquires two incompatible narrators. The narrator who argues against . . . representational realism destroys the credibility of the other narrator, for whom Dionysian insight is the tragic perception of original truth" (98).

12. Nietzsche opens his "Attempt at a Self-Criticism" by evoking this capital question: "Whatever may be at the bottom [*Grunde*] of this questionable book, it must have been an exceptionally significant and fascinating question" (17). If the Apollo/Dionysus question is indeed the *Grunde* of the book, then presumably it is the Dionysus of the book. This chapter demonstrates how this is in fact the case.

13. Both this citation and the previous one about Schopenhauer are examples of the book's ostensible polemic against science, philosophy, and epistemology. What Nietzsche calls Dionysus is equated in both passages with the destruction or the exposed limitation of logic. This critique is also taken up in somewhat similar terms in Nietzsche's essay "On Truth and Lie in an Extra-moral Sense."

At the same time that Nietzsche critiques science and logic, however, the Dionysian art of tragedy is itself also a mode of knowing, and Nietzsche's book reproduces the very epistemological forms it would critique, as Nietzsche acknowledges in *Ecce Homo*. As de Man notes, "in *The Birth of Tragedy*, Nietzsche advocates the use of epistemologically rigorous methods as the only possible means to reflect on the limitations of these methods" (86).

14. Cf. de Man: "The one who has reached [Dionysian insight] is, like Hamlet, frozen forever in the madness of inaction" (93).

15. Carol Jacobs points out that "*Schauer* . . . also means shudder, spasm" (5). Her reading concentrates on the *Schauer* as the birthspasm of tragedy in the ideal spectator (*Schauer*), the Dionysian chorus. My own reading focuses on the link Nietzsche implies between seeing Dionysus and being struck with terror and awe.

16. Besides the figure of the mirror, Nietzsche uses the figure of the veil in a similar capacity:

> That overwhelming dismay in the face of the titanic powers of nature, the Moira enthroned inexorably over all knowledge, the vulture of the great lover of mankind, Prometheus, the terrible fate of the wise Oedipus, the family curse of the Atridae which drove Orestes to matricide: in short, that entire philosophy of the sylvan god, with its mythical exemplars, which caused the downfall of the melancholy Etruscans— all this was again and again overcome by the Greeks with the aid of the Olympian *middle world* of art; or at any rate it was veiled and withdrawn from sight. (42)

In the manuscript version of *The Birth of Tragedy*, Nietzsche includes "Gorgons and Medusas" in the list of mythical exemplars. See *Kritische Studienausgabe* (hereafter abbreviated KSA), 14:47.

On the figure of the protective veil, cf. also section 3: "The Homeric 'naiveté' can be understood only as the complete victory of Apollinian illusion. . . . The true goal is veiled by a phantasm [*Wahnbild*]" (44) and section 2: "it was only [the Greek's] Apollinian consciousness which, like a veil, hid this Dionysian world from his vision" (41).

17. What protects the epic poet from being fused with his creations is that he takes pleasure in the illusion as such, in the image as such. This is the pleasure of the Apollonian *par excellence*, the pleasure of dreamers. "In our dreams," Nietzsche writes in section 1, "we delight in the immediate understanding of

figures . . . . But even when this dream reality is most intense, we still have, glimmering through it, the sensation that it is *mere appearance*" (34). The protective effect of the Apollonian mirror is due to this sensation.

As the poet's identification with his figures (in what Nietzsche calls the pain and contradiction of a primal oneness) is here said to be a sign of the true Dionysian artist (specifically the lyrist, as opposed to the epic poet and the sculptor), in later texts the artist's identification with his characters is said to be a sign of decadence—for example, Wagner's in section 4 of the "Third Essay" of the *Genealogy of Morals.*

18. This formulation is repeated almost verbatim in another 1870 preparatory text, "Die Geburt des tragischen Gedankens" [The Birth of Tragic Thought]. See KSA, 1:589.

19. On the use of the Medusa motif in Nietzsche's writings, see Bernard Pautrat, "Nietzsche Medused," and Sarah Kofman, *Nietzsche et la scène philosophique*, 63–76. Pautrat's essay discusses the Medusa figure that appears in preparatory drafts and sketches for *Thus Spake Zarathustra*, while Kofman discusses the Medusa who appears in and around *The Birth of Tragedy.*

20. See Books 24 and 47 of the *Dionysiaca* and Book 2 of *Description of Greece.* Nietzsche makes reference to Pausanias and *Description of Greece* in his text "Homer's Contest," though not to the episode in which Perseus turns the satyrs to stone.

21. Feldman, "Origin," 221. On this episode, see Feldman ("Origin," 220–221) and Vernant (136).

Feldman reads the figure of Perseus as a moral enforcer, since he uses Medusa's head not for personal aggrandizement, but for moral purposes. For instance, he uses the head to petrify Phineus, who makes unjust claims on Andromeda after the latter's rescue by Perseus, as well as Polydectes, who desires and pursues Perseus's mother, Danae, against her will. Similarly, Feldman argues, Perseus functions as a moral defense against the Dionysian cult. One could add that Perseus functions in the Medusa myth as an emissary of Greek culture in general, and of Athena specifically, sent to the edge of the known world to defeat a strange, monstrous power.

Vernant maintains that the satyr cult confronted by Perseus "contained a gorgonlike element in its madness" (136), suggesting that Perseus is holding up Medusa's head at a version of Medusa herself. This is also the case in Nietzsche's passage, the implications of which I discuss in the paragraphs immediately following.

22. As indicated earlier, Nietzsche makes explicit use of Medusa as a figure for the Dionysian in drafts and preparatory texts for *The Birth of Tragedy.* Besides the examples cited above, see KSA, 1:568 and 1:596. In the passage itself, he describes the Dionysian festivals as "grotesquely [*fratzenhaft*] uncouth." The word *fratzenhaft* is the standard term used in nineteenth-century German classical scholarship to describe the original *gorgoneion*, the figure from which Medusa is a derivation. (*Gorgoneia* are decorative masks that frontally depict a contorted face made up of glaring eyes, snaky hair, a protruding tongue, horns, long teeth or tusks, and a beard. They emblematize fear or the cause of fear, and were apotropaically placed by the Greeks on buildings, tools, pottery, weapons, and shields to avert evil.) See for example Furtwängler (1721) and Schauenburg

(78). On iconographic parallels between the Gorgon and the Satyrs and Silenoi, see Vernant (113).

23. The Apollonian emblem of this victory, of the transfiguration of a frenzied Dionysus into the calmness of sculpture, might be the so-called "beautiful type" of Gorgon, which in the fourth century BC comes to replace the earlier *fratzenhaft*, grotesque type, the *gorgoneion* (Furtwängler, 1721). The beautiful Medusa is characterized by its human face, smoothness of contours, slightly downcast eyes, and serenity. Furtwängler describes it as "tranquilly beautiful" and as a type of "flawless, but cold, rigid beauty" (1721–24), recalling the kind of language Nietzsche uses to describe the Apollonian artwork. The prototype of the beautiful Medusa is the so-called Medusa Rondanini, a marble icon dating to 400–350 BC, commented on by Goethe and George Eliot, among others, and now most recognizable as the logo of the fashion designer Gianni Versace.

24. This is true of Freud's apotropaic gesture in "Medusa's Head" as well, as I demonstrate in the final section of the previous chapter.

25. Nietzsche also maintains, moreover, that Apollo's power is enhanced by his creating the illusion that the Dionysian is a subservient aspect of his own art: "What can the healing magic of Apollo not accomplish when it can even create the illusion that the Dionysian is really in the service of the Apollinian and capable of enhancing its effects—as if [Dionysian] music were essentially the art of presenting an Apollinian content?" (128). Apollo's healing power, in short, relies on creating the illusion that the fundamental order of things has been reversed.

26. Cf. also the following formulation: "With what astonishment must the Apollinian Greek have beheld [the dithyrambic votary of Dionysus]! With an astonishment that was all the greater the more it was mingled with the shuddering suspicion that all this was actually not so very alien to him after all, in fact, that it was only his Apollinian consciousness which, like a veil, hid this Dionysian world from his vision" (41). Here too the Dionysian is related rather than opposed to the Apollonian, a kinship that is revealed to the Apollonian Greek by his glimpse into the Dionysian. In this sentence, Apollonian consciousness fulfills the veiling function Nietzsche elsewhere assigns to the Apollonian artwork.

27. The genetic model eventually arrives at a "reconciliation" of Apollo and Dionysus that occurs when the Dionysian begins to appear not as an invasion from outside of Greece, but as a native plant growing from roots in the Hellenic nature itself. At this stage, which represents a step toward the dialectical model and the dialectical union of Apollo and Dionysus in Attic tragedy, Dionysus is allowed to take root in Hellenic culture but remains safely mitigated by Apollo: "The opposition between Apollo and Dionysus became more hazardous and even impossible, when similar [Dionysian] impulses finally burst forth from the deepest roots of the Hellenic nature and made a path for themselves: the Delphic god, by a seasonably effected reconciliation [*Versöhnung*], now contended himself with taking the destructive weapons from the hands of his powerful antagonist" (39).

28. Warminski, "Terrible Reading," 391. Warminski associates the destructive meaning of Apollo with the radically semiotic functioning of language as such.

29. Cf. Warminski: "One could call that meaning 'Dionysian' but it is 'Dionysian' in a new, re-inscribed sense: one that has nothing to do with the existential

pathos of human suffering" ("Terrible Reading," 391). Cf. also: "In the case of de Man's reading of *The Birth of Tragedy*, the disjunction is not the trivial and clichéd distinction bequeathed to us by intellectual history—i.e., between the Apollinian serenity of the surface and the Dionysian existential horror underneath—but rather the disjunction proper to the Apollinian itself" (Ibid.).

30. Nietzsche's shift away from an existential pathos is analogous to the shift I trace in Freud's "Medusa's Head" away from the sexual pathos of male castration anxiety toward an anxiety that is epistemological and rhetorical in nature.

31. For an exemplary account of this predicament, see Sarah Kofman: "One can understand why Nietzsche should have sung and not spoken when writing *The Birth of Tragedy*, or should have expressed himself as a poet: philosophical language [Apollo] is the most unsatisfactory there is, for it petrifies the 'music of the world' [Dionysus] into concepts" (*Nietzsche and Metaphor*, 13). According to this version of the Apollo/Dionysus relationship, Dionysus is for Nietzsche the privileged term over Apollo, as poetry and music are privileged over philosophical language and concepts. The petrification of music by philosophical language is akin to the figure of Apollo holding up Medusa's head at Dionysus, only here petrification designates not only the containment but also the compromising of Dionysus. As noted earlier, Kofman goes on to critique what she regards as Nietzsche's logocentrism that is implied in the very notion of a Dionysus compromised by Apollo.

32. Cf. also the almost verbatim variation of this sentence in "Die dionysische Weltanschauung," KSA, 1:568.

33. Critics who have found the Freudian logic of fetishism at work in texts by Nietzsche include Pautrat, "Nietzsche Medused"; Derrida, *Spurs*; and Kofman, "Baubô" and chapter 3 of *Camera Obscura*.

CHAPTER THREE. TWO IMPRESSIONS OF MEDUSA

1. For a useful summary of Swinburne's highly subjective and impressionistic style of criticism, see McGann, *Swinburne*, 14–23.

2. Pater's allusion is to Matthew Arnold, specifically to the 1864 essay "The Function of Criticism at the Present Time."

3. The word *aesthetic* derives from the Greek *aisthanestai*, to perceive. Aesthetic criticism is so called because of its stated emphasis on the critic's perceptions of the work (rather than the work's objective elements). As Swinburne notes in his essay on the painter James McNeill Whistler, "Not merely the only accurate meaning but the only possible meaning of [*aesthete*] is nothing more but nothing less than this: an intelligent, appreciative, quick-witted person; in a word, as the lexicon has it, 'one who perceives'" (16:27). On the importance of perception in Swinburne's criticism, see McGann (*Swinburne*, 18) and Morgan (325). On the centrality of perception in Pater's criticism, see Bloom (164–65). On the importance of the senses in aesthetic criticism more generally, see Peters (100–01).

4. Cf. for example the following sentence from Pater's essay on Leonardo: "a lover of strange souls may still analyse for himself the impression made on him by those works, and try to reach through it a definition of the chief elements of Leonardo's genius" (78).

5. This excerpt from Swinburne's introductory remarks on Michelangelo is perhaps the most well known passage in "Notes on Designs." It is cited whole or in part by, among others, McGann ("Beauty," 15), Lang (xvii), Bloom (167–68), Levey (108), and Donoghue (142). Yet these critics have little or nothing to say about the excerpt they quote, besides noting a stylistic influence on Pater. Harold Bloom does point to the theme of knowledge with which Swinburne is preoccupied in the passage (168).

6. "Leonardo da Vinci" was first published sixteen months after "Notes and Designs," and in the same journal, the *Fortnightly Review*. Swinburne remarks on the stylistic influence of his art criticism on Pater's Leonardo essay in an 1869 letter to Rossetti (Lang, 2:58). And in an 1873 letter to John Morley, editor of the *Fortnightly Review*, he claims that Pater had personally acknowledged his influence during a conversation at Oxford (Lang, 2:240–41).

For accounts of Swinburne's stylistic influence on Pater, see Morgan (325–30), Chew (265–67), and Levey (107–09). This influence is noted in passing by virtually everyone writing on Swinburne's art criticism, on "Leonardo da Vinci," or on the Swinburne–Pater relationship, among them Rooksby (3), McGann (*Swinburne*, 14), Henderson (81–82), Welby (210), Lang (xvii), Bloom (167–68), Crawford (850–52), Donoghue (140–42), and Donald Hill's editorial notes in *The Renaissance* (371–72, 380). See also Wellek (382), Praz (249–54), and McGann ("Beauty," 14–15).

Swinburne himself seems to have recognized the historical importance of "Notes on Designs," since it was one of only two essays on visual art he chose to reprint in his 1875 volume, *Essays and Studies*.

7. In his own essay on Michelangelo in *The Renaissance*, Pater also describes Michelangelo in terms that allude to Swinburne's essay, for example in the essay's opening remarks:

> Critics of Michelangelo have sometimes spoken as if the only characteristic of his genius were a wonderful strength, verging . . . on what is singular or strange. A certain strangeness . . . is indeed an element in all true works of art: that they shall excite or surprise us is indispensable. But that they shall give pleasure and exert a charm over us is indispensable too; and this strangeness must be sweet also—a lovely strangeness. And to the true admirers of Michelangelo this is the true type of the Michelangelesque—sweetness and strength.

Pater goes on to say that "people have for the most part been attracted or repelled by the strength" of Michelangelo's art, adding that "few have understood his sweetness" (57–58).

8. Commenting on Pater's well-known passage about *La Gioconda* in "Leonardo da Vinci," Oscar Wilde in "The Critic as Artist" proposes that Pater has himself projected the secrets he finds in Leonardo's works onto those works: "And so the picture becomes more wonderful to us than it really is, and reveals to us a secret of which, in truth, it knows nothing" (1029). Wilde's broader point is that aesthetic criticism enriches the artwork by adding to its meaning: "the meaning of any beautiful created thing is, at least, as much in the soul of him who looks at it as it was in his soul who wrought it" (1029). My purpose in this chapter is to

show how aesthetic criticism also attempts rhetorically to manipulate the secrets and revelations it finds in—or projects onto—the artworks it discusses.

9. Pater dwells on the theme of a secret knowledge throughout "Leonardo da Vinci," as in the following remarks: "[Leonardo] seemed to [his contemporaries] rather the sorcerer or the magician, possessed of curious secrets and hidden knowledge, living in a world of which he alone possessed the key" (84) and "Beneath [Verrocchio's] cheerful exterior of the mere well-paid craftsman . . . lay the ambitious desire to expand the destiny of Italian art by a larger knowledge and insight into things, a purpose in art not unlike Leonardo's still unconscious purpose" (80). In "Notes on Designs," Swinburne's description of Leonardo's drawings anticipates Pater's theme of Leonardo's mystery: "Of Leonardo the samples [in the Uffizi basement] are choice and few; full of that indefinable grace and grave mystery which belong to his slightest and wildest work" (1:156).

10. In his essay on Michelangelo in *The Renaissance*, Pater explicitly identifies writing as a potential means of containing intense emotions: "We know how Goethe escaped from the stress of sentiments too strong for him by making a book about them; and for Michelangelo, to write down his passionate thoughts at all, to express them in a sonnet, was already in some measure to command, and have his way with them" (66–67).

11. The problematic I am building here is somewhat analogous to a problematic constructed by James Heffernan under the name "Medusa model of ekphrasis" (108). Ekphrasis is the verbal representation of a visual representation, or, more narrowly defined by Leo Spitzer, "the poetic description of a pictorial or sculptural work of art" (Krieger, xiii). According to Heffernan, ekphrasis is "a literary mode that turns on the antagonism . . . between verbal and visual representation" (7). He maintains that this antagonism manifests itself in the verbal representation's attempt to limit and control the power of the visual representation: "Ekphrasis commonly reveals a profound ambivalence toward visual art, a fusion of iconophilia and iconophobia, of veneration and anxiety. To represent a painting or a sculpted figure in words is to evoke its power—the power to fix, excite, amaze, entrance, disturb, or intimidate the viewer—even as language strives to keep that power under control" (7). Heffernan derives the name "Medusa model of ekphrasis" from W. J. T. Mitchell, for whom Shelley's 1819 fragmentary poem "On the Medusa of Leonardo da Vinci in the Florentine Gallery" represents the "primal scene" of ekphrastic poetry. See Mitchell, 709.

Swinburne's and Pater's essays are not, strictly speaking, works of ekphrasis, since they are verbal representations of subjective visual impressions rather than of visual objects. But they do exude a "profound ambivalence" toward the works they discuss, and they exemplify the fusion of veneration and anxiety, of iconophilia and iconophobia, that Heffernan associates with ekphrasis. And their descriptions of those works do work rhetorically to limit and to contain the works' powers.

12. This is the painting described by Shelley in "On the Medusa of Leonardo da Vinci in the Florentine Gallery," a poem to which Pater makes reference in the original version of "Leonardo da Vinci" published in the *Fortnightly Review*, as well as in the 1873, 1877, 1888, and 1900 editions of *The Renaissance*. Swinburne makes reference to the poem in his essay "Notes on the Text of Shelley" (15:365–66) and saw the Medusa painting on the same trip to Florence on which

he saw the Uffizi's collection of uncatalogued drawings. See Edmund Gosse, *Life of Algernon Charles Swinburne*, in Swinburne, *Complete Works*, 19:97–98.

On Pater's description of the Medusa painting, see Donoghue (140–42), McGann ("Beauty," 10–14), Dellamora (130–46), and Miller ("Walter Pater," 77–80).

13. On the analogy between Leonardo and Perseus, see Monsman, 59–61. Monsman defines the analogy in terms of Perseus and Leonardo both creating a reflection of a frightening reality that should not be looked at directly (Perseus by means of his mirror shield, Leonardo by means of his painting). He does not extend the analogy, however, to Perseus and Leonardo both cutting to their subject's center.

14. Over the course of the essay, Pater makes references to Vasari, Goethe, Michelet, Gautier, Carlo Amoretti, Raffaelle du Fresne, Charles Clément, and Alexis-François Rio.

15. Although many critics have remarked upon Pater's identification with the person of Leonardo, only two commentators on "Leonardo da Vinci" have to my knowledge noted Pater's identification of his own *text* with Leonardo's art. James Eli Adams argues that Pater mobilizes in his essay the fascination said to be aroused in the viewer by Leonardo's mysteriousness: "Pater's technique . . . not only describes but attempts to reproduce the erotic 'fascination' of Leonardo's art" (450). According to Adams, Pater does this by intimating but ultimately keeping Leonardo's secrets: "Pater's reserve in regard to Leonardo's secrets also encourages the reader to respond to Pater's own works in precisely the way that he responds to Leonardo's: as a seductive veil to the secret" (451). Adams reads Pater's transfer of seductive power from Leonardo's secretive works to his own secretive text as a rhetorical means of self-empowerment and self-authorization: "this public withholding of private information works in turn to enforce a peculiar authority in the author" (451). He accounts for this authority in historical terms, in the cultural context of a late Victorian "obsession with secrecy and exposure" (450) diagnosed in Michel Foucault's *History of Sexuality* and D. A. Miller's *The Novel and the Police*, a context in which the very act of having and keeping an erotic secret would constitute a socially sanctioned form of power, even as it also constitutes a form of social vulnerability.

The other critic who has noticed the transfer between Leonardo's art and Pater's writing is Elaine Scarry: "[Leonardo] draws [any given face] over and over, just as Pater (who tells us this about Leonardo) replicates—now in sentences—Leonardo's acts, so that the essay reenacts its subject, becoming a sequences of faces" (3).

16. Mario Praz discusses the unique type of beauty Pater finds in the Medusa painting and in Leonardo's work more generally, and identifies it as a romantic innovation. He calls the association of beauty with horror or terror, pain, fascination, repulsion, corruption, or death "Medusean" beauty (43) because he locates its original version in Shelley's poem "On the Medusa of Leonardo da Vinci in the Florentine Gallery." He calls the poem "a manifesto of the conception of Beauty peculiar to the Romantics" (25) and finds examples of this type of beauty in both Pater's "Leonardo da Vinci" and Swinburne's "Notes on Designs," as well as in texts by Keats, Poe, Baudelaire, Flaubert, and D'Annunzio (25–52). On "Medusean" beauty in nineteenth-century literature, see also McGann

("Beauty"), Patterson, and Hyles. McGann points out that combinations of beauty and horror, pleasure and pain, and life and death in nineteenth-century texts like Shelley's poem and Swinburne's and Pater's essays are not a romantic innovation, as Praz maintains, but are derived from the "equivocal mythology of the ancient figure" of Medusa, which already combines these kinds of opposite aspects (3–4). One example noted in the previous chapter is the distinction in classical Greek sculpture between the Dionysian *gorgoneion* and the Apollonian "beautiful Medusa" types of Gorgon.

17. "About the dainty lines of the cheek the bat flits unheeded" (83). In the first version of "Leonardo da Vinci" published in the *Fortnightly Review*, the "dainty lines of the cheek" are contrasted with the image of a creeping rabbit (*The Renaissance*, 229). In all subsequent versions, the rabbit is replaced with the bat. Whatever the reason for the substitution, the bat's juxtaposition with the "dainty lines" of Medusa's cheek becomes one version of a contrast between beautiful elements and terrifying elements that is developed throughout the passage on the Medusa painting.

18. On the association of Medusa with death in classical literature and art, see Jean-Pierre Vernant, "Death in the Eyes: Gorgo, Figure of the *Other*," in *Mortals and Immortals*, especially 121–25.

19. One well-known example of this turn from horror to beauty is the famous passage on *La Gioconda*, in which all the maladies of the soul, the combined thoughts and experiences of the world going back to Pagan antiquity (the animalism of Greece, the lust of Rome, the sins of the Borgias, and so on) are said to be sublimated into a face of perfect beauty.

20. Next to Swinburne's introductory remarks about Michelangelo's drawings, quoted earlier, this passage about the three female portraits is the most frequently cited portion of "Notes on Designs." In *The Romantic Agony*, Mario Praz identifies one of the three portraits (292n66A). See Berenson, *The Drawings of the Florentine Painters*, catalogue entry 1626, plate 781 (Figure 6). For another drawing of a strikingly similar motif, now in the British Museum, see Berenson, catalogue entry 1689, plate 786 (Figure 7).

Berenson attributes the drawing Praz identifies not to Michelangelo himself, but to an unknown pupil whom he names "Andrea di Michelangelo." Assuming that he is correct, and that Praz is correct in identifying the actual image Swinburne saw, and also that Swinburne's descriptions do in fact refer to actual drawings, it is possible that Swinburne's remarks are not about works actually by Michelangelo, just as Pater's remarks on the Leonardo Medusa, a painting he sees as representative of Leonardo's art in general, are not about an image actually by Leonardo. Among other things, this coincidence would reiterate the motif of the autonomous work of criticism shared by both writers.

21. On the motif of the Fatal Woman in the passage about the three portraits, see Praz (249), Levey (109), Boyer (164), Gitter (952), Patterson (118), and Dellamora (138). On Medusa as a variant of the nineteenth-century Fatal Woman, see Praz, Gitter, Richards, McGann ("Beauty"), Patterson, Boyer, Dellamora, Hyles, Dijkstra, and Kestner. Swinburne frequently makes use of Medusa as an image in his poetry, often in the context of the Fatal Woman theme, as for example in "Laus Veneris," "Fragoletta," and "Hesperia" in the 1866 *Poems and Ballads*, and in the 1866 poem "Cleopatra." On Swinburne's use of the Medusa

motif in his poetry and prose, see Gitter (952) and Boyer (178–89). On Swinburne's allusion in the passage on the Michelangelo female portraits to Shelley's Medusa poem, see McGann ("Beauty," 15). On the general influence of Shelley's poem on Swinburne's use in his poetry and prose of the Medusa figure, see Patterson (117–19).

Some of the formulations of Swinburne's passage anticipate Pater's well-known description in "Leonardo da Vinci" of *La Gioconda*, another Fatal Woman prototype.

22. For example, the description of the woman as "beautiful always beyond desire and cruel beyond words; fairer than heaven and more terrible than hell" echoes the description of Michelangelo's drawings in general, which are said to be "terrible and exquisite" and "delightful beyond words." And the "tragic attraction" Swinburne finds in the three portraits echoes the "tragic beauty" Swinburne attributes to the entire Michelangelo catalogue.

23. My argument here is that Swinburne's description of the drawings is implicitly a means to protect Swinburne from the threat of the drawings and of the woman depicted in the drawings. But conversely Swinburne also uses the threat as an occasion and as a foundation for his unique style of criticism, a double gesture that is similar to Pater's in "Leonardo da Vinci." For a very different reading of how Swinburne constructs his aestheticism on the basis of female figures (and more specifically figures of dangerous or transgressive women), see Kathy Psomiades, *Beauty's Body*, 59–83. Psomiades focuses on the poetry in the 1866 *Poems and Ballads*. Her discussion of the relation between aestheticism and threatening female figures concentrates on a shared theme of resistance to bourgeois norms.

24. See Swinburne, *Complete Works*, 15:161. Swinburne compares Michelangelo's portrait of Cleopatra (Figure 8) to Flaubert's description in *Salammbo* of Salammbo's ritualistic dance with her snake. The dance with the snake occurs in chapter 10 of *Salammbo*.

The continuity between a woman's body and her ornaments or clothes is also a prominent motif in Baudelaire's 1863 essay "The Painter of Modern Life," but for Baudelaire this continuity is a source of pleasure and titillation for men, rather than the interpretative problem it is for Swinburne and, as I discuss in this paragraph, for Flaubert's protagonist Mâtho.

25. Naomi Schor argues that the scene in Mâtho's tent serves to break down a common distinction made by Flaubert's critics about *Salammbo*, namely the distinction between the "accessory" narrative and the "essential" narrative. The accessory narrative, she claims, is coded by the critics as feminine and sexual, while the essential narrative is coded as masculine and political; the Salammbo plot is an example of the former, while the mercenaries' war with Carthage is an example of the latter. She claims that, unlike his critics, Flaubert sets up the relationship between the two narratives "in terms other than those of mutual exclusion" (115). One of her supporting examples is the blending of Salammbo's ornaments and body—that is, the blending of an accessory and an essence—in the tent scene.

Schor's argument is suggestive for a reading of Swinburne's passage on the Michelangelo portraits, which also establishes an opposition between an accessory (the woman's ornaments) and an essence (her body), and which also rewrites this relation in terms other than mutual exclusion, as the rest of this chapter section goes on to demonstrate.

26. Nor does the monstrosity lie in the many conventional Fatal Woman attributes that appear in Swinburne's description of the Michelangelo portraits— attributes like the cold stare, the cruel mouth, the proud eyes, the hieratic bearing, the combination of beauty and terror, and the combination of beauty and cruelty. However frightening these elements are said to be, they are ultimately reassuring to the (male) critic in their visibility and legibility.

27. In the shared context of a dangerous artwork and a would-be protective verbal representation of that artwork, the shared image of a woman depicted in the artwork can be interpreted as a figure for the dangerous artwork itself, as suggested by the continuity Swinburne and Pater both imply between the danger of the woman and the danger of the artwork.

In the related context of ekphrasis, discussed in endnote 11 of this chapter, James Heffernan and W. J. T. Mitchell analyze the relationship between verbal representation and visual representation as a gendered conflict between a male writer (or a masculine text) and a feminine or feminized visual image. Mitchell, for example, reads Shelley's ekphrastic Medusa poem as a prototype of a conflict between a masculine subject and a feminine visual object. The Medusa painting is for him a version of what he calls the graphic Other of language. It both entices and threatens to petrify the male writer's attempt to represent—and thereby to overcome—it. Because the painting is an image of a woman, the poem dramatizes this conflict in gendered terms, as a conflict between a male writer's desire to represent a feminized Other and his fear of being paralyzed, castrated, or silenced by that Other (709–10). Heffernan follows Mitchell's attention to gender in his own definition of ekphrasis as "a mode of writing in which the male poet ambivalently responds to an image typically viewed as female: an image that excites both 'ekphrastic hope'—the desire for union—and the 'ekphrastic fear' of being silenced, petrified, and thus unmanned by the Medusan 'other.' . . . This Medusa model of ekphrasis can be plausibly invoked wherever the conflict between word and image demonstrably becomes a conflict between male authority and the female power to enchant, subvert, or threaten it" (108). Heffernan assigns a gender to verbal and visual representations as such, and explicitly represents the ekphrastic relationship as a conflict between the sexes.

In regard to assigning categorically a gender to formal entities like texts and paintings, Mitchell makes the very significant point that verbal and visual representations are not inherently, essentially masculine or feminine. Such gender assignments, he maintains, are due to ideological associations, often motivated by fears of sexual and social forms of otherness. The assumption that verbal representations (and temporal forms more generally) are inherently masculine, or that visual representations (and spatial forms more generally) are inherently feminine, is an example of this kind of an ideological transfer of gendered properties onto purely formal structures and materials.

28. Recent commentators working on Pater's and Swinburne's early critical writings have focused largely on a different point of overlap between the two, one that is more thematic and less structural. Richard Dellamora and Thaïs Morgan, for example, both note a shared homoeroticism in texts like *The Renaissance* and "Notes on Designs." Morgan argues that certain passages in both texts construct

new definitions of masculinity through images of androgynous and explicitly masculine beauty. Dellamora concentrates on images in both texts that allow homosexual desires and homoerotic fantasies to emerge. One of his examples is the image of Medusa, which he interprets "as a figure of male–male desire" (130). This particular relationship between Pater and Swinburne could be suggestively elaborated, I think, by way of the shared figures of Leonardo and Michelangelo.

29. On aesthetic criticism as an autonomous form of creation, see McGann (*Swinburne*, 14–23), Monsman (9–36), and Buckler (36–55).

CHAPTER FOUR. SYMPATHY AND TELEPATHY

1. See Haight, 428. On *The Renaissance*, see also 464.

2. The figure of an expanded sympathy is indebted to Wordsworth: "Thus daily were my sympathies enlarged." See *The Prelude*, 74. For Wordsworth, an enlarged capacity for sympathy is made possible by contact with nature and, more significantly to Eliot, with his rural neighbors: "I read, without design, the opinions, thoughts, / Of those plain-living people, in a sense / Of love and knowledge" (134).

3. *The George Eliot Letters*, 2:299, hereafter abbreviated L and cited parenthetically by volume and page number.

4. The citation of Pater is from the "Preface" to *The Renaissance*, xix–xx. On the relation between aesthetics and sympathy, see in particular chapter 17 of *Adam Bede*: "All honour and reverence to the divine beauty of form. . . . But let us love that other beauty too, which lies in no secret of proportion, but in the secret of deep human sympathy" (224). On the ethics of sympathy in *Adam Bede*, see J. Hillis Miller, *The Ethics of Reading*, 61–80.

5. See Flint (455–73), Bull (244–61), Menke (629–30), and Shuttleworth (xi–xxxii). Much of this line of inquiry is indebted to B. M. Gray's 1982 essay "Pseudoscience and George Eliot's 'The Lifted Veil.'"

6. *The Lifted Veil and Brother Jacob*, 15. All further references to *The Lifted Veil* are hereafter abbreviated LV and cited parenthetically by page number.

7. *The Lifted Veil* was originally published anonymously in *Blackwood's* magazine in July 1859, six months after the publication of *Adam Bede*. Its composition coincided with Eliot's beginning work on what would eventually become her second novel, *The Mill on the Floss*. Eliot did not republish the novella until 1878, two years before her death. On the biographical circumstances of the text's composition and publication, see Haight (295–97) and Knoepflmacher (128–39). Critics consider the work an anomaly because its formal and thematic elements are unusual for Eliot: the use of an "unreliable" first-person narrator, the heightened tone and diction, the lurid imagery, the Continental settings, the sensationalist plot, the arbitrary plot structure, and the use of supernatural and gothic motifs. See Rubinstein (177), Hurley (259), Gilbert and Gubar (445–46), Royle (86), and Swann (40–42). On parallels between *The Lifted Veil* and Eliot's other fiction, see Handley.

My argument in this chapter that an ostensibly marginal and minor text addresses problems that are central to Eliot's work and thought is similar to the argument I make in the first chapter about the exemplarity of Freud's short essay "Medusa's Head." And just as Freud disavowed "Medusa's Head" by declining to publish or even to finish it, Eliot disavowed *The Lifted Veil* by publishing it anonymously and then declining to republish it for nineteen years. My explanation for Eliot's disavowal of her text is similar to my explanation for Freud's disavowal of his. There is something implicitly threatening in these texts, something that threatens the authors themselves.

8. My claims in this paragraph are based on some points in Charles Swann's essay "Déjà Vu: Déjà Lu," especially pages 46–49. Swann defines the ethical problem in *The Lifted Veil* as follows:

> [Latimer] has "direct experience of the inner states of others." Yet—with all these advantages—he does not feel for others as a reader should. . . . Latimer is in literal possession of what Eliot normally offers as metaphors for how to be a moral agent: but he is paralyzed into passivity by his insights. If Latimer is an example of a reader trapped in the book of life, then there is the horrific possibility for Eliot that her key value of sympathy doesn't open the door into the fully moral life. Her theories about the relationship between her art and life may be entirely wrong. (47)

While Swann here identifies Latimer as Eliot's reader, other critics and Swann himself have also interpreted him as a stand-in for Eliot herself or for the novelist as such. See Beer (94–101), Gilbert and Gubar (470–71), Hertz (*George Eliot's Pulse*, 42–62), and Swann (46–49). These critics equate Latimer's telepathy with the novelist's power to imagine the thoughts and feelings of a great variety of different characters. Whether Latimer is interpreted as the reader, the writer, or both at once, he points to a similar ethical problem: a lack of sympathy for those to whose thoughts and feelings he has access. His responses to his clairvoyant visions contradict Eliot's moral injunctions about creating and responding to art.

9. Christopher Lane also finds a threat to Eliot's ethics of sympathy in *The Lifted Veil* but defines it somewhat differently than Swann and myself. He locates the crisis not in Latimer's antipathy but in the duplicity, egotism, and treachery that Latimer's clairvoyance reveals in the people around him. He argues that Latimer's misanthropy is a product of his insights into the minds of his friends and neighbors. For Lane, the threat implicit in *The Lifted Veil* is therefore not that the human insights afforded by art will fail to elicit an ethical response in the viewer or reader, but rather the demonstrable absence of any sympathy between the characters in the fictional world. According to this reading, the danger Eliot confronts in *The Lifted Veil* is that her ethics of sympathy remains an abstraction and lacks efficacy when translated into the concrete terms of her fiction, that is, into the thoughts and actions of actual characters like the ones into whom Latimer has insight. See *Hatred and Civility*, 107–16.

10. My claims about the novella's negative implications for Eliot's aesthetics and ethics are complementary to a critical tradition that has read *The Lifted Veil* as an allegorical text about writing and the creative process. See, for example, Redinger (403), Knoepflmacher (137–61), Hertz (*George Eliot's Pulse*, 42–62), Swann (42), Beer (94–101), Jacobus (254–74), and Gilbert and Gubar (470). See also Vierra (749–67). Vierra reads the novella in the context of Marian Evans's critical writings about art and aesthetics from the 1840s and 1850s. Many critics locate the allegory at the level of an autobiographical identification they find

between the emerging writer George Eliot and her protagonist Latimer, who identifies himself as a failed poet. Both the young Marian Evans and Latimer, they
maintain, are characterized by intense self-doubt, self-consciousness, insecurity,
feelings of guilt vis-à-vis their fathers and families, and "feminine" sensitivity.
See, for example, Knoepflmacher (137, 150–52, 160–61), Redinger (401–05),
and Gilbert and Gubar (450). Jacobus moves beyond a narrow autobiographical
approach to read the story as a commentary on the predicaments of the Victorian woman writer (254–74). Other critics focus specifically on the problem of
Latimer's misanthropy and selfishness but do not discuss these character traits in
terms of their potentially negative implications for Eliot's aesthetics or her ethics
of sympathy. See Rubinstein (180–82), Hurley (260–62), and Knoepflmacher
(154–59). It is only a few critics, in particular Charles Swann and Gillian Beer,
who have brought the theme of Latimer's misanthropy into a relation with Eliot's
allegorical reflections in *The Lifted Veil* on art and writing as such.

11. Latimer's conversion to sympathy anticipates that of Philip Wakem
in *The Mill on the Floss*, a text written concurrently with and after *The Lifted
Veil*. There are notable parallels between the two characters, as both are inse-
cure, solipsistic, overly self-conscious, deeply alienated from society, selfish, and
devoid of sympathy for others. Philip indicates his conversion in a letter he writes
to Maggie late in the novel:

> The new life I have found in caring for your joy and sorrow more than
> for what is directly my own, has transformed the spirit of rebellious
> murmuring into that willing endurance which is the birth of true sym-
> pathy. I think nothing but such complete and intense love could have
> initiated me into that enlarged life which grows and grows by appropri-
> ating the life of others; for before I was always dragged back from it by
> ever-present painful self-consciousness. (634)

12. The doubling of Bertha and Latimer is emphasized in the two characters' reciprocal gazes: "I saw myself in Bertha's thought as she lifted her cutting
grey eyes, and looked at me: a miserable ghost-seer." Grammatically, the word
ghost-seer refers equally to Bertha and to Latimer, who has earlier described himself as having a "half-ghostly beauty" (LV 14). The mutual mirroring of Bertha
and Latimer is also reiterated at the level of the sentence: "we were *front* to *front*
with *each other* and judged *each other*" (my emphases). This doubling has gone
largely unnoticed by critics, an oversight that works in the interest of Eliot's
ethical agenda, since ultimately she wants to disassociate the two characters in
order to redeem Latimer and to sacrifice Bertha. Only Neil Hertz has recognized
Bertha as Latimer's clone. See *George Eliot's Pulse*, 55–56, 62. For Hertz, the
doubling of Eliot's surrogate Latimer is a step toward safely distancing Eliot
(and, by extension, Marian Evans) from any direct implication in the potentially
harmful powers of her own language. Gilbert and Gubar also note that Bertha
and Latimer are "mutually reciprocal characters." They interpret the "effeminate
Latimer" and the "castrating Bertha" autobiographically, as two aspects of Eliot's
allegedly divided self (465).

13. On Bertha as a version of the conventional Fatal Woman figure, see
Knoepflmacher (148–49), Gilbert and Gubar (459–61), Vierra (755), and Gray
(Afterword, 74). Gilbert and Gubar specifically compare Eliot's description of

Bertha to the Michelangelo female portraits described in Swinburne's "Notes on Designs" (460). Jacobus reads Bertha in Freudian terms, as a Medusa-like castration figure (257–58, 264–65).

14. Consider, for example, Freud's statements on women and ethics. In his essay "Some Psychical Consequences of the Anatomical Distinction between the Sexes," he writes, "I cannot evade the notion (though I hesitate to give it expression) that for women the level of what is ethically normal is different from what it is in men" (19:257). In the lecture on "Femininity," he makes this point in a less roundabout way: "we attribute a larger amount of narcissism to femininity" (22:132).

15. Throughout her novels, Eliot shows great interest in—and ambivalence about—female characters who somehow transgress against the social order, characters like Hetty Sorrel in *Adam Bede*, Maggie Tulliver in *The Mill on the Floss*, Rosamond Vincy in *Middlemarch*, and Gwendolen Harleth in *Daniel Deronda*. Critics maintain that she uneasily identifies with aspects of each of these characters, the most obvious object of her identification being Maggie. Bertha is much less complex and multifaceted than these characters but she too is a transgressive woman and an object of identification for Eliot. If she is Latimer's double, and Latimer is Eliot's proxy, then Eliot also identifies herself with Bertha. In exorcizing Bertha, she would exorcize an aspect of herself that she finds threatening.

16. Some of Eliot's commentators identify Latimer's solipsism as the reason for his initial failure as poet. See Swann (44) and Beer (96–97). In making this point, they draw on Eliot's dictum that successful writing necessitates entering into an open and interactive relation with others. As Latimer puts this, "A poet pours forth his song and *believes* in the listening ear and answering soul" (LV 7). Early on in his narrative, Latimer himself does not have this belief, but he is ultimately converted to it by his father's death. His clairvoyant witnessing of his father's suffering enables him to enter for the first time into a reciprocal relation with another person and thus, eventually, to write. The proof is the completed manuscript we are reading. The culmination of Latimer's conversion is his appeal in the frame narrative to the reader's sympathy and his complementary promise that he will fully "unbosom" himself to the reader.

17. The citation is from chapter 15 of *Middlemarch*. The full sentence, which refers to Lydgate, runs as follows: "For surely all must admit that a man may be puffed and belauded, envied, ridiculed, counted upon as a tool and fallen in love with, or at least selected as a future husband, and yet remain virtually unknown—known merely as a cluster of signs for his neighbours' false suppositions" (171). I am arguing that *The Lifted Veil* explicitly depicts Bertha as such a cluster of signs, and Latimer's unveiling of her as one interpretation of those signs. For a discussion of the characters in *Middlemarch* as texts open to numerous and potentially conflicting interpretations by other characters, see J. Hillis Miller, "Narrative and History," 465–68.

18. J. Hillis Miller makes a similar argument about perceptions in *Middlemarch*. He proposes that the optical metaphors in the novel, and the kinds of knowledge they make possible, are always subverted by other metaphors that qualify any (literal or figurative) perceptions as interpretations, which is to say as having a subjective investment in what is seen and in particular ways of seeing. See "Optic and Semiotic," 109.

19. According to George Henry Lewes's journal, Marian Evans and he attended a performance of Donizetti's opera *Lucrezia Borgia* in August 1857, not long before the writing of *The Lifted Veil*. See Haight, 241. On Lucrezia Borgia as part of the standard catalogue of nineteenth-century Fatal Women, see Praz (115, 226). In her editorial notes for *The Lifted Veil*, Helen Small points out that the painting Latimer describes was for much of the nineteenth century attributed to Giorgione in error, and she identifies it as a copy of Lorenzo Lotto's *A Lady with a Drawing of Lucretia* (LV 93n18).

20. See Eagleton, "Power and Knowledge in 'The Lifted Veil,'" 58–59. Eagleton maintains that the revelation scene in *The Lifted Veil* provides the reader with no means by which to verify its truth, but he lays out the predicament very differently than I do. On one hand, he argues, the conventions of realist fictions demand that Latimer's report be taken literally because he is the narrator and as such is the most reliable index of truth in the novella. On the other hand, he maintains, it is equally possible that "Latimer has rigged his tale to frame his wife, impudently concocting an event as he may have previously, perhaps more permissably, falsified perceptions" (58). For Eagleton, this ambiguity undermines the narrative's restoration of truth, which is generically the aim of realist fiction. My own reading of the scene does not attribute its ambiguity to character psychology or intention (Latimer's untrustworthiness, for instance) but rather to the content and form of the truth that is revealed.

21. Eliot famously makes reference to Aristotle's theory of metaphor in book 2, chapter 1 of *The Mill on the Floss*.

22. In the same essay, she writes that art is a mode of "extending our contact with our fellow-men *beyond the bounds of our personal lot*" (271, my emphasis).

23. This is true even for critics who do not endorse Eliot's ethics of sympathy and focus, rather, on her questioning of the possibility or viability of sympathetic identifications, as for instance John Kucich in *Repression in Victorian Fiction*, J. Hillis Miller in *The Ethics of Reading*, and D. A. Miller in *Narrative and Its Discontents*. One notable exception to the general pattern of critics overlooking Eliot's ethical emphasis on otherness and difference is Elizabeth Deeds Ermath, "George Eliot's Conception of Sympathy."

24. On the motif of telepathy in *The Lifted Veil*, see Nicholas Royle, *Telepathy and Literature*, chapter 5, especially 84–87.

25. On the other in *Middlemarch* and in Eliot's work in general as an epistemological problem, see J. Hillis Miller, *Others*, 67–79.

26. In the revivification scene, Latimer writes, "we all felt that the dark veil had completely fallen." His remark is thoroughly ambiguous, since it could be taken to mean Bertha's complete obfuscation as much as her full exposure.

27. The ethics of sympathy is evoked explicitly by the epigraph Eliot wrote for *The Lifted Veil* fourteen years after its original publication: "Give me no light, great heaven, but such as turns / To energy of human fellowship; / No powers save the growing heritage / That makes completer manhood." This epigraph first appears in a letter of February 1873 to John Blackwood (L 5:380). It has been attached to all subsequently published versions the novella, including the one in the 1878 Cabinet edition of Eliot's works. Ostensibly, the epigraph serves to counter the threat of Latimer's lack of sympathy, as Helen Small has argued in her introduction to the novella: "[the motto] is also an attempt to close down the

threat of what [Eliot] has allowed herself to imagine. . . . [It] courts our compassionate insight into the narrator while he himself mocks us with the impossibility of sympathy" (LV xxx). I would add that Eliot's evocation of human fellowship also covers over and defends against the impossibility of telepathy.

28. On the success and failure of telepathy in *The Lifted Veil*, see Marc Redfield, *Phantom Formations*, 160–70. Complementary to my juxtaposition of sympathy and telepathy, Redfield reads the figure of telepathy as itself indicative of both identification and difference. He discusses telepathy as a metaphor for reading the materiality of language, and, at the same time, as "a particularly appropriate metaphor for an aesthetic of sympathy, grounded in a predicament of reading it must disavow" (162). So on one hand he equates the distance (*tele*) in telepathy with the other's irreducible difference as the otherness of language: "this difference and distance is that of language in its materiality" (162). At the same time, he takes the *pathos* in telepathy as a figure for feeling, for sympathy, for aesthetically bringing the other close to oneself. These two figures are for him in a relation of mutual disavowal, wherein feeling must disavow the necessity of reading in order to succeed. Telepathy (as a figure for feeling with the other) figuratively designates the possibility of sympathy, but (as a figure for reading the material signs of language) it also designates sympathy's destruction. It insists that one cannot feel with the other, one only reads the material signs that constitute the other's otherness from oneself. Telepathy thus designates an irreducible difference within sympathy that is also the ground of sympathy.

For Eliot, I would add, the other's otherness from oneself designates not only the epistemological destruction of any grounds on which sympathy could take place but also an ethical imperative that is heterogeneous to the ethical imperative called sympathy. Certainly the other's otherness is for Eliot a metaphor for the materiality of language, as Redfield points out; but this figurative relationship also functions in reverse, thereby supplementing the epistemological problematic with an ethical one.

29. Insofar as this move to sympathy is at best a consolation, however, it also relegates sympathy to a questionable status. As D. A. Miller has argued, Eliot's ostensible endorsement of an ethics of sympathy coincides with an implicit questioning of sympathy. See *Narrative and Its Discontents*, 152–94. For Miller's reading of Eliot, sympathy is on one hand a genuine ethical transcendence of egotism, of the separation between self and other, and of the ambiguous material signs through which the other becomes intelligible. At the same time, Miller argues, sympathy is shown by Eliot to be impossible insofar as any moment of transcendence is subverted by the very material signs that narrate it, signs which are demonstratively as much indicative of egotism and obfuscation as of fellow feeling and transparency. Hence Eliot leaves us in a kind of double bind: sympathetic transcendence would negate the problem of interpersonal differences, but is in turn also negated by difference (in the form of material signs). Miller's reading of sympathy as a structure of mutual negation is not unlike the structure of mutual disavowal identified in Marc Redfield's double reading of telepathy, discussed in the previous endnote. Both Redfield and Miller see the materiality of signs as a difference Eliot would overcome in the name of a sympathetic ethics. In *The Lifted Veil*, however, the association of Bertha with texts, writing, and signs not only questions and potentially subverts the possibility of sympathetic

identifications. It is also a reminder of an entirely different ethical imperative, of an ethics that would not transcend otherness but would maintain it (this relation is what I am calling telepathy). My emphasis on telepathy as a second ethical imperative (besides sympathy) refutes received ideas about the formal impasse in which deconstructive readings of Eliot are often said to terminate. Telepathy is for Eliot a figure for a genuine ethical value, not only a figure for the simultaneous possibility and impossibility of interpersonal identifications.

30. This phrase is excerpted from a telling remark Lewes makes about *The Lifted Veil* to the writer Edith Simcox: "the moral is plain enough . . . the one-sided knowing of things in relation to the self" (Eliot, *Letters*, 9:220). Lewes is presumably referring to Latimer's egotism, but Latimer's sympathy, and perhaps any sympathy, is similarly unilateral, similarly one-sided.

31. As John Kucich has pointed out, egotism in Eliot's work is not an indifference to other people. Rather, it is a dependence on others. For Kucich, Eliot's egotists (such as Tito in *Romola*, Hetty in *Adam Bede*, Godfrey in *Silas Marner*, and Gwendolen and Grandcourt in *Daniel Deronda*) depend on the thoughts and opinions of the people around them to constitute themselves as selves, to have desires and motives, and to feel valuable (181–200).

32. "We are all of us born in moral stupidity, taking the world as an udder to feed our supreme selves" (*Middlemarch*, 243). According to J. Hillis Miller, this narcissistic feeding on the world often takes the form in Eliot's writings of a particular way of seeing objects and people:

> Seeing, then, is for Eliot not a neutral, objective, dispassionate, or passive act. It is the creative projection of light from an egotistic center motivated by desire and need. This projected radiance orders the field of vision according to the presuppositions of the seer. The act of seeing is the spontaneous affirmation of a will to power over what is seen. This affirmation of order is based on the instinctive desire to believe that the world is providentially structured in a neat pattern of which one is oneself the center, for "we are all of us born in moral stupidity, taking the world as an udder to feel our supreme selves." ("Optic and Semiotic," 105)

Miller's analysis is particularly relevant to *The Lifted Veil*, where moral judgments repeatedly take the form of seeing.

33. It is on this point that my reading dovetails momentarily with John Kucich's compelling and counterintuitive critique of sympathy as a moral value in Eliot's work (114–200). Kucich too finds an unexpected and ironic similarity between sympathy and egotism in Eliot's writings; both sympathy and egotism, he claims, represent a dangerous dependence on, and vulnerability to, other people, and both represent an implicit submission of the self to the other (172, 181). As such, Kucich argues, both pose a threat to the autonomy of the self (150). I would argue, by contrast, that neither sympathy nor egotism poses a threat to the self (what they threaten, rather, is Eliot's ethics). Both are fundamentally confirming and constitutive of the self, insofar as both are relations to the other in which the other is defined in terms of the self (and not vice versa, as Kucich maintains), and in which the self constructs itself out of an appropriation of the other. According to Kucich, Eliot's solution to the problem of otherness is to

bypass any relation to the other altogether, and to advocate a model of selfhood and an ethics that are constituted by an exclusively inner dialectic between desire and internalized repression (117). On the contrary, I do not see Eliot advocating a turn inward and away from the other but rather see her as advocating a qualitatively different relationship to the other, one I am calling telepathy (as an alternative to both egotism and sympathy). It seems to me significant that Kucich's critique of sympathy, a value which he understands as a fusion with the other and as a renunciation of all individuation, does not acknowledge Eliot's insistence on respecting and engaging with the other's otherness. Kucich cites part of a sentence from "The Natural History of German Life" about the obligatory movement from selfishness to moral sentiment, but tellingly elides Eliot's call in that sentence for an "attention to what is apart from [ourselves]" (see Kucich, 114, and Eliot, *Essays*, 270).

34. There is a general critical consensus that Eliot felt somehow anxious about or threatened by *The Lifted Veil*, an assumption based partly on her decision to publish the work anonymously and on her later unwillingness to republish it (L 5:380). On Eliot's anxiety, see in particular Gilbert and Gubar (446, 470), Beer (94–95), and Swann (55–56). Critics like Gilbert and Gubar (450), Knoepflmacher (137, 150–52, 160–61), and Redinger (401–05) account for this anxiety autobiographically, via parallels between Marian Evans's life and Latimer's story. Jacobus frames the anxiety in the Freudian terms of hysteria and melancholia, as the paralyzing return in the figure of the feminized, hysterical Latimer of Eliot's awareness of her own femininity and her awareness of Victorian women's literary and cultural dispossession (both of which, she asserts, are repressed in Marian Evans's male pseudonym and in her male-identified realist novels) (254–74).

It is of course impossible to say reliably whether or not Eliot was indeed anxious about this text, or whether her readers are conflating her with elements from her story (the avowedly anxious Latimer, for instance). And not all readers of *The Lifted Veil* share in the consensus about Eliot's anxiety. Henry James reads the story "as the *jeux d'esprit* of a mind that is not often—perhaps not often enough—found at play" (131). James notes the "woefully sombre" (131) plot, but he is careful not to confuse the story or its protagonist with its author. The image of Eliot at play provides a welcome contrast to the ubiquitous images of an anxious Eliot that pervade most commentaries on *The Lifted Veil*.

It should be pointed out that to read Eliot's text and then to talk about Eliot being somehow anxious or threatened is to reproduce the move from telepathy to sympathy that is performed within the text itself. Just as there is a movement in the novella from "reading" the other to "seeing into" or "feeling with" the other, we perform, as soon as we hypothesize Eliot's awareness of a threat, a movement from reading the text to psychologizing and anthropomorphizing it. John Blackwood, for instance, writes to Eliot about the manuscript version, "Others like me are thrilled [with the story], but wish the author in a happier frame of mind" and elsewhere, "I think you must have been worrying and disturbing yourself about something when you wrote" (Eliot, *Letters*, 3:112, 67). Blackwood's attention moves from the writing to a speculation about how the author must have been feeling when she wrote. This interest in Marian Evans's mindset is the move from reading the manuscript to psychologizing it. The moment we ask about how Eliot might have been feeling, and the moment we speculate about her awareness of one or another threat emerging in her work, we respond at a level of similarity, of metaphor, of aesthetic ideology. We reproduce an ethics of sympathy, not an ethics of telepathy. As Eliot suggests, this move is epistemologically unavoidable, but it also places us into an ethical predicament that is similar to the one dramatized in her text.

35. Eliot's suspicion of sympathy, and her shifting of the ethical dilemma away from an opposition between sympathy and egotism, distinguish her project from ethical theories that equate morality with individual conscience, intention, or character psychology. Those theories commonly base their definition of ethics on psychology, typology, the traditional subject, or the categorical valorization of some form of alterity. They also tend to construct simple oppositions between good and bad, moral and immoral, and self and other. Eliot's own conclusions demonstrate how such projects can succeed ethically only through celebrations and condemnations of the other (and of the self) that are ultimately arbitrary and, in a manner of speaking, narcissistic.

CONCLUSION.

1. Cf. Jacques Derrida, commenting on this apotropaic function in Freud's essay "Medusa's Head": "And what if the 'assumption' or denial of castration should also, strangely enough, amount to the same, as one can *affirm*? In that case, apotropaics would always have more than one surprise up its sleeve" (*Dissemination*, 40).

On the "strict equivalence between the affirmation and the denial of castration, between castration and anti-castration, between assumption and negation," see also Derrida, *Spurs*, 58–63.

2. See Heffernan (91–134), Mitchell, and Hertz, "Medusa's Head: Male Hysteria under Political Pressure" (*End*, 160–93). Heffernan and Mitchell both write about Shelley's poem "On the Medusa of Leonardo da Vinci in the Florentine Gallery," among other texts, while Hertz writes about what he calls "Medusa fantasies" (179) in texts by Victor Hugo, Maxime du Camp, Alexis de Tocqueville, and Freud. Hertz takes as his point of departure for examining "the representation of what would seem to be a political threat as if it were a sexual threat" (161) the question, "How is what one sees shaped by what one thinks one has or fears to lose?" (173).

Bibliography

Adams, James Eli. "Gentleman, Dandy, Priest: Manliness and Social Authority in Pater's Aestheticism." *ELH* 59 (1992): 441–66.

Ainsworth, Maryan Wynn, ed. *Dante Gabriel Rossetti and the Double Work of Art.* New Haven: Yale University Art Gallery, 1976.

Anger, Suzy, ed. *Knowing the Past: Victorian Literature and Culture.* Ithaca: Cornell UP, 2001.

Apollodorus. *The Library.* Trans. James George Frazer. Vol. 1. Cambridge: Harvard UP, 1939.

Aristotle. *Poetics.* Trans. and ed. Stephen Halliwell. Chapel Hill: U of North Carolina P, 1987.

———. *Rhetoric.* Trans. W. Rhys Roberts. *The Rhetoric and the Poetics of Aristotle.* New York: Modern Library, 1984.

Becker-Leckrone, Megan. "Pater's Critical Spirit." *Walter Pater: Transparencies of Desire.* Ed. Laurel Brake, Lesley Higgins, and Carolyn Williams. Greensboro: ELT P, 2002. 286–97.

Beer, Gillian. "Myth and the Single Consciousness: *Middlemarch* and *The Lifted Veil.*" *This Particular Web: Essays on* Middlemarch. Ed. Ian Adam. Toronto: U of Toronto P, 1975. 91–115.

Belfiore, Elizabeth S. *Tragic Pleasures: Aristotle on Plot and Emotion.* Princeton: Princeton UP, 1992.

Berenson, Bernard. *The Drawings of the Florentine Painters.* 3 vols. Chicago: U of Chicago P, 1938.

Bloom, Harold. "Walter Pater: The Intoxication of Belatedness." *Yale French Studies* 50 (1974): 163–89.

Bowers, Susan R. "Medusa and the Female Gaze." *NWSA Journal* 2 (1990): 217–35.

Boyer, Patricia E. "The Body of Death: Medusan Transfigurations of Betweenness in Keats and Swinburne." Diss. Yale U, 1992.

Buckler, William E. *Walter Pater: The Critic as Artist of Ideas.* New York: New York UP, 1987.

Bull, Malcolm. "Mastery and Slavery in *The Lifted Veil.*" *Essays in Criticism* 48 (1998): 244–61.

Chew, Samuel. *Swinburne.* Boston: Little, Brown, 1929.

Cixous, Hélène. "The Laugh of the Medusa." Trans. Keith Cohen and Paula Cohen. *Critical Theory Since 1965*. Ed. Hazard Adams and Leroy Searle. Tallahassee: UP of Florida, 1986. 308–20.

Crawford, Robert. "Pater's *Renaissance*, Andrew Lang, and Anthropological Romanticism," *ELH* 53 (1986): 847–77.

Creed, Barbara. *The Monstrous Feminine: Film, Feminism, Psychoanalysis*. New York: Routledge, 1993.

Danahay, Martin A. "Mirrors of Masculine Desire: Narcissus and Pygmalion in Victorian Representation." *Victorian Poetry* 32 (1994): 35–54.

Deleuze, Gilles, and Felix Guattari. *A Thousand Plateaus: Capitalism and Schizo-phrenia*. Trans. Brian Massumi. Minneapolis: U of Minnesota P, 1987.

Dellamora, Richard. *Masculine Desire: The Sexual Politics of Victorian Aestheticism*. Chapel Hill: U of North Carolina P, 1990.

De Man, Paul. *Allegories of Reading: Figural Language in Rousseau, Nietzsche, Rilke, Proust*. New Haven: Yale UP, 1979.

Derrida, Jacques. *Dissemination*. Trans. Barbara Johnson. Chicago: U of Chicago P, 1981.

———. *Margins of Philosophy*. Trans. Alan Bass. Chicago: U of Chicago P, 1982.

———. *Memoirs of the Blind: The Self-Portrait and Other Ruins*. Trans. Pascale-Anne Brault and Michael Naas. Chicago: U of Chicago P, 1993.

———. *Spurs: Nietzsche's Styles*. Trans. Barbara Harlow. Chicago: U of Chicago P, 1979.

Dijkstra, Bram. *Idols of Perversity: Fantasies of Feminine Evil in Fin-de-Siècle Culture*. New York: Oxford UP, 1986.

Donoghue, Denis. *Walter Pater: Lover of Strange Souls*. New York: Knopf, 1995.

DuBois, Page. *Sowing the Body: Psychoanalysis and Ancient Representations of Women*. Chicago: U of Chicago P, 1988.

Eagleton, Terry. "Power and Knowledge in 'The Lifted Veil.'" *Literature and History* 9 (1983): 52–61.

Eliot, George. *Adam Bede*. Ed. Stephen Gill. Harmondsworth: Penguin, 1980.

———. *Daniel Deronda*. Ed. Terence Cave. Harmondsworth: Penguin, 1996.

———. *Essays of George Eliot*. Ed. Thomas Pinney. New York: Columbia UP, 1963.

———. *The George Eliot Letters*. 9 vols. Ed. Gordon S. Haight. New Haven: Yale UP, 1954–78.

———. *The Lifted Veil and Brother Jacob*. Ed. Helen Small. Oxford: Oxford UP, 1999.

———. *Middlemarch*. Ed. W. J. Harvey. Harmondsworth: Penguin, 1985.

———. *The Mill on the Floss*. Ed. A. S. Byatt. Harmondsworth: Penguin, 1979.

Ermath, Elizabeth Deeds. "George Eliot's Conception of Sympathy." *Nineteenth-Century Fiction* 40 (1985): 23–42.

Euripides. *Ion*. Trans. Ronald Frederick-Willetts. *Four Tragedies*. Ed. David Grene and Richmond Lattimore. Chicago: U of Chicago P, 1958.

Feldman, Thalia Phillies. "Gorgo and the Origin of Fear." *Arion* 4 (1965): 484–94.

———. "The Origin and Function of the Gorgon-Head." *American Journal of Archaeology* 58 (1954): 209–21.

Ferenczi, Sandor. "Zur Symbolik des Medusenhaupts." *Internationale Zeitschrift für Psychoanalyse* 9 (1923): 69.

Feuerbach, Ludwig. *The Essence of Christianity.* Trans. George Eliot. New York: Harper, 1957.

Flaubert, Gustave. *Salammbo.* Trans. A. J. Krailsheimer. Harmondsworth: Penguin, 1977.

Flint, Kate. "Blood, Bodies, and *The Lifted Veil.*" *Nineteenth-Century Literature* 51 (1997): 455–73.

Foucault, Michel. *The History of Sexuality: An Introduction.* Trans. Robert Hurley. Harmondsworth: Penguin, 1984.

Freud, Sigmund. *The Standard Edition of the Complete Psychological Works of Sigmund Freud.* Trans. and ed. James Strachey et al. 24 vols. London: The Hogarth P, 1953–74.

Furtwängler, A. "*Gorgones* und *Gorgo.*" *Ausführliches Lexikon der griechischen und römischen Mythologie.* Ed. W. H. Roscher. Leipzig: Teubner, 1896–1910.

Garber, Marjorie. *Shakespeare's Ghost Writers: Literature as Uncanny Causality.* New York: Methuen, 1987.

Gilbert, Sandra, and Susan Gubar. *The Madwoman in the Attic: The Woman Writer and the Nineteenth-Century Literary Imagination.* New Haven: Yale UP, 1979.

Gitter, Elisabeth G. "The Power of Women's Hair in the Victorian Imagination." *PMLA* 99 (1984): 936–54.

Gray, B. M. Afterword. *The Lifted Veil.* By George Eliot. London: Virago/Penguin, 1985. 69–91.

———. "Pseudoscience and George Eliot's 'The Lifted Veil.'" *Nineteenth-Century Fiction* 36 (1982): 407–23.

Haight, Gordon S. *George Eliot: A Biography.* Harmondsworth: Penguin, 1968.

Handley, Graham. "'The Lifted Veil' and Its Relation to George Eliot's Fiction." *The George Eliot Fellowship Review* 15 (1984): 64–69.

Heffernan, James. *Museum of Words: The Poetics of Ekphrasis from Homer to Ashberry.* Chicago: U of Chicago P, 1993.

Heinrich, Klaus. "Das Floss der Medusa." *Faszination des Mythos: Studien zu antiken und modernen Interpretationen.* Ed. Renate Schlesier. Frankfurt: Stroemfeld / Roter Stern, 1985. 335–69.

Henderson, Philip. *Swinburne: The Portrait of a Poet.* London: Routledge, 1972.

Hertz, Neil. *The End of the Line: Essays on Psychoanalysis and the Sublime.* New York: Columbia UP, 1985.

———. *George Eliot's Pulse.* Stanford: Stanford UP, 2003.

Hurley, Edward. "'The Lifted Veil': George Eliot as Anti-Intellectual." *Studies in Short Fiction* 5 (1968): 257–62.

Hyles, Vernon. "Medusa and the Romantic Concept of Beauty." *The Shape of the Fantastic: Selected Essays from the Seventh International Conference on the Fantastic in the Arts.* Ed. Olena H. Saciuk. Westport: Greenwood, 1990. 143–47.

Jacobs, Carol. *The Dissimulating Harmony: The Image of Interpretation in Nietzsche, Rilke, Artaud, and Benjamin.* Baltimore: The Johns Hopkins UP, 1978.

Jacobus, Mary. *Reading Woman: Essays in Feminist Criticism.* New York: Columbia UP, 1986.

Jakobson, Roman. *Language in Literature*. Ed. Kristina Pomorska and Stephen Rudy. Cambridge: Harvard UP, 1987.

James, Henry. "'The Lifted Veil' and 'Brother Jacob.'" *A Century of George Eliot Criticism*. Ed. Gordon S. Haight. Boston: Houghton Mifflin, 1965. 130–31.

Kahn, Laurence. "Le monde serein des dieux d'Homère." *L'Écrit du Temps* 2 (1982): 117–40.

Kestner, Joseph. *Mythology and Misogyny: The Social Discourse of Nineteenth-Century British Classical-Subject Painting*. Madison: U of Wisconsin P, 1989.

Knoepflmacher, U. C. *George Eliot's Early Novels: The Limits of Realism*. Berkeley: U of California P, 1968.

Kofman, Sarah. "Baubô: Theological Perversion and Fetishism." Trans. Tracy B. Strong. *Nietzsche's New Seas: Explorations in Philosophy, Aesthetics, and Politics*. Ed. Michael Allen Gillespie and Tracy B. Strong. Chicago: U of Chicago P, 1988. 175–202.

———. *Camera Obscura: Of Ideology*. Trans. Will Straw. Ithaca: Cornell UP, 1999.

———. *The Enigma of Woman: Woman in Freud's Writings*. Trans. Catherine Porter. Ithaca: Cornell UP, 1985.

———. "'It's Only the First Step that Costs.'" Trans. Sarah Wykes. *Speculations after Freud: Psychoanalysis, Philosophy, and Culture*. Ed. Sonu Shamdasani and Michael Münchow. New York: Routledge, 1994. 97–131.

———. *Freud and Fiction*. Trans. Sarah Wykes. Boston: Northeastern UP, 1991.

———. *Nietzsche and Metaphor*. Trans. Duncan Large. Stanford: Stanford UP, 1993.

———. *Nietzsche et la scène philosophique*. Paris: Galilée, 1986.

Krieger, Murray. *Ekphrasis: The Illusion of the Natural Sign*. Baltimore: The Johns Hopkins UP, 1992.

Kucich, John. *Repression in Victorian Fiction: Charlotte Brontë, George Eliot, and Charles Dickens*. Berkeley: U of California P, 1987.

Lacoue-Labarthe, Philippe. *The Subject of Philosophy*. Ed. Thomas Trezise. Trans. Thomas Trezise et al. Minneapolis: U of Minnesota P, 1993.

Lane, Christopher. *Hatred and Civility: The Antisocial Life in Victorian England*. New York: Columbia UP, 2004.

Lang, Cecil Y., ed. *The Swinburne Letters*. 6 vols. New Haven: Yale UP, 1959.

Laplanche, Jean. *Problématiques II: Castration/Symbolisations*. Paris: PUF, 1980.

Laplanche, Jean, and J.-B. Pontalis. *The Language of Psychoanalysis*. Trans. Donald Nicholson-Smith. New York: Norton, 1973.

Levey, Michael. *The Case of Walter Pater*. London: Thames and Hudson, 1978.

Levine, George. *Dying to Know: Scientific Epistemology and Narrative in Victorian England*. Chicago: U of Chicago P, 2002.

Macleod, Dianne Sachko. *Art and the Victorian Middle Class: Money and the Making of Cultural Identity*. Cambridge: Cambridge UP, 1996.

Marin, Louis. *To Destroy Painting*. Trans. Mette Hjort. Chicago: U of Chicago P, 1995.

Marsh, Jan. *Dante Gabriel Rossetti: Painter and Poet*. London: Weidenfeld & Nicolson, 1999.

McGann, Jerome J. "The Beauty of the Medusa: A Study in Romantic Literary Iconology." *Studies in Romanticism* 2 (1972): 3–25.

————, ed. *Dante Gabriel Rossetti: Collected Poetry and Prose*. New Haven: Yale UP, 2003.

————. *Swinburne: An Experiment in Criticism*. Chicago: U of Chicago P, 1972.

Menke, Richard. "Fiction as Vivisection: G. H. Lewes and George Eliot." *ELH* 67 (2000): 617–53.

Miller, D. A. *Narrative and Its Discontents: Problems of Closure in the Traditional Novel*. Princeton: Princeton UP, 1981.

Miller, J. Hillis. *The Ethics of Reading: Kant, de Man, Eliot, Trollope, James, and Benjamin*. New York: Columbia UP, 1987.

————. "The Mirror's Secret: Dante Gabriel Rossetti's Double Work of Art." *Victorian Poetry* 29 (1991): 333–49.

————. "Narrative and History." *ELH* 41 (1974): 455–73.

————. "Optic and Semiotic in *Middlemarch*." *George Eliot: Modern Critical Views*. Ed. Harold Bloom. New York: Chelsea House, 1986. 99–110.

————. *Others*. Princeton: Princeton UP, 2001.

————. "Walter Pater: A Partial Portrait." *Walter Pater: Modern Critical Views*. Ed. Harold Bloom. New York: Chelsea House, 1985. 75–95.

Mitchell, W. J. T. "Ekphrasis and the Other." *South Atlantic Quarterly* 91 (1992): 695–719.

Monsman, Gerald. *Walter Pater's Art of Autobiography*. New Haven: Yale UP, 1980.

Morgan, Thaïs E. "Reimagining Masculinity in Victorian Criticism: Swinburne and Pater." *Victorian Studies* 36 (1993): 315–32.

Morris, William. "The Doom of King Acrisius." *The Earthly Paradise: A Poem*. Boston: Roberts, Brothers, 1868.

Nietzsche, Friedrich. *The Birth of Tragedy*. Trans. Walter Kaufmann. *The Birth of Tragedy and The Case of Wagner*. New York: Vintage, 1967.

————. *Ecce Homo*. Trans. Walter Kaufmann. *On the Genealogy of Morals and Ecce Homo*. Ed. Walter Kaufmann. New York: Vintage, 1967.

————. *Sämtliche Werke: Kritische Studienausgabe*. Ed. Giorgio Colli and Mazzino Montinari. 15 vols. Berlin: De Gruyter, 1967–88.

Nonnos. *Dionysiaca*. Trans. W. H. D. Rouse. 3 vols. Cambridge: Harvard UP, 1940.

Ovid. *Metamorphoses*. Trans. Mary Innes. New York: Penguin Books, 1955.

Pater, Walter. *The Renaissance: Studies in Art and Poetry. The 1893 Text*. Ed. Donald L. Hill. Berkeley: U of California P, 1980.

————. *Selected Writings of Walter Pater*. Ed. Harold Bloom. New York: Columbia UP, 1982.

Patterson, Kent. "A Terrible Beauty: Medusa in Three Victorian Poets." *Tennessee Studies in Literature* 17 (1972): 111–20.

Pausanias. *Description of Greece*. Trans. W. H. S. Jones. 6 vols. London: Heinemann, 1918.

Pautrat, Bernard. "Nietzsche Medused." Trans. Peter Connor. *Looking After Nietzsche*. Ed. Laurence A. Rickels. Albany: State U of New York P, 1990. 159–73.

Peters, Robert. *The Crowns of Apollo: A Study in Victorian Criticism and Aestheticism*. Detroit: Wayne State UP, 1965.

Phinney, Edward. "Perseus' Battle with the Gorgons." *Transactions of the American Philological Association* 102 (1971): 445–63.

Plato. *The Republic*. Trans. G. M. A. Grube. Rev. C. D. C. Reeve. Indianapolis: Hackett, 1992.

———. *Symposium*. Trans. Michael Joyce. *Collected Dialogues*. Ed. Edith Hamilton and Huntington Cairns. Princeton: Princeton UP, 1989.

Poulson, Christine. "Death and the Maiden: The Lady of Shalott and the Pre-Raphaelites." *Re-framing the Pre-Raphaelites: Historical and Theoretical Essays*. Ed. Ellen Harding. Aldershot: Scolar P, 1996. 173–94.

Praz, Mario. *The Romantic Agony*. Trans. Angus Davidson. New York: Oxford UP, 1970.

Psomiades, Kathy Alexis. *Beauty's Body: Femininity and Representation in British Aestheticism*. Stanford: Stanford UP, 1997.

Rauch, Alan. *Useful Knowledge: The Victorians, Morality, and the March of the Intellect*. Durham: Duke UP, 2001.

Redfield, Marc. *Phantom Formations: Aesthetic Ideology and the Bildungsroman*. Ithaca: Cornell UP, 1996.

Redinger, Ruby. *George Eliot: The Emergent Self*. New York: Knopf, 1975.

Richards, Sylvie F. "The Conceits of Eyes and Hair in the French Decadence." *West Virginia University Philological Papers* 28 (1982): 41–48.

Riede, David G. "Aestheticism to Experience: Revisions for *Poems* (1870)." *Critical Essays on Dante Gabriel Rosetti*. Ed. David G. Riede. New York: G. K. Hall & Co., 1992. 128–48.

———. *Dante Gabriel Rossetti Revisited*. New York: Twayne, 1992.

Rooksby, Rikky. *A. C. Swinburne: A Poet's Life*. Aldershot: Scolar P, 1997.

Rossetti, Dante Gabriel. *The Correspondence of Dante Gabriel Rossetti*. Ed. William E. Fredeman. 6 vols. Cambridge: D. S. Brewer, 2002–06.

———. *The Works of Dante Gabriel Rossetti*. Ed. William Michael Rossetti. London: Ellis, 1911.

Roussillon, Laurence. "*Aspecta Medusa*: The Many Faces of Medusa in the Painting and the Poetry of Dante Rossetti." *The Journal of Pre-Raphaelite Studies* 11 (2002): 5–18.

Royle, Nicholas. *Telepathy and Literature: Essays on the Reading Mind*. Oxford: Basil Blackwell, 1990.

Rubinstein, Eliot L. "A Forgotten Tale by George Eliot." *Nineteenth-Century Fiction* 17 (1962): 175–83.

Scarry, Elaine. *On Beauty and Being Just*. Princeton: Princeton UP, 1999.

Schauenburg, Konrad. *Perseus in der Kunst des Altertums*. Bonn: Rudolf Habelt, 1960.

Schlesier, Renate. *Konstruktionen der Weiblichkeit bei Sigmund Freud: Zum Problem der Entmythologisierung und Remythologisierung in der psychoanalytischen Theorie*, Frankfurt: Europäische Verlangsanstalt, 1981.

Schor, Naomi. *Breaking the Chain: Women, Theory, and French Realist Fiction*. New York: Columbia UP, 1985.

Shaw, W. David. *The Lucid Veil: Poetic Truth in the Victorian Age*. London: The Athlone P, 1987.

———. *Victorians and Mystery: Crises of Representation*. Ithaca: Cornell UP, 1990.

Shelley, Percy Bysshe. *The Major Works*. Ed. Zachary Leader and Michael O'Neill. Oxford: Oxford UP, 2003.

Shuttleworth, Sally. Introduction. *The Lifted Veil and Brother Jacob*. By George Eliot. Ed. Sally Shuttleworth. New York: Penguin, 2001. xi-l.

Siebers, Tobin. *The Mirror of Medusa*. Berkeley: U of California P, 1983.

Spackman, Barbara. *Decadent Genealogies: The Rhetoric of Sickness from Baudelaire to D'Annunzio*. Ithaca: Cornell UP, 1989.

———. *Fascist Virilities: Rhetoric, Ideology, and Social Fantasy in Italy*. Minneapolis: U of Minnesota P, 1996.

Starobinski, Jean. *The Living Eye*. Trans. Arthur Goldhammer. Cambridge: Harvard UP, 1989.

Surtees, Virginia. *The Paintings and Drawings of Dante Gabriel Rossetti (1828–1882): A Catalogue Raisoné*. 2 vols. Oxford: Clarendon P, 1971.

Suther, Judith D. "The Gorgon Medusa." *Mythical and Fabulous Creatures: A Source Book and Research Guide*. Ed. Malcolm South. New York: Greenwood, 1987.

Swann, Charles. "Déjà Vu: Déjà Lu: 'The Lifted Veil' as an Experiment in Art." *Literature and History* 5 (1979): 40–57.

Swinburne, Algernon Charles. *The Complete Works*. Ed. Edmund Gosse and Thomas J. Wise. 19 vols. London: Heinemann, 1926.

Vernant, Jean-Pierre. *Mortals and Immortals: Collected Essays*. Ed. Froma I. Zeilin. Princeton: Princeton UP, 1991.

Vickers, Nancy. "'The Blazon of Sweet Beauty's Best': Shakespeare's *Lucrece*." *Shakespeare and the Question of Theory*. Ed. Patricia Parker and Geoffrey Hartman. New York: Methuen, 1985. 95–115.

Vierra, Carroll. "'The Lifted Veil' and George Eliot's Early Aesthetic." *Studies in English Literature* 24 (1984): 749–67.

Warminski, Andrzej. *Readings in Interpretation: Hölderlin, Hegel, Heidegger*. Minneapolis: U of Minnesota P, 1987.

———. "Terrible Reading (preceded by 'Epigraphs')." *Responses: On Paul de Man's Wartime Journalism*. Ed. Werner Hamacher et al. Lincoln: U of Nebraska P, 1989. 386–96.

Welby, T. Earle. *A Study of Swinburne*. Port Washington: Kennikat, 1968.

Wellek, René. *A History of Modern Criticism, 1750–1950*. Vol. 4. New Haven: Yale UP, 1977.

Wilde, Oscar. *The Complete Works of Oscar Wilde*. New York: Harper Perennial, 1989.

Woodward, Jocelyn M. *Perseus: A Study in Greek Art and Legend*. London: Cambridge UP, 1937.

Wordsworth, William. *The Prelude: 1799, 1805, 1850*. Ed. Jonathan Wordsworth et al. New York: Norton, 1979.

Index